高等学校工程管理专业规划教材

FIDIC 合同条款概论（双语）

Introduction of FIDIC Conditions of Contract

李德智　刘亚臣　编著

中国建筑工业出版社

图书在版编目（CIP）数据

FIDIC 合同条款概论（双语）/李德智，刘亚臣编著. —北京：
中国建筑工业出版社，2017.8（2023.8 重印）
高等学校工程管理专业规划教材
ISBN 978-7-112-20916-3

Ⅰ.①F… Ⅱ.①李… ②刘… Ⅲ.①建筑工程-经济合同-中国-
双语教学-高等学校-教材 Ⅳ.①D923.6

中国版本图书馆 CIP 数据核字（2017）第 152309 号

本书主要以 FIDIC "新红皮书" 的结构为框架，阐述了 FIDIC "新红皮书" 合同条款的主要内容。全书共分为 20 章，对应了 FIDIC "新红皮书" 的 20 章内容，每一章内容均按照英文论述、疑难词汇、疑难语句以及中文综述进行编排，对 FIDIC "新红皮书" 合同条款进行了归纳和总结。本书内容力求反映 FIDIC 合同条款的最新研究成果，在注重理论体系完备的同时，也具备了实用性。

本书既可以作为高等学校工程管理专业、土木工程专业、建设法专业的双语教材或教学参考用书，也可作为国际留学生的 FIDIC 课程用书。同时，本书也可供政府建设主管部门、律师、工程咨询及监理单位、施工单位相关从业人员参考使用。

为更好地支持相应课程的教学，我们向采用本书作为教材的教师提供教学课件，有需要者可与出版社联系，邮箱：jckj@cabp.com.cn，电话：(010)58337285，建工书院 https://edu.cabplink.com（PC 端）。

* * *

责任编辑：刘晓翠 张 晶 王 跃
责任校对：李欣慰 党 蕾

高等学校工程管理专业规划教材
FIDIC 合同条款概论（双语）
李德智 刘亚臣 编著

*

中国建筑工业出版社出版、发行（北京海淀三里河路 9 号）
各地新华书店、建筑书店经销
北京红光制版公司制版
建工社（河北）印刷有限公司印刷

*

开本：787×1092 毫米 1/16 印张：14 字数：346 千字
2017 年 9 月第一版 2023 年 8 月第三次印刷
定价：**32.00** 元（赠教师课件）
ISBN 978-7-112-20916-3
(30561)

前　言

　　近年来，我国建筑企业在境外承包各类工程的数量有逐年上升趋势，特别是我国"一带一路"战略为对外承包工程的发展注入了新的活力，这就需要更多既懂国际工程管理，也懂国际工程英语的专门人才，以适应建筑产业国际化的要求。

　　本书以 FIDIC（First Edition 1999）（"新红皮书"）为蓝本，在参考 FIDIC 1999 版"黄皮书"、"银皮书"等相关规定的基础上，结合国际工程实践，以及各国有关 FIDIC 的著述与研究成果，考虑了中国学生阅读英文的习惯，编写而成。

　　本书每章内容均由 FIDIC 合同条款英文论述、疑难词汇短语、疑难语句，以及中文综述四部分组成。本书内容共 20 章，依据 FIDIC（First Edition 1999）"新红皮书"的 20 个条款次序进行编排，对 FIDIC "新红皮书"的每个条款逐一进行阐述、归纳和总结。本书力求反映 FIDIC 合同条款的最新研究成果，在注重理论体系完备的同时，也注重内容的实用性。同时，为了便于读者学习和理解 FIDIC，对文中出现的疑难词汇和语句进行了中文解读，并对每一章节作了中文综述，以期读者在阅读英文内容时易于读懂与掌握。

　　本书可以作为高等学校工程管理专业、土木工程专业和建设法专业的双语教材或教学参考用书，也可作为国际留学生学习工程管理专业 FIDIC 课程的用书。同时，本书也可供政府建设主管部门、律师、工程咨询及监理单位、施工单位等有关工程管理人员工作和学习参考使用。

编者

2017 年 5 月

目　　录

Chapter 1　Introduction of the FIDIC ··· 1

　1.1　The Construction Contract ··· 1

　1.2　What is FIDIC? ·· 1

　1.3　A Brief History of FIDIC ·· 2

　1.4　The New FIDIC Forms 1999 ·· 3

　1.5　The Consist of the New Red Book ·· 6

　1.6　The Main Contents of the New Red Book ···································· 8

　疑难词汇 ·· 8

　疑难语句 ·· 9

　中文综述 ·· 9

　Questions ·· 13

Chapter 2　The Employer ·· 14

　2.1　Introduction ··· 14

　2.2　Appointment of Engineer ·· 15

　2.3　Right of Access to the Site ·· 15

　2.4　Permits，Licences or Approvals ·· 17

　2.5　Employer's Personnel ··· 17

　2.6　Employer's Financial Arrangements ·· 18

　疑难词汇 ·· 19

　疑难语句 ·· 19

　中文综述 ·· 20

　Questions ·· 23

Chapter 3　The Engineer ··· 24

　3.1　Introduction ··· 24

　3.2　Engineer's Duties and Authority ·· 24

　3.3　Delegation by the Engineer ·· 26

　3.4　Instructions of the Engineer ··· 27

　3.5　Replacement of the Engineer ·· 28

　3.6　Determinations ··· 29

　疑难词汇 ·· 31

　疑难语句 ·· 31

　中文综述 ·· 32

　　Questions ·· 35

Chapter 4　The Contractor ··· 36

　4.1　Introduction ·· 36

　4.2　Contractor's General Obligations ·· 36

　4.3　Contractor's Representative ··· 37

　4.4　Progress Reports ··· 38

　4.5　Safety Procedures ·· 40

　4.6　Sufficiency of the Accepted Contract Amount ······················· 40

　4.7　Unforeseeable Physical Conditions ··· 41

　疑难词汇 ·· 43

　疑难语句 ·· 43

　中文综述 ·· 44

　　Questions ·· 47

Chapter 5　The Subcontractors ·· 48

　5.1　Introduction ·· 48

　5.2　Clause 4.4 Subcontractor (The New Red Book 1999) ··············· 49

　5.3　FIDIC Subcontract 2011 ·· 49

　5.4　Main Features of the FIDIC Subcontract ································· 50

　5.5　Nominated Subcontractors ·· 51

　疑难词汇 ·· 54

　疑难语句 ·· 54

　中文综述 ·· 55

　　Questions ·· 58

Chapter 6　Staff and Labour ·· 59

　6.1　Introduction ·· 59

　6.2　Engagement of Staff and Labour ·· 59

　6.3　Rates of Wages and Conditions of Labour ···························· 60

　6.4　Persons in the Service of Employer ······································ 60

　6.5　Labour Laws ·· 60

　6.6　Working Hours ··· 61

　6.7　Facilities for Staff and Labour ··· 61

　6.8　Health and Safety ·· 62

　6.9　Contractor's Superintendence ··· 62

　6.10　Contractor's Personnel ·· 63

　6.11　Records of Contractor's Personnel and Equipment ················· 63

　6.12　Disorderly Conduct ·· 64

　疑难词汇 ·· 64

　疑难语句 ·· 64

　　中文综述 ·· 65
　　Questions ··· 68
Chapter 7　Plant, Materials and Workmanship ····················· 69
　7.1　Introduction ·· 69
　7.2　Manner of Execution ·· 69
　7.3　Samples ·· 70
　7.4　Inspection ··· 70
　7.5　Testing ··· 71
　7.6　Rejection ··· 73
　7.7　Remedial Work ··· 73
　7.8　Ownership of Plant and Materials ··································· 74
　　疑难词汇 ·· 74
　　疑难语句 ·· 75
　　中文综述 ·· 75
　　Questions ··· 78
Chapter 8　Commencement, Delays and Suspension ············· 79
　8.1　Introduction ·· 79
　8.2　Commencement of Work ·· 79
　8.3　Time for Completion ··· 80
　8.4　Extension of Time for Completion ··································· 81
　8.5　Delay Damages ·· 82
　8.6　Suspension ··· 83
　8.7　Resumption of Work ··· 85
　　疑难词汇 ·· 85
　　疑难语句 ·· 86
　　中文综述 ·· 86
　　Questions ··· 90
Chapter 9　Tests on Completion ····································· 91
　9.1　Introduction ·· 91
　9.2　Contractor's Obligations ·· 91
　9.3　Delayed Tests ·· 92
　9.4　Retesting ·· 93
　9.5　Failure to Pass Tests on Completion ································ 93
　　疑难词汇 ·· 94
　　疑难语句 ·· 94
　　中文综述 ·· 95
　　Questions ··· 96
Chapter 10　Employer's Taking Over ······························· 97

10. 1　Introduction ･･ 97

10. 2　Taking-Over of the Works and Sections ･･････････････････････ 98

10. 3　Taking-Over of Parts of the Works ･･･････････････････････････ 99

10. 4　Interference with Tests on Completion ･･･････････････････････ 101

10. 5　Surfaces Requiring Reinstatement ･････････････････････････････ 102

疑难词汇･･ 102

疑难语句･･ 102

中文综述･･ 103

Questions ･･ 105

Chapter 11　Defects and Liability ･･･････････････････････････････････････ 106

11. 1　Introduction ･･ 106

11. 2　Completion of Outstanding Work and Remedying Defects ･･････････ 107

11. 3　Extension of Defects Notification Period ･･････････････････････ 108

11. 4　Failure to Remedy Defects ･･････････････････････････････････････ 108

11. 5　Removal of Defective Work and Further Tests ･･･････････････ 109

11. 6　Performance Certificate ･･ 110

11. 7　Clearance of Site ･･ 110

疑难词汇･･ 111

疑难语句･･ 111

中文综述･･ 112

Questions ･･ 114

Chapter 12　Measurement and Evaluation ･･･････････････････････････････ 115

12. 1　Introduction ･･ 115

12. 2　Works to be Measured ･･ 115

12. 3　Method of Measurement ･･ 116

12. 4　Evaluation ･･ 117

12. 5　Omissions ･･ 118

疑难词汇･･ 119

疑难语句･･ 119

中文综述･･ 119

Questions ･･ 121

Chapter 13　Variations and Adjustments ･･･････････････････････････････ 122

13. 1　Introduction ･･ 122

13. 2　Right to Vary ･･ 122

13. 3　Value Engineering ･･ 124

13. 4　Variation Procedure ･･ 125

13. 5　Provisional Sums ･･ 125

13. 6　Daywork ･･ 126

疑难词汇 ……………………………………………………………………… 127

疑难语句 ……………………………………………………………………… 128

中文综述 ……………………………………………………………………… 129

Questions …………………………………………………………………… 132

Chapter 14　Contract Price and Payment …………………………………… 133

14.1　Introduction ……………………………………………………………… 133

14.2　The Contract Price ……………………………………………………… 133

14.3　Advance Payment ……………………………………………………… 134

14.4　Application for Interim Payment Certificates ………………………… 135

14.5　Schedule of Payments …………………………………………………… 136

14.6　Payment …………………………………………………………………… 137

14.7　Delayed Payment ………………………………………………………… 138

14.8　Statement at Completion ………………………………………………… 138

14.9　Final Payment Certificate ……………………………………………… 139

疑难词汇 ……………………………………………………………………… 141

疑难语句 ……………………………………………………………………… 141

中文综述 ……………………………………………………………………… 142

Questions …………………………………………………………………… 146

Chapter 15　Termination ……………………………………………………… 147

15.1　Introduction ……………………………………………………………… 147

15.2　Termination by Employer ……………………………………………… 148

15.3　Suspension and Termination by Contractor ………………………… 150

疑难词汇 ……………………………………………………………………… 153

疑难语句 ……………………………………………………………………… 153

中文综述 ……………………………………………………………………… 154

Questions …………………………………………………………………… 156

Chapter 16　Risk and Responsibility ……………………………………… 157

16.1　Introduction ……………………………………………………………… 157

16.2　Indemnities ……………………………………………………………… 158

16.3　Contractor's Care of the Works ……………………………………… 159

16.4　Employer's Risks ………………………………………………………… 160

16.5　Consequences of Employer's Risks …………………………………… 160

16.6　Intellectual and Industrial Property Rights ………………………… 161

16.7　Limitation of Liability …………………………………………………… 162

疑难词汇 ……………………………………………………………………… 162

疑难语句 ……………………………………………………………………… 163

中文综述 ……………………………………………………………………… 163

Questions …………………………………………………………………… 165

Chapter 17　Insurance ································· 166

17.1　Construction Risks ································· 166

17.2　The Insurance Policy ······························ 166

17.3　Insurance Clauses under FIDIC ····················· 167

17.4　General Requirements for Insurances ················· 167

17.5　Insurance for Works and Contractor's Equipment ········ 169

17.6　Insurance against Injury to Persons and Damage to Property ··· 169

17.7　Insurance for Contractor's Personnel ················· 170

疑难词汇 ··· 170

疑难语句 ··· 171

中文综述 ··· 172

Questions ·· 174

Chapter 18　Force Majeure ···························· 175

18.1　Introduction ···································· 175

18.2　Definition of Force Majeure ······················· 176

18.3　Notice of Force Majeure ··························· 177

18.4　Consequences of Force Majeure ····················· 178

18.5　Optional Termination，Payment and release ············ 179

18.6　Release from Performance Under the Law ·············· 180

疑难词汇 ··· 180

疑难语句 ··· 181

中文综述 ··· 181

Questions ·· 183

Chapter 19　Claims ·································· 184

19.1　Introduction ···································· 184

19.2　Claims and the Conditions of Contract ··············· 184

19.3　Contractor's Claims ······························ 185

19.4　Claims by the Employer ··························· 189

疑难词汇 ··· 190

疑难语句 ··· 191

中文综述 ··· 191

Questions ·· 199

Chapter 20　The Dispute Adjudication Board ·············· 200

20.1　Different Methods of Dispute Resolution in Construction Disputes ··· 200

20.2　Introduction to DAB ····························· 203

20.3　Appointment of the Dispute Adjudication Board ········· 204

20.4　Obtaining Dispute Adjudication Board's Decision ········ 205

20.5　Notice of dissatisfaction ··························· 206

20.6　Arbitration: selecting the applicable pathway ·················· 207

疑难词汇 ··· 208

疑难语句 ··· 208

中文综述 ··· 209

　Questions ·· 211

参考文献 ··· 212

Chapter 1   Introduction of the FIDIC

1. 1   The Construction Contract

1. 1. 1   A construction contract is made between two parties:

(1) An Employer who is referred to as the Employer, who has decided that he needs the project and who will pay for the project. The Employer will need to establish his requirements, decide who will prepare the detailed design and check that the construction meets his requirements, and

(2) A Contractor who will prepare all or any part of the design as required by the employer and who will actually construct the works.

The project organization for the design, supervision and construction may vary but the tasks must be carried out by someone, either on behalf of the Employer or on behalf of the Contractor. The FIDIC Conditions of Contract for Construction are based on design by the Employer, the actual design is usually carried out by a Consulting Engineer, on behalf of the Employer. The Conditions of Contract for Plant and Design-Build and the Conditions of Contract for EPC/Turnkey Projects are based on design by the Contractor, again, the actual design may be carried out by a Consulting Engineer, but on behalf of the Contractor.

1. 1. 2   International Contracts

An international contract may be defined as a contract in which one of the parties is from a different country to the country of the project. In many cases the requirements outlined in the Conditions of Contract for international contracts are similar to those for domestic contracts, but there are additional matters such as different legal systems, or local customs and procedures, currency which must be considered.

1. 2   What is FIDIC?

FIDIC is an acronym for Fédération Internationale Des Ingénieurs Conseils-i. e. the French for the International Federation of Consulting Engineers. The organization was founded in 1913 by three countries each wholly or partly francophone (being Belgium, France and Switzerland). There are now almost 100 Member Associations from all over the world, and FIDIC is currently located in the World Trade Centre in Geneva, Switzerland.

1

FIDIC represents globally the consulting engineering industry by promoting the business interests of firms supplying technology-based intellectual services for the built and natural environment. FIDIC is particularly well known for its work in drafting standard form conditions of contract which are used on higher value international construction projects, and are endorsed by many multilateral development banks. FIDIC also organizes conference, seminars and training courses.

1. 3 A Brief History of FIDIC

The form of the early FIDIC contracts followed closely the fourth edition of the ICE Conditions of contract. In fact so closely did the FIDIC form mirror its English counterpart that Ian Duncan Wallace commented that: *"as a general comment, it is difficult to escape the conclusion that at least one primary object in preparing the present international contract was to depart as little as humanly possible from the English conditions"*.

One difficulty with the original FIDIC Red Book was that it was based on the detailed design being provided to the Contractor by the Employer or his Engineer. It was therefore best suited for civil engineering and infrastructure projects such as roads, bridges, dams, tunnels and water and sewage facilities. It was not so suited for contracts where major items of plant were manufactured away from site. This led to the first edition of the "Yellow Book" being produced in 1963 by FIDIC for mechanical and electrical works. This had an emphasis on testing and commissioning and so was more suitable for the manufacture and installation of plant. The second edition was published in 1980.

Both the Red and Yellow Books were revised by FIDIC and new editions published in 1987. A key feature of the 4th edition of the Red Book was the introduction of an express term which required the Engineer to act impartially when giving a decision or taking any action which might affect the rights and obligations of the parties, whereas the previous editions had assumed this implicitly.

A supplement was published in November 1996 which provided the user with the ability to incorporate alternative arrangements comprising an option for a Dispute Adjudication Board to go with modelled terms of appointment and procedural rules, and an option for payment on a lump sum basis rather than by reference to bills of quantities.

In 1995 a further contract was published (known as the Orange Book). This was for use on projects procured on a design and build or turnkey basis, dispensing with the Engineer entirely, and provided for an "Employer's Representative", who, when determining value, costs or extensions of time, had to *"determine the matter fairly, reasonably and in accordance with the Contract"*.

Consequently the need to submit matters to the Engineer for his "Decision" was eliminated. In its place an Independent Dispute Adjudication Board was introduced consisting of either one or three members appointed jointly by the Employer and the Contractor at the commencement of the contract, with the cost being shared by the parties. This provision mirrored a World Bank amendment to the FIDIC Red Book.

Although People concentrate on the new FIDIC forms, it should be remembered that the FIDIC 4th edition 1987 ("The Old Red Book") remains the contract of choice throughout much of the Middle East, particularly the UAE. However, this is slowly changing, as the government in Abu Dhabi introduced its own version of the 1999 FIDIC Red Book under cover of Law 21 of 2006.

1. 4　The New FIDIC Forms 1999

In 1994 FIDIC established a task force to update both the Red and the other colour Books in the light of developments in the international construction industry, including the development of the Orange Book. The key considerations included:

(i) The role of the Engineer and in particular the requirement to act impartially in the circumstances of being employed and paid by the Employer.

(ii) The desirability for the standardization of the FIDIC forms.

(iii) The simplification of the FIDIC forms in light of the fact that the FIDIC conditions were promulgated in English but in very many instances were being utilized by those whose language background was other than English.

(iv) The New books would be suitable for use in both common law and civil law jurisdictions.

The 1994 Task force led to the publication of four new contracts in 1999:

(1) Conditions of Contract for Construction, for Building and Engineering Works, Designed by the Employer: The Construction Contract (The New Red Book).

The Red Book is intended for projects where the main responsibility for design rests with the Employer (or its Engineer). Thus, the works are usually completed by the Contractor in accordance with the Employer's design. However, the works may also include elements of civil, mechanical, electrical and/or construction works designed by the Contractor. The work done is quantified, with payment made on the basis of a bill of quantities (although it is also possible for payment to be made on a lump sum basis) . The Red Book is the most commonly used standard form of construction and engineering contract where most (or all) of the works are to be designed by (or on behalf of) the Employer.

(2) Conditions of Contract for Plant and Design-Build for Electrical and Mechanical Plant, and for Building and Engineering Works, Designed by the Contractor (The New Yellow Book).

The Yellow Book is intended for projects where responsibility for design rests with the Contractor. The Contractor will design the project in accordance with requirements specified by the Employer. The testing procedures prescribed by the Yellow Book are usually more complicated than those in the Red Book. Payment is made on a lump sum basis, usually against a schedule of payments.

(3) Conditions of Contract for EPC Turnkey Projects (First Edition, 1999) (The Silver Book).

The Silver Book is intended for Engineering Procurement and Construction (EPC) arrangements. Under an EPC contract, the Contractor is responsible for the entirety of the works and design required to provide the Employer with a facility that is ready for operation at the "turn of a key". Accordingly, the Contractor's risk for time and cost is considerably greater than the risk it would assume under the Yellow Book.

(4) Short Form of Contract (The Green Book).

The Green Book is intended for engineering and building work of relatively small capital value. Accordingly, the Green Book is suitable for relatively simple or repetitive work, or work that will not require input from specialist sub contractors.

FIDIC is also aware of the need to develop new contract forms in order to adapt to changing conditions. Since the original publication of the 1999 suite of contracts, FIDIC has also introduced the following:

(1) Conditions of Contract for Construction for Building and Engineering Works Designed by the Employer, for bank-financed projects only (The Pink Book).

The Pink Book is intended for projects funded by Multilateral Development Banks, such as the World Bank or the European Bank for Reconstruction and Development. Indeed, The World Bank is clear that:

"These SBDW ❶are mandatory for use in major works contracts (those estimated to cost more than US$10 million, including contingency allowance) unless the Bank agrees to the use of other Bank Standard Bidding Documents on a case-by-case basis."

The SBDW notes that the use of the Conditions of Contract for Construction for Building Engineering Works Designed by the Employer, Multilateral Development Bank Harmonized Edition, prepared by FIDIC, is compulsory. The User's Guide makes it clear that: "The provisions in Section I (Instructions to Bidders) and Section VII (General Conditions of Contract) must be used with their text unchanged."

(2) Conditions of Contract for Design, Build and Operate Projects (The Gold Book).

The Gold Book combines design, construction, operation and maintenance of a facility into a single contract, and is intended for "Design, Build and Operate" projects. The project's commissioning testing is followed by a 20 year operation and maintenance period, during which the Contractor must achieve various operational targets and then hand over the project to the Employer in an agreed condition. The DBO form was a response to the call for a standard concession contract for the transport and water/waste sectors. The

---

❶　SBDW means "Standard Bidding Documents for Works" which prepared by the World Bank for use by borrowers in the procurement of admeasurement (unit price or rate) type of works contracts through international competitive bidding.

market had been using the existing FIDIC Yellow Book with operations and maintenance obligations tacked on. FIDIC recognised this unsatisfactory state of affairs and the need to tailor a form to meet the demand.

Under the DBO form, the Contractor (who, given the size of these projects, will typically be in the form of joint venture or consortium) will be responsible for:

(a) designing and constructing the works during the design-build period; and

(b) operating and maintaining the facilities for a 20 year period once the facility has been handed over with the issue of the Commissioning Certificate.

However, the Contractor will have no responsibility for the financing and ultimate commercial success of the project.

(3) Conditions of Contract for Design-Build and Turnkey 1995 (The Orange Book)

The Orange book was published in 1995 to provide a design and build option to the current FIDIC suite. This standard form was the first FIDIC contract to adopt the current FIDIC style of drafting and was used as a template for the drafting teams when preparing the 1999 suite of contracts.

(4) Dredgers Contract (The Blue Book).

The Blue Book is intended for dredging and reclamation work and ancillary construction. The Employer undertakes the design of the project.

(5) Consultant Model Agreements, including the Model Representative Agreement (The White Book).

The White Book is an agreement to be used by the Employer and its consultant. In common with other contracts a new version is being prepared.

(6) Conditions of Subcontract for Construction for Building and Engineering Works Designed by the Employer (the "2011 Subcontract").

Sub-contracts for all the main forms will be prepared as part of the current review.

In addition, there are a number of other forms, based on the FIDIC terms. For example, in 2007 the Abu Dhabi Executive Affairs Authority General Conditions of Contract, introduced for construction of projects undertaken in Abu Dhabi on behalf of Public Entities.

FIDIC also introduced a Procurement Procedures Guide in 2011.

There are also steps being taken to revise the entire suite, starting with the Yellow Book and followed next by the Red and Silver Books, although it is not anticipated that FIDIC will be in a position to release a test edition until some time towards the end of 2016 at the earliest. In a progress report issued in October 2014 the FIDIC Contracts Committee listed the following revisions as being "on the drawing board":

a. Task Group 4A-Update of Joint Venture Model Agreement and Sub-Consultant Model Agreement;

b. Task Group 4B-Update of Client / Consultant Model Agreement (White Book);

c. Task Group 6-Update of 1999 Rainbow Suite (Red, Yellow and Silver book);

    d. Task Group 7-Update of Dredgers Contract;

    e. Task Group 9-New Yellow Book / Silver Book Sub-contract Forms;

    f. Task Group 10-New Tunnelling/Underground Contract;

    g. Task Group 11-New Operate, Design& Build (ODB) Form of Contract; and

    h. Task Group 12-New Contract & Agreement-Glossary of Terms.

1.5 The Consist of the New Red Book

1.5.1 In General

The Conditions of Contract of The New Red Book include:

    (1) General Conditions;

    (2) Particular Conditions.

FIDIC General Conditions of Contract are intended to be used unchanged for every project. The Particular Conditions are prepared for the particular project taking account of any changes or additional clauses to suit the local and project requirements. Some employers have their own versions of the General Conditions available which incorporate some changes to suit their own requirements.

Normally General Conditions include the Appendix to Tender which gives essential project information some of which must be completed by the Employer before issuing the tender documents, together with some information which must be added by the tenderer upon submission of the tender.

In any project in order to overcome problems it will often be necessary to carry out additional work and this will take time and money. The most common situation is that the Contractor spends money and claims it back from the Employer. It is then necessary to decide whether the Employer must pay, or whether the Contractor must bear the additional cost. The initial decision will normally be made by the Employer's Representative or Engineer. However this can only be an interim decision and is subject to appeal to the Engineer or the Dispute Adjudication Board and ultimately to an arbitrator or the courts. The actual dispute resolution processes vary in different FIDIC forms of contract.

The basis on which such decisions must be made is laid down in the Conditions of Contract. The Conditions of Contract deals with the roles of the parties to the Contract and lays down their rights and obligations under the Contract.

1.5.2 The Consist of the FIDIC Forms

In keeping with the desire for standardization, each of the new books includes General Conditions together with guidance for the preparation of the Particular Conditions, and a Letter of Tender, Contract Agreement and Dispute Adjudication Agreements.

The FIDIC forms consist of a number of documents. The contract forms will typically comprise of the following:

    (1) Letter of Acceptance—the Red, Yellow and Gold Books define the Letter of Ac-

ceptance as the "letter of formal acceptance, signed by the Employer, of the Letter of Tender, including any annexed memoranda comprising agreements between and signed by both Parties".

(2) Memoranda annexed to the Letter of Acceptance—the memoranda recording the technical and commercial aspects of the works.

(3) Letter of Tender—under the Red, Yellow and Gold Books, this is a letter from the Contractor in response to the Employer's invitation to tender, setting out its offer for the works. Under the Red and Yellow books, the Letter of Tender is deemed to include the Appendix to Tender.

(4) Appendix to Tender—this document specifies the key terms of the contract between the parties. Usually, the Employer will complete parts of the Appendix to Tender with which it requires the bidder to comply. The bidder subsequently completes the remainder of the Appendix to Tender by specifying the details of its offer.

(5) General Conditions of Contract; Particular Conditions of Contract—the Conditions of Contract set out the core terms of the contract between the parties. In doing so, the Conditions of Contract set forth the rights, obligations and responsibilities of the parties arising in connection with the design and construction of the works. The Conditions of Contract also prescribe procedures for the management of the project, such as the role of the Engineer under the Red and Yellow Books.

(6) Specification—under the Red Book, the specification sets out the technical requirements of the works, and how those works are to be executed.

(7) Drawings—under the Red Book, the drawings supplement the Specification by setting out the design of the project.

(8) Employer's Requirements—the Employer's Requirements are used in the Yellow, Silver and Gold Books to set out the purpose, scope, design and technical aspects of the works. This may comprise a detailed design specification or certain performance requirements for the end product.

(9) Contractor's Proposal—in the Yellow and Gold Books, the Contractor's Proposal details the Contractor's proposals for the works.

(10) Schedules—in the Red, Yellow and Gold Books, Schedules are defined as documents "completed by the Contractor and submitted with the Letter of Tender, as included in the Contract". The Schedules may therefore consist of bills of quantities, data, and price lists.

(11) Tender—under the Silver Book, the Tender is used instead of the Letter of Tender and documents that support it (Contractor's Proposals, Schedules, etc). The Silver Book defines the Tender as the "Contractor's signed offer for the Works and all other documents which the Contractor submitted therewith (other than these Conditions and the Employer's Requirements, if so submitted), as included in the Contract".

(12) Addenda—the Addenda are issued by the Employer if it wishes to amend any of

the tender documents after commencement of the tendering process. The Addenda may amend the tendering procedure, as well as the tender documents that comprise the contract between the parties.

1.6　The Main Contents of the New Red Book

From a practical point of view, the key to reading and understanding the New Red Book is to understand its structure. The New Red Book has 20 clauses which are perhaps best viewed as chapters covering the key project topics. Those clauses are as follows:

(1) Clause 1　General provisions;

(2) Clause 2　The Employer;

(3) Clause 3　The Engineer or Employer's representative;

(4) Clause 4　The Contractor;

(5) Clause 5　Design (Silver Book) or Nominated sub-Contractor (Red Book);

(6) Clause 6　Staff and Labour;

(7) Clause 7　Plant, materials and workmanship;

(8) Clause 8　Commencement, delays and suspension;

(9) Clause 9　Tests on completion;

(10) Clause 10　Taking over;

(11) Clause 11　Defects liability;

(12) Clause 12　Tests after completion;

(13) Clause 13　Variations and adjustments;

(14) Clause 14　Contract price and payment;

(15) Clause 15　Termination by Employer;

(16) Clause 16　Suspension and termination by Contractor;

(17) Clause 17　Risk and responsibility;

(18) Clause 18　Insurance;

(19) Clause 19　Force majeure;

(20) Clause 20　Claims, disputes and arbitration.

In the Gold book, there is a slightly different order, with the insurance clause having been moved to clause 19, whilst clause 17 has been renamed "risk allocation" and the force majeure clause has been dropped and replaced with a new clause 18 headed "exceptional risks". This may well represent the way forward for any future amendment of the remaining four FIDIC contracts.

☞ 疑难词汇 ☜

1. dispensing with the Engineer entirely 完全免除或省掉了工程师

2. EPC/Turnkey Projects 交钥匙总承包合同

3. task force 特别小组

4. common law 习惯法，不成文法（主要指以英美为代表的英美法系国家法律体系）

5. civil Law 民法，欧陆法系（主要指以德法为代表的大陆法系国家法律体系）

6. a lump sum 一次性支付

7. EPC：Engineering Procurement and Construction

8. SBDW：The World Bank Standard Bidding Documents 世界银行标准招标文件

9. commissioning testing 运行试验

10. DBO：The Design-Build-Operate Form of Contract 设计—建造—运营合同格式

11. annexed memoranda 附加备忘录

12. substantial bundle of documents 大量的文件

13. bear the consequences 承担后果或结果，在这里 Bear 是动词，有承担，负担之意

14. addenda 附录，规范增补

15. ICE：The Institution of Civil Engineers（England）英国土木工程师学会

16. on the drawing board 处于设计阶段

☞ **疑难语句** ☜

1. In fact so closely did the FIDIC form mirror its English counterpart that Ian Duncan Wallace commented that：*"as a general comment，it is difficult to escape the conclusion that at least one primary object in preparing the present international contract was to depart as little as humanly possible from the English conditions"*.

事实上，FIDIC 合同形式紧密地借鉴了英国的建筑合同条款（ICE），正如 Ian Duncan Wallace 所说的，一般来说，很难回避这样一个结论，就是准备国际合同的初衷几乎不能脱离英国合同条件（ICE 作为参考）。

2. A supplement was published in November 1996 which provided the user with the ability to incorporate alternative arrangements comprising an option for a Dispute Adjudication Board to go with modelled terms of appointment and procedural rules, and an option for payment on a lump sum basis rather than by reference to bills of quantities.

（FIDIC）在 1996 年 11 月发布了增补版本，为用户增加了可选择性的安排，即争端裁决委员会的任命和程序规定，同时增加了一次性支付的付款选项，而不仅仅参考工程量清单支付。

3. "These SBDW are mandatory for use in major works contracts (those estimated to cost more than US＄10 million, including contingency allowance) unless the Bank agrees to the use of other Bank Standard Bidding Documents on a case-by-case basis."

除非世界银行同意根据不同的项目使用其他银行标准招标文件，在一些主要工程项目上（包括应急准备金在内的，预估花费超过 1000 万美元的项目），世界银行标准招标文件是强制性使用的合同文件。

☞ **中文综述** ☜

一、国际工程合同概述

国际工程合同是指个人或企业（作为承包商），在国际承包市场上通过投标、接受委

托或其他途径承揽国际组织、外国政府或私人雇主（作为雇主）的工程建设项目、物资采购及其他方面的承包业务，就双方的权利和义务，包括但不限于资金、支付、技术、设备、工期、变更、劳务、责任风险承担和纠纷解决等多方面内容的约定达成的合意。国际工程合同一般有如下特点。

（1）当事人主体结构复杂。这主要表现在投资主体的多样化和不同国籍的合同主体的文化差异。

（2）合同内容的复杂性。国际工程合同由通用条款和特殊条款组成，若就条款性质划分，它既包括技术条款、经济条款、文化条款，也包括法律条款。

（3）合同风险大，风险分配复杂。工程建设过程包含着政治风险、自然风险、项目风险、人员风险等诸多风险因素，这就要求在订立合同之初，合同各方应将各种风险分配责任及保险约定清楚。因此，风险分配是国际工程合同条款约定的主要内容，通用条款无法定义的风险及风险分配，一般由特殊条款加以补充。

（4）政府的支持和政策对合同履行影响重大。很多国际工程项目都是政府作为特许人或者投资人出现的。投资项目所在地政策的稳定、投资环境的完善、项目所在国与本国的关系等都是国际工程合同顺利执行的重要保证。

（5）国际工程一般使用国际通用的合同文本。目前，FIDIC 合同文本为世界各国政府、投资人、世界银行和组织等广泛使用。除此以外，美国的 AIA（The American Institute of Architects）、AGC（Associated General Contractors）、EJCDC（Engineers Joint Contract Documents Committee），英国的 ICE（Institution of Civil Engineers）、JCT（Joint Contracts Tribunal）和 NEC（New Engineering Contract）等合同文本在英语国家也不同程度地得到应用。

二、FIDIC 简介

FIDIC 是以法语为官方语言的三个欧洲国家——比利时、法国和瑞士，于 1913 年在比利时根特发起设立的，它的全称是国际咨询工程师联合会（Fédération Internationale Des lngénieurs-Conseils），FIDIC 是其法文第一个字母的缩写合拼。目前已有近百个成员国加入 FIDIC，分属于四个地区性组织，即亚洲及太平洋地区会员协会（ASPAC）、欧洲共同体会员协会（CEDIC）、非洲会员协会组织（CAMA）、北欧会员协会组织（RINORD）。FIDIC 是最具有权威性的咨询工程师组织，自建立以来，有效地推动了全球范围内高质量工程咨询服务业的发展。目前，FIDIC 总部设在瑞士洛桑，主要职能机构有：执行委员会、土木工程合同委员会、雇主与咨询工程师关系委员会、职业责任委员会以及秘书处。1996 年，中国工程咨询协会代表我国加入了 FIDIC，成为其正式成员。

三、FIDIC 合同文本

1994 年，FIDIC 成立特别工作小组，根据国际建筑工业发展现状，决定升级"红皮书"和"黄皮书"，同时进一步发展"橘皮书"。通过特别工作小组的努力使得其在 1999 年发布了四个新的合同文本。

1.《建筑工程合同条款》（Conditions of Contract for Construction）（"新红皮书"）

在 1999 以前，FIDIC 组织分别在 1957 年、1963 年、1977 年和 1987 年出版了"红皮书"第一版、第二版、第三版和第四版。从第三版起，"红皮书"就得到了欧洲建筑业国际联合会、亚洲及西太平洋承包商协会国际联合会、美洲国家建筑业联合会、美国普通承包商联合会、国际疏浚公司协会的共同认可。经世界银行推荐将 FIDIC "红皮书" 第三版也纳入了世界银行与美洲开发银行共同编制的《工程采购招标文件样本》。正因存在前四个版本的红皮书，所以 1999 年修订出版的红皮书被称为 "新红皮书"。"新红皮书" 是 FIDIC 组织推荐的适用于由雇主负责设计的建筑施工工程，其最大特点体现在以下两个方面：其一是雇主支付承包商的依据是工程量清单；其二，工程师的纠纷解决职能被 DAB 机构所取代。

2.《生产设备和设计—建造合同条款》(Conditions of Contract for Plant and Design-Build for Electrical and Mechanical Plant，and for Building and Engineering Works，Designed by the Contractor)（"新黄皮书"）。

黄皮书适用于大型工程的设备提供和施工安装，承包工作范围包括设备的制造、运送、安装和保修几个阶段。这个合同是在土木工程施工合同基础上编制的，针对相同情况制定的条款完全照搬土木工程施工合同的规定。与土木工程施工合同的区别主要表现为：一是该合同涉及的不确定风险的因素较少，但实施阶段管理程序较为复杂；二是支付管理程序与责任划分基于总价合同。这个合同一般适用于大型项目中的部分工程。"黄皮书" 于 1963 年出第一版，并在 1980 年和 1987 年出版第二版和第三版。因此，1999 年出版的 "黄皮书" 被称为 "新黄皮书"。

3.《设计采购施工（EPC）/交钥匙项目合同条款》(Conditions of Contract for EPC/Turnkey Projects)（"银皮书"）。该合同可适用于以交钥匙方式提供工厂或类似设施的加工或动力设备、基础设施项目或其他类型的开发项目，一般采用总价合同的形式。该合同适用于建设项目规模大、复杂程度高、承包商提供设计、承包商承担绝大部分风险的情况。"银皮书" 主要针对工程采购和建筑而设计。根据 "银皮书" 的条款，承包商将负责工程包括设计在内的全部工作，（在工程完工后）向雇主提交拿钥匙即可进驻的设施。在 "银皮书" 条件下，承包商承担的时间和费用风险要比 "黄皮书" 合同条件下大得多。

4.《简明合同格式》(Short Form of Contract)（"绿皮书"）。"绿皮书" 的宗旨在于使该合同范本适用于投资规模相对较小的民用土木工程，如：①造价在 50 万美元以下以及工期在 6 个月以下；②工程相对简单，不需专业分包合同；③重复性工作；④施工周期短。

同时，FIDIC 也意识到，为了适应不断变化的工程条件，发布新的合同文本已经成为一种客观需要。除了上述四个合同文本，FIDIC 在 1999 年前后又分别发布了一些其他合同文本。

1.《施工合同条件——多边开发银行协调版》(Multilateral Development Banks，MDBS)

"粉皮书" 是 "红皮书" 的协调版，2005 年 5 月初版，修订于 2006 年 3 月和 2010 年 6 月。"粉皮书"(Pink book) 是 FIDIC 与世界银行等国际金融组织合作专门编制的用于国际多边金融组织出资的建设项目，其条款并不是很适合其他资金来源的项目，例如，MBD 合同对于采购地就有明确而严格的限制。

2.《设计—建造和运营项目合同条款》(Conditions of Contract for Design-Build and Operate Projects)（"金皮书"）。

"金皮书" 将设计、建设、运营和维护于一体，项目的运行要经受 20 年运营与维护的考验，在此期间，承包商要实现运作目标，并根据合同条件，将项目的运营权转移给雇主。FIDIC声明起草"金皮书"的目的在于减少项目移交后由于项目设计、工艺和材料质量问题引起的风险。因此，"金皮书"适用于需要长时间使用的，并需要长期维护的基础设施项目，例如，PPP项目和BOT项目。

3.《设计—建造与交钥匙工程合同条款》（Conditions of Contract for Design-Build and Turnkey，1st Edition 1995）（"橘皮书"）

"橘皮书"发布于1995年，为FIDIC合同的工作小组起草合同提供样本。1999年FIDIC发布了"新红皮书"和"新黄皮书"后，就很少使用"橘皮书"了。

4.《招标程序》（Tendering Procedure）（"蓝皮书"）

FIDIC在1982年出版了《招标程序》，反映了国际建设行业当今招标投标的通行做法，并提供了一个完整、系统的国际建设项目招标程序，具有实用性和灵活性。

5.《委托人与咨询工程师标准服务协议书》（Conditions of the Client/Consultant Model Services Agreement）（"白皮书"）

"白皮书"是雇主为了工程项目的顺利进行与咨询机构签订的关于工程咨询服务的合同。

6.《土木工程施工分包合同》

FIDIC编制的《土木工程施工分包合同》是与FIDIC施工合同条款配套使用的分包合同范本。施工分包合同制定于1994年，2011年进行了修订。

四、FIDIC"新红皮书"的主要内容

FIDIC"新红皮书"的主要内容由通用条款和特殊条款组成。通用条款是对每个项目都适用的条款。特殊条款是合同当事人根据项目的特殊性或雇主方提出的特殊要求，或者根据当地的风俗习惯等因素订立的条款。

FIDIC"新红皮书"的通用条款包括：

(1) Clause 1   General Provisions 一般规定；

(2) Clause 2   The Employer 雇主；

(3) Clause 3   The Engineer or Employer's representative 工程师及雇主代表；

(4) Clause 4   The Contractor 承包商；

(5) Clause 5   Nominated Sub Contractor 指定分包商；

(6) Clause 6   Staff and Labour 职员和劳工；

(7) Clause 7   Plant，Materials and Workmanship 永久设备、材料和工艺；

(8) Clause 8   Commencement，Delays and Suspension 开工、延误和暂停；

(9) Clause 9   Tests on Completion 竣工检验；

(10) Clause 10   Employer's Taking Over 雇主的接收；

(11) Clause 11   Defects Liability 缺陷责任；

(12) Clause 12   Measurement and Evaluation 测量和估价；

(13) Clause 13   Variations and Adjustments 变更和调整；

(14) Clause 14   Contract Price and Payment 合同价格与支付；

(15) Clause 15   Termination by Employer 雇主提出终止；

(16) Clause 16   Suspension and Termination by Contractor 承包商提出暂停和终止；

(17) Clause 17　　Risk and Responsibility 风险与责任；

(18) Clause 18　　Insurance 保险；

(19) Clause 19　　Force Majeure 不可抗力；

(20) Clause 20　　Claims，Disputes and Arbitration 索赔、争议与仲裁。

Questions

1. What is the unique feature of New Red Book?

2. Please introduce the functions of each Clause of New Red Book?

(17) *Clause 17　Risk and Responsibility* 风险与职责;
(18) *Clause 18　Insurance* 保险;
(19) *Clause 19　Force Majeure* 不可抗力;
(20) *Clause 20　Claims, Disputes and Arbitration* 索赔、争议与仲裁。

Questions
1. What is the unique feature of New Red Book?
2. Please introduce the construction period of Chinese and New Red book?

Chapter 2　The Employer

2. 1　Introduction

The FIDIC standard form for the Contract Agreement includes the statement that the Employer covenants to pay the Contractor the Contract Price in consideration of the execution and completion of the Works and the remedying of defects therein. However, this does not mean that the Employer is only required to appoint an Engineer to administer the project and then sign the payment cheques. The development of Conditions of Contract over the years has imposed additional tasks on the Employer, involving both rights and obligations. In some countries the law also imposes duties on the Employer in a construction Contract.

The Conditions of Contract require the Employer, as distinct from the Engineer, to take certain actions during the construction period. Even though the Engineer is now classed as "Employer's Personnel" there are some tasks that are allocated to the Employer. Whilst the Employer could delegate the paperwork to the Engineer, particularly if the designated Engineer is an employee of the Employer, the actual tasks require the Employer to be involved. It is important that the Employer designates a staff member, separate from the Engineer, to represent him whenever the Contract requires notice to, or action by, the Employer.

Under the FIDIC Conditions of Contract, the developer of a project will have taken a number of specific actions before reaching the stage where he is involved in the role of employer. He will already have received professional advice and have taken a number of decisions in connection with the following:

(1) The choice of professional advisers for the planning, engineering and other aspects of the construction project;

(2) The most suitable contractual arrangements for the employment of these professional advisers;

(3) The design of the project, the site, assessment of budget costs, choice of financial arrangements and any services which must be obtained to permit construction to start on site;

(4) The most appropriate procurement and contractual arrangements for the purpose of constructing the project;

(5) The criteria to be adopted for selecting the contractor who will be responsible for

construction of the project;

(6) The most appropriate arrangements for the day-to-day control over the quality of the construction and final completion of the project;

(7) The manner in which any legislative or governmental approvals are to be obtained; and

(8) The relevant information required in respect of the various clauses of the conditions of contract chosen to govern the construction of the works.

2. 2   Appointment of Engineer

The role of the engineer during the construction of a project in Red Book is extremely complex and involves:

(1) a continuing design role;

(2) an administrative role as the employer's agent;

(3) a supervisory role;

(4) a certifying role; and

(5) an adjudicating role.

Whilst it is recommended and highly desirable that the Employer appoint the Engineer from the beginning of the project so that he would be the person responsible for carrying out the pre-contract duties of design, this is not an absolute requirement. The obvious disadvantages of appointing someone different for these two distinct roles, i. e. pre-contract and post-contract roles, would have to be considered very carefully before adopting that course.

Where the Employer wishes to restrict the authority of the Engineer in such a way that he is required to obtain the specific approval of the Employer before exercising any such authority, the Employer must set out such restrictions in the terms of appointment of the Engineer and in the Articles of any agreement with him. Attention must be given by the Employer to two aspects: first, to Sub-Clause 3. 1 where the engineer shall have no authority to amend the Contract; secondly, throughout the Red Book, the Engineer is required to duly consult with the Employer and the Contractor, but having so consulted, he is entitled to form his own opinion regardless of what the Employer or the Contractor may say to him.

2. 3   Right of Access to the Site

The Employer shall give the Contractor right of access to, and possession of, all parts of the Site within the time (or times) stated in the Appendix to Tender. The right and possession may not be exclusive to the Contractor. If, under the Contract, the Employer is required to give (to the Contractor) possession of any foundation, structure, plant or means of access, the Employer shall do so in the time and manner stated in the Specification. However, the Employer may withhold any such right or possession until the Performance Security has been received.

If no such time is stated in the Appendix to Tender, the Employer shall give the Contractor right of access to, and possession of, the Site within such times as may be required to enable the Contractor to proceed in accordance with the programme submitted under Sub-Clause 8. 3 [Programme].

If the Contractor suffers delay and/or incurs Cost as a result of a failure by the Employer to give any such right or possession within such time, the Contractor shall give notice to the Engineer and shall be entitled subject to Sub-Clause 20. 1 [Contractor's Claims] to:

(a) an extension of time for any such delay, if completion is or will be delayed, under Sub-Clause 8. 4 [Extension of time for Completion]; and

(b) payment of any such Cost plus reasonable profit, which shall be included in the Contract Price.

After receiving this notice, the Engineer shall proceed in accordance with Sub-Clause 3. 5 [Determinations] to agree or determine these matters.

However, if and to the extent that the Employer's failure was caused by any error or delay by the Contractor, including an error in, or delay in the submission of, any of the Contractor's Documents, the Contractor shall not be entitled to such extension of time, Cost or profit.

In the Red Book, Sub-Clause 2. 1 states that possession does not necessarily mean exclusive possession, but shared possession requires clarification in the Particular Conditions. When the Contractor takes possession of the Site he assumes responsibility for matters such as safety, security and insurance. If the Contractor does not have full control of the Site and the activities on the Site, or if these powers are to be shared, then the extent of the Contractor's responsibilities must be clearly stated.

The "Site" is defined at Sub-Clause 1. 1. 6. 7 as including not just the area of land on which the Works are to be executed, but also any other places which are specified in the Contract. These may include areas that have been set aside for the Contractor to use for storage or for obtaining excavated materials or for any other purpose. It is important that the Site area is delineated clearly in the Contract Drawings or Specification.

If the Employer Fails to give right of access to and possession of the Site within the stated period then the Contractor will be entitled to an extension of time, plus his Costs and a reasonable profit, subject to his following the correct procedures as detailed at Sub-Clauses 2. 2 and 20. 1 and the delay not being attributable to a failure on the part of the Contractor.

2. 4 Permits, Licences or Approvals

The Employer shall (where he is in a position to do so) provide reasonable assistance to the Contractor at the request of the Contractor:

(a) by obtaining copies of the Laws of the Country which are relevant to the Contract but are not readily available; and

(b) for the Contractor's applications for any permits, licences or approvals required by the Laws of the Country: (ⅰ) which the Contractor is required to obtain under Sub-Clause 1. 13 [Compliance with Laws], (ⅱ) for the delivery of goods, including clearance through customs, and (ⅲ) for the export of Contractor's Equipment when it is removed from the Site.

Sub-Clause 2. 2 obliges the Employer to assist the Contractor to obtain copies of the Laws of the Country and with applications for any permits, licenses or approvals required by these Laws, in the circumstances which are listed in the Sub-Clause. This refers to the Laws of the Country, which are not necessarily the governing law as stated in the Appendix to Tender, but are documents to which the Employer can be assumed to have access.

The obligation is qualified as reasonable and the Employer being in the position to give assistance. The Contractor will also rely on his local partner, agent or representative before calling on the assistance of the Employer. Co-operation and assistance should always be given when possible, but it must be doubtful whether, if the assistance fails to achieve the desired result, this would reduce the Contractor's obligations or give grounds for a claim. However, a delay in any of these operations could result in a claim under Sub-Clause 8. 5 for Delays by Authorities.

The Sub-Clause does not refer to the Employer being able to charge the Contractor for providing this service. The provision of reasonable assistance must be assumed to be free of any charge. However, if the Contractor is asking for excessive unreasonable assistance then the Employer might give notice under Sub-Clause 2. 5 that he intends to make a charge. The Contractor might then decide to withdraw his request and obtain the information elsewhere.

2. 5 Employer's Personnel

The Employer shall be responsible for ensuring that the Employer's Personnel and the Employer's other contractors on the Site:

(a) cooperate with the Contractor's efforts under Sub-Clause 4. 6 [Cooperation]; and

(b) take actions similar to those which the Contractor is required to take under subparagraphs (a), (b) and (c) of Sub-Clause 4. 8 [Safety Procedures] and under Sub-Clause

4. 18 [Protection of the Environment].

Employer's Personnel are defined at Sub-Clause 1. 1. 2. 6 as being people so notified to the Contractor, including: the Engineer and his assistants; all staff, labour and employees of the Employer and the Engineer; any other person who the Employer or the Engineer has decided to designate as Employer's Personnel.

Sub-Clause 4. 6 has a separate requirement for the Contractor to cooperate with other Contractors and public authority personnel. They are not normally Employer's Personnel, but presumably some individuals could be designated and notified to the Contractor as Employer's Personnel.

Sub-Clause 2. 3 obliges the Employer to take responsibility for Employer's Personnel and for other Contractors' reciprocal co-operation under Sub-Clause 4. 6, Safety Procedures similar to Sub-Clause 4. 8 (a), (b), (c) and Protection of the Environment as Sub-Clause 4. 1. It is important that the Employer includes similar Clauses in his Contracts with all the Contractors who will be working on the Site.

When two or more Contractors are working on the same Site the possibilities of delays and Costs from failures of co-operation, or other problems, can have serious consequences. If the Contractor incurs Costs as a consequence of an action by another Contractor then he may wish to claim against the Employer, but the liability is not clear and may depend on the applicable law. The FIDIC Clauses may be adequate when this Contractor is carrying out a high percentage of the total work on the Site. However, if the work is more evenly divided between two or more Contractors it is necessary to review provisions of the Contract.

2. 6   Employer's Financial Arrangements

The Employer shall submit, within 28 days after receiving any request from the Contractor, reasonable evidence that financial arrangements have been made and are being maintained which will enable the Employer to pay the Contract Price (as estimated at that time) in accordance with Clause 14 [Contract Price and Payment]. If the Employer intends to make any material change to his financial arrangements, the Employer shall give notice to the Contractor with detailed particulars.

Sub-Clause 2. 4 is a new provision which could be reassuring to Contractors. The Sub-Clause requires the Employer to provide evidence that he has the finance available to pay the Contractor in accordance with the Contract. The evidence must be provided within 42 days of a request by the Contractor. If the project is financed by an international development agency or similar organization then it may be advisable to state this fact in the Particular Conditions to reassure tenderers and avoid the subsequent request. Any representative of the finance institution could then be declared as Employer's Personnel and visit the Site if necessary.

If the Employer fails to comply with this Sub-Clause then the Contractor can give 21 day' notice to suspend work, or reduce the rate of work, under Sub-Clause 16. 1, If he does not receive reasonable evidence within 42 days of giving notice under Sub-Clause 16. 1, then he is entitled to terminate the Contract under Sub-Clause 16. 2. The procedures of Sub-Clauses 16. 3 and 16. 4 will then apply.

The protracted time periods are necessary to give the Employer a reasonable time to make arrangements and satisfy the Contractor. However, they make a total period of 105 days or three and a half months from the initial request to the entitlement to terminate the Contract. During this period the Contractor may have spent substantial sums of money on the Contract, perhaps with little chance of recovery.

The Sub-clause is not clear as to who provides the estimate of the Contract Price and what would constitute reasonable evidence. If the Contractor has already submitted claims, which have been rejected by the Engineer, then they may have very different estimates of the figure which should be taken as the estimated Contract Price. The matter of what constitutes reasonable evidence will depend on the circumstances and could require a statement from the bank, financing authority, Ministry of Finance, or whoever is providing the finance for the project. A payment guarantee by the Employer, on the standard form at Annex G at the back of the FIDIC document, would presumably meet the requirement. The consequences that can arise if the Employer fails to comply with the request are so serious that this situation could result in a dispute, which could be referred to the DAB.

☞ **疑难词汇** ☜

1. covenant 订立契约
2. access to 通往，通向
3. be exclusive to 为……所独有
4. proceed in accordance with the programme 根据规划或程序进行工作
5. clarification 澄清（明确）
6. set aside 留出（用于……）
7. excavated materials 挖出物（工程进行中挖出的土石等物）
8. clearance through customs 清关（雇主帮助承包商的进口货物通过海关）
9. give grounds for a claim 为索赔创造条件
10. excessive 过度的，过分的
11. withdraw 收回
12. be reassuring to 可靠的，使……放心的
13. with discretion 谨慎的，慎重的
14. reciprocal co-operation 相互合作

☞ **疑难语句** ☜

1. The Conditions of Contract require the Employer, as distinct from the Engineer, to

take certain actions during the construction period. Even though the Engineer is now classed as "Employer's Personnel" there are some tasks that are allocated to the Employer. Whilst the Employer could delegate the paperwork to the Engineer, particularly if the designated Engineer is an employee of the Employer, the actual tasks require the Employer to be involved.

有别于工程师，合同条件要求雇主在建筑工程施工期间实施一定的行动。虽然工程师被归类为雇主人员，但是仍有一些工作需要雇主来完成。当雇主将书面文字工作委托给工程师的时候，特别是当指定的工程师是雇主雇员时，需要雇主对这些工作承担责任。

2. It is important that the Site area is delineated clearly in the Contract Drawings or Specification.

在合同图纸和规范中清晰地描述（承包商）现场占有是非常重要的。

3. Co-operation and assistance should always be given when possible, but it must be doubtful whether, if the assistance fails to achieve the desired result, this would reduce the Contractor's obligations or give grounds for a claim.

如果有可能，（雇主）会尽力合作与帮助（承包商），但是如果这种帮助没有达到期望的结果，雇主必须确定这是否会减轻承包商的责任，并为索赔创造条件。

☞ 中文综述 ☜

一、雇主的含义

在国际工程实践中，雇主是投资方，也是工程施工合同的招标方和达成合同的承诺方。1987 年版 FIDIC 合同条款比 1977 年版强调了雇主的作用，突出了雇主的权力，特别是在工程管理方面强调了雇主的直接介入权。FIDIC 合同条款（1999 版）在此基础上则是进一步强化了雇主的权力与地位，例如对工程师权力的限制，以及相对于承包商，雇主索赔的非时限性等。

根据 FIDIC "新红皮书"第 1.1.2.2 款规定，雇主（the Employer 或 the Owner）是指工程项目的所有者和拥有者以及其财产的合法继承人。在美国大多称之为 "The Owner"或者 "Building Owner"，指对其工程使用的土地和对地上建筑物拥有所有权的含义，而在英国和其他英语国家的建筑工程领域，雇主被称为 "The Employer"，具有 "雇主"的含义。

二、雇主与承包商及工程师之间的法律关系

1. 雇主与承包商之间的法律关系及利益冲突

雇主和承包商之间是互相合作、互相监督的合同法律关系。合同是一种民事法律行为，其基本特征之一便是行为主体的法律地位平等。在合同中，合同双方的权利和义务是互为前提条件的，雇主的义务是提供施工的外部条件及支付工程款，这是承包商享有的权利；承包商的义务是按合同规定的工期及质量要求对工程项目进行施工、竣工及修复缺陷，这是雇主享有的权利。在施工过程中，雇主一般不直接与承包商接触，而是通过工程师来下达指令、行使权力、管理工程的。但是，作为施工合同的主体，雇主和承包商必然行使最终权利。当双方发生争端时，工程师可以调解，调解不成而履行仲裁和诉讼程序时，工程师的意见只具有一般的参考价值。

作为合作者，雇主和承包商在各自利益方面又是对立的两方。雇主希望以最少的成本获得最大的工程价值，而承包商既要完成项目，又要争取最大效益。承包商的行为会对雇主构成风险，雇主的行为也会威胁承包商的利益，双方利益冲突的结果就是索赔和反索赔行为的产生。如果雇主违约，承包商可以降低施工速度或中止工程，提出索赔，甚至撤销合同。如果承包商违约，雇主可以索赔，可以终止合同，也可以授权其他人去完成工作。

2. 雇主和工程师之间的法律关系

雇主和工程师之间是委托合同法律关系，确切地说是一种雇用关系。雇主聘用工程师代其进行工程管理，工程师的任务和职权是由雇主与承包商之间签订的施工合同及雇主与工程师签订的监理服务合同两种文件确定的。工程师在行使工程管理的监理权时，是雇主的代理人，应维护雇主的利益。工程师的良好服务，能为雇主带来巨大的利益：如工程师对承包商完成的工程量进行严格地计量和审核、控制变更工程和额外工程费用、处理索赔事宜等工作，能直接降低工程成本；工程师促使承包商按时或提前完工，能使工程项目早日产生效益；工程师严格控制质量，能使工程的未来维护费用、运行费用降低；工程师提出的改进建议能节省投资等。

三、雇主的主要权利

1. 雇主任命工程师的权利

在工程管理实践中，大多数投资人或开发商并不具备丰富的工程管理经验。在确定由哪个承包商承建工程前，发现一个有工程设计和管理经验的工程师，并得到其帮助是必不可少的。因此，聘用工程师代理雇主管理和监督承包商的工作是十分必要的。任命工程师是雇主在 FIDIC 合同条款中的基本权利。根据 FIDIC 合同条款（1999 版）第 3.1 款规定："雇主应任命工程师，该工程师应履行合同中赋予他的职责。工程师的人员包括有恰当资格的工程师以及其他有能力履行上述职责的专业人员。"

2. 雇主发布指示的权利

为了使工程按期完工，雇主有权向承包商发布指示、任命、信息、计划和细节。如需要，雇主或雇主代表或其代理人，如建筑师或工程师必须在适当的时间内向承包商发出指示，以使承包商能够履行合同义务。如果合同没有明确规定发布指示的时间，则雇主应在合理的时间内发出指示。合理时间取决于合同的明示规定或具体情况，但并不单独取决于承包商的方便和金钱利益。另一方面，除非合同另有规定，否则，如果雇主未能在适当的时间内签发施工所需的计划、图纸和其他信息，则雇主的行为构成了违约。

3. 雇主指定分包商的权利

FIDIC 合同条款规定，雇主有指定分包商（Nominated Subcontractor）的权利。

四、雇主的主要义务

1. 安排承包商进入现场的义务

提供承包商现场占有权是雇主的一项主要义务。关于"占有"的定义，对承包商而言，"占有"是指允许承包商占有现场，直至项目竣工日期为止。在项目竣工时，这种许可将终止。进入现场（access to site）具有多重含义，可以指进入现场区域的方式和可能性，也可以指占有现场的能力。进入现场意味着允许承包商的人员、设备、材料、车辆、服务能够到达现场区域，履行施工合同项下的义务。为了有效地进入现场，应允许承包商采用各种运输方式，并且雇主必须准备妥当，使现场具备进入的条件。

　　FIDIC"新红皮书"第2.1款规定：雇主应在投标函附录中注明的时间（或各时间段）内给予承包商进入和占用现场所有部分的权利。此类进入和占用权可不为承包商独享。如果合同要求雇主赋予（承包商）对基础、结构、永久设备或通行手段的占用权，则雇主应在规范注明的时间内按照规定的方式履行该职责。但是在收到履约保证之前，雇主可以不给予任何此类权利或占用。如果投标函附录中未注明时间，则雇主应在合理的时间内给予承包商进入现场和占用现场的权利，此时间应能使承包商可以按照第8.3款〔进度计划〕提交的进度计划顺利开始施工。

　　2. 合作义务

　　合作是雇主的另一项义务。在每一个建筑和土木工程施工合同中，雇主应尽一切必要的努力使工程得以完成，这是合同的一项默示条款。在FIDIC合同条款中，很多条款都体现了这一原则。例如第3.1款规定，工程师可行使合同中明确规定的或必然隐含的赋予他的权力。如果要求工程师在行使其规定权力之前需获得雇主的批准，则此类要求应在合同专用条件中注明。雇主不能对工程师的权力加以进一步限制，除非与承包商达成一致。又如，第5.2款关于承包商对指定分包商的反对也体现了雇主与承包商的合作义务。

　　3. 资金安排义务

　　资金是工程项目的血液，资金安排不充分会直接影响工程项目的顺利进行，也会导致索赔或纠纷的产生。FIDIC合同条款第2.4款对雇主的资金安排进行了明示规定如下："在收到承包商的任何要求后的28天内，雇主应提交其已做的并将予以保持的资金安排的合理证据，以便雇主有能力按照第14条〔合同价格和付款〕的规定，支付合同价格（按当时估算）。如雇主拟对其资金安排作出任何重要的变更，应将有关变更细节通知承包商。"

　　4. 支付义务

　　支付或许诺支付是雇主的一项最重要的义务。施工合同的本质是承包商实施工程项目，而雇主为此支付工程价款。施工合同的性质不同，支付方式也有所不同。FIDIC"新红皮书"第14.7款规定，雇主应向承包商支付：

　　（1）首期预付款，支付时间在中标函颁发后42天，或在收到按照第4.2款〔履约担保〕和第14.2款〔预付款〕规定提交的文件后21天，二者中较晚的日期内；

　　（2）各期中付款证书确认的金额，支付时间在工程师收到报表和证明文件后56天内；

　　（3）最终付款证书确认的金额，支付时间在雇主收到该付款证书后56天内。

　　每种货币的应付款额应汇入合同（为此货币）指定的付款国境内的承包商指定的银行账户。

　　5. 帮助承包商获得许可的义务

　　帮助承包商获得开工许可是雇主的一项重要义务。一般而言，在申请只有雇主才能获得的有关许可时，雇主应积极承担获得许可的义务和责任。在需要承包商获得有关许可时，雇主负有协助承包商获得许可的义务。FIDIC"新红皮书"第2.2款规定：雇主应根据承包商的请求，为以下事宜向承包商提供合理的协助（如果他的地位能够做到），以帮助承包商：①获得与合同有关的但不易取得的工程所在国的法律的副本，以及②申请法律所要求的许可、执照或批准，包括（ⅰ）依据第1.13款〔遵守法律〕要求承包商必须获得的，（ⅱ）为了货物的运送，包括清关所需的，以及（ⅲ）当承包商的设备运离现场而出口时所需的。

6. 披露信息的义务

FIDIC "新红皮书"、"新黄皮书"和"银皮书"中的多项条款对雇主披露信息的义务作了明示规定，主要包括：

（1）文件的照管和提供。对文件中的错误或缺陷，确保文件文字的准确。

（2）雇主的资金安排。资金安排应能确保工程项目建设的顺利进行，任何资金安排的变动，对于承包商都有着重大的影响。因此，资金安排的任何变更都需要进行信息披露，使相关利益者及时掌握。

（3）雇主的索赔。雇主对其他合同主体提出的索赔，应披露索赔细节。

（4）工程师的替换。更换工程师的细节需要披露。

（5）现场数据。主要包括地质、水文、环境等数据的披露。

（6）完成扫尾工作和修补。主要包括缺陷通知期内缺陷信息的披露。

（7）修补缺陷的费用。主要包括非承包商自费负责的缺陷、未能修补缺陷的日期信息披露。

（8）雇主终止。雇主有终止合同的权利，但对终止的原因应进行披露。

（9）知识产权和工业产权。对侵犯知识产权和工业产权的事件进行披露。

（10）不可抗力的通知。对不可抗力事件的具体情况进行披露，对因不可抗力实际引发的终止合同事宜进行披露。

（11）取得争议裁决委员会的决定。对不满争议裁决委员会的决定进行披露。

Questions

1. What are relationships between the Employer and the Engineer?

2. Describe the contractor's rights of access to the Site?

Chapter 3   The Engineer

3. 1   Introduction

The Engineer is defined at FIDIC Sub-Clause 1. 1. 2. 4 as the person appointed by the Employer and named in the Appendix to Tender. Under the introductory paragraph to Sub-Clause 1. 1 the word person can mean a company, so the Engineer may be named as a firm of Consulting Engineers rather than an individual. If the Engineer is a company then the company should designate an individual to carry out the role of the Engineer. Alternatively, the Engineer may be an individual or a member of the Employer's own staff. If the Employer wishes to change the Engineer from the person named in the Appendix to Tender then he must follow the procedures of Sub-Clause 3. 4.

One of the most important changes from the FIDIC Fourth Edition to the FIDIC Conditions of Contract for construction (1999) is in the role of the Engineer. The (1987) FIDIC Fourth Edition required the Engineer to exercise his discretion impartially within the terms of the Contract and having regard to all the circumstances. The 1999 Conditions stated that the Engineer shall be deemed to act for the Employer, but, when he is making a decision under Sub-Clause 3. 5, shall make a fair determination in accordance with the Contract, taking due regard of all relevant circumstances. Whether this change means that the Engineer would make a different decision on any particular claim and the extent to which this change of role will influence the Engineer when he is making decisions will emerge in time. The Engineer must also remember that any decision can be overruled by the DAB within a very short period of time. A series of adverse decisions by the DAB may cause an Employer to question the competence of the Engineer.

Furthermore, the previous FIDIC Contracts had a clear distinction between the tasks and procedures that are the duty of the Engineer and those that are matters for the Employer. The 1999 Conditions have omitted the requirement that some notices which are sent to the Engineer must be copied to the Employer. However, the distinction has been maintained in other provisions, although some of these are likely in practice to be carried out by the Engineer now that he is deemed to act for the Employer.

3. 2   Engineer's Duties and Authority

The Employer shall appoint the Engineer who shall carry out the duties assigned to him in the Contract. The Engineer's staff shall include suitably qualified engineers and other professionals who are competent to carry out these duties.

The Engineer shall have no authority to amend the Contract.

The Engineer may exercise the authority attributable to the Engineer as specified in or necessarily to be implied from the Contract. If the Engineer is required to obtain the approval of the Employer before exercising a specified authority, the requirements shall be as stated in the Particular Conditions. The Employer undertakes not to impose further constraints on the Engineer's authority, except as agreed with the Contractor.

However, whenever the Engineer exercises a specified authority for which the Employer's approval is required, then (for the purposes of the Contract) the Employer shall be deemed to have given approval.

Except as otherwise stated in these Conditions:

(a) whenever carrying out duties or exercising authority, specified in or implied by the Contract, the Engineer shall be deemed to act for the Employer;

(b) the Engineer has no authority to relieve either Party of any duties, obligations or responsibilities under the Contract; and

(c) any approval, check, certificate, consent, examination, inspection, instruction, notice, proposal, request, test, or similar act by the Engineer (including absence of disapproval) shall not relieve the Contractor from any responsibility he has under the Contract, including responsibility for errors, omissions, discrepancies and noncompliances.

The Engineer has an extremely important role in the administration of the Contract and the way in which he carries out his duties will have a major impact on the work of the Contractor and the success of the project.

The Particular Conditions must include details of any requirements for the Engineer to obtain the Employer's approval before exercising any authority which is given to him under the Contract. When writing the Particular Conditions it is important that the Employer considers the implications on the whole sequence of project management events and does not just consider isolated Sub-Clauses. This Sub-clause recognizes that having to obtain such approval is a constraint on the Engineer's authority and his freedom to make fair decisions. Any additional constraint imposed on the Engineer after the Contract has been agreed would be a breach of Contract by the Employer, for which the Contractor would be entitled to claim damages.

The approvals that are required will vary dependent on whether the Engineer is an independent consultant or a member of the Employer's own staff. An Engineer who is a member of the Employer's staff may have limits on his authority such that additional expenditure, or certifying payment, requires approval from a senior person or a different department. If a named individual is the Engineer any limits on his authority must be stated. A consultant working for a private Employer may have been given the necessary authority, but a consultant working for a Government Employer will probably have limits placed on his authority. The Contractor does not see the contract between the Engineer and the Employer so a clear statement of his authority is essential.

Approval could reasonably be required before issuing variations under Clause 13 which would involve changes to the design or result in additional cost greater than a designated figure. Some Employers require the Engineer to obtain approval before certifying any additional cost or extension of time. However, under Sub-Clause 3. 5, the Engineer is required to consult with the Employer before making a fair determination in accordance with the Contract on a claim for time or money. To require approval of the action after this consultation would imply that the Employer may wish to prevent the Engineer from giving a determination based on his technical and contractual assessment of the claim.

In accordance with Sub-Clause 3. 1 (a) the Engineer is deemed to act for the Employer except as otherwise stated in these Conditions. However, it is not clear which Sub-Clauses comply with this otherwise stated exception. Several Sub-Clauses, such as Sub-Clause 3. 5 and the payment provisions require the Engineer to be fair and it must be assumed that he will always act in accordance with the requirements of the Contract. Furthermore, whether acting for the Employer or under Sub-Clause 3. 5 he will presumably discuss any approval, certificate or action with the Employer if he wishes to obtain the Employer's point of view before deciding what action to take.

A problem will arise if the Employer persuades the Engineer to take some action which is clearly against the provisions of the Contract. This situation would be exposed if a dispute is referred to the DAB and their decision so clearly contradicts the action of the Engineer that no reasonable Engineer could have been expected to act in that way.

3. 3　Delegation by the Engineer

The Engineer may from time to time assign duties and delegate authority to assistants, and may also revoke such assignment or delegation. These assistants may include a resident engineer, and/or independent inspectors appointed to inspect and/or test items of Plant and/or Materials. The assignment, delegation or revocation shall be in writing and shall not take effect until copies have been received by both Parties. However, unless otherwise agreed by both Parties, the Engineer shall not delegate the authority to determine any matter in accordance with Sub-Clause 3. 5 [Determinations].

Assistants shall be suitably qualified persons, who are competent to carry out these duties and exercise this authority, and who are fluent in the language for communications defined in Sub-Clause 1. 4 [Law and language].

Each assistant, to whom duties have been assigned or authority has been delegated, shall only be authorized to issue instructions to the Contractor to the extent defined by the delegation. Any approval, check, certificate, consent, examination, inspection, instruction, notice, proposal, request, test, or similar act by an assistant, in accordance with the delegation, shall have the same effect as though the act had been on act of the Engineer. However:

(a) any failure to disapprove any Work, Plant or Materials shall not constitute approval, and shall therefore not prejudice the right of the Engineer to reject the Work, Plant or Materials;

(b) if the Contractor questions any determination or instruction of an assistant, the Contractor may refer the matter to the Engineer, who shall promptly confirm, reverse or vary the determination or instruction.

The Engineer, either as an individual or a designated member of a company, will require assistance to carry out all the duties assigned to him under the Contract. Details of the delegation must be sent in writing to both parties. If a company designated as Engineer then all the individuals who will be exercising authority by checking or instructing the Contractor, as Engineer or as assistance to the Engineer, should be named and their authority confirmed.

FIDIC conditions of contract included specific reference to the "Engineer's Representative", who was normally resident on the Site, acted as the representative of the Engineer and to whom most of the daily administration was delegated. Reference to this position has now been deleted and seems to be replaced by the phrase " These assistants may include a resident engineer". The implication is that the Engineer no longer needs a deputy who is permanently on the Site. Possibly the Engineer himself is expected to spend more time on the Site and so be able to supervise the work of a number of assistants to whom particular duties have been delegated. This would mean that the Engineer would be a less senior person within his organization. Sub-Clause 4. 3 requires the Contractor to designate a Contractor's Representative who will be employed full time on the Contract, so it would be logical for the Engineer to designate someone to act as resident engineer on the Site.

In practice, for a major project, the Engineer will need a large team of engineers, inspectors and other specialists. A detailed organization chart should be issued to the Contractor at the start of the project and updated whenever there are changes in personnel. All such people are designated by definition as Employer's Personnel.

3. 4　Instructions of the Engineer

The Engineer may issue to the Contractor (at any time) instructions and additional or modified Drawings which may be necessary for the execution of the Works and the remedying of any defects, all in accordance with the Contract. The Contractor shall only take instructions from the Engineer, or from an assistant to whom the appropriate authority has been delegated under this Clause. If an instruction constitutes a Variation, Clause 13 [Variations and Adjustments] shall apply.

The Contractor shall comply with the instructions given by the Engineer or delegated assistant, on any matter related to the Contract. Whenever practicable, their instructions shall be given in writing. If the Engineer or a delegated assistant:

(a) gives an oral instruction,

(b) receives a written confirmation of the instruction, from (or on behalf of) the individuals who will be exercising authority by checking or the Contractor, within two working days after giving the instruction, and

(c) does not reply by issuing a written rejection and/or instruction within two working days after receiving the confirmation; then the confirmation shall constitute the written instruction of the Engineer or delegated assistant (as the case may be).

The Engineer, either as an individual or a designated member of a delegated assistant will require assistance to carry out all the duties assigned to him under the Contract. Details of the delegation must be sent in writing to both Parties.

Sub-Clause 3.3 requires the Contractor to comply with any instruction from the Engineer, or an assistant to whom authority has been delegated under Sub-Clause 3.2, with a procedure for the confirmation of oral instructions. If the Contractor considers that an instruction will result in additional Costs or delay to completion then he should confirm receipt as a Variation, in accordance with Sub-Clause 13.3.

The Sub-Clause gives the Engineer the power to issue additional or modified Drawings. This is an important power because many Contracts under the FIDIC Conditions of Contract rely on a very small number of Drawings in the Tender documents. The majority of the detailed Drawings are issued as and when required during construction. It is for the Engineer to ensure that the Drawings are issued to suit the progress requirements and he will rely on the Contractor's programme as Sub-Clause 8.3, the monthly progress reports as Sub-Clause 4.21, information on any design which is the responsibility of the Contractor as Sub-Clauses 4.1 (a) and (b) and any requests from the Contractor as Sub-clause 1.9.

3.5   Replacement of the Engineer

If the Employer intends to replace the Engineer, the Employer shall, not less than 42 days before the intended date of replacement, give notice to the Contractor of the name, address and relevant experience of the intended replacement Engineer. The Employer shall not replace the Engineer with a person against whom the Contractor raises reasonable objection by notice to the Employer, with supporting particulars.

The Employer is entitled to change the Engineer provided he gives 42 days' notice with details of the proposed replacement. However, a change to the named individual, when the Engineer is a company, does not require this notification, although reasonable notice and discussion would assist in efficient administration. The Employer does not have to give any reason for the change, but should take into account that to change the Engineer will have serious consequences for the administration of the Contract, whether the change is made at the start or during the progress of the Works.

The 42 day notice period must be considered in relation to the other time periods stated in the Conditions of Contract. For example, at the start of the project, if the Employer gave notice in the Letter of Acceptance, the Engineer named in the Appendix to Tender would still be obliged to give the notice of the Commencement Date, unless the 42 days stated at Sub-Clause 8.1 had been changed in the Particular Conditions. Similarly, whenever the notice is given, the original Engineer will issue at least one monthly Interim Payment Certificate under Sub-Clause 14.6 during the notice period. A change of Engineer could also mean changes to the resident engineer and other assistants appointed under Sub-Clause 3.2. The Contractor should indicate as quickly as possible whether he intends to object to the replacement Engineer so that the 42 day period can be used as a changeover period as well as a notice period. If the Engineer should die, or otherwise cease to be available, then the notice period should be waived, by agreement between the Parties.

3.6 Determinations

Whenever these Conditions provide that the Engineer shall proceed in accordance with this Sub-Clause 3.5 to agree or determine any matter, the Engineer shall consult with each Party in an endeavour to reach agreement. If agreement is not achieved, the Engineer shall make a fair determination in accordance with the Contract, taking due regard of all relevant circumstances.

The Engineer shall give notice to both Parties of each agreement or determination, with supporting particulars. Each Party shall give effect to each agreement or determination unless and until revised under Clause 20 [Claims, Disputes and Arbitration]. Throughout the Conditions of Contract, whenever the Contractor submits a claim for an extension of time or reimbursement of costs, the Engineer is required to proceed in accordance with Sub-Clause 3.5. This Sub-Clause requires the Engineer to consult with each Party in an endeavour to reach agreement. To comply with this requirement the Engineer must act as a mediator and try to help the Parties towards agreement.

If agreement is not achieved, the Engineer must make a fair determination in accordance with the Contract, taking due regard of all relevant circumstances. The key phrase here is "in accordance with the Contract". The determination must express the rights and obligations of the Parties, in accordance with the Contract and the applicable law, regardless of the preferences of either Party. Under Sub-Clause 3.2 the Engineer cannot delegate this task without the agreement of both Parties. This Sub-Clause does not impose a time limit on the Engineer for making his determination, but the situation would be covered by the requirement of Sub-Clause 1.3 that a determination "shall not be unreasonably withheld".

The FIDIC Guidance for the Preparation of Particular Conditions includes an example

Sub-Clause for either the Engineer or the Contractor's representative to call a management meeting. This is a very useful provision and should be included in any FIDIC Contract. A definition of "Management Meeting" should be added to Sub-Clause 1.1.6. FIDIC procedures rely on the exchange of notices and written information whereas from a practical project management point of view a meeting to discuss a problem is far more effective than an exchange of paperwork. Whilst most Contractors and Engineers arrange meetings when necessary without any provision in the Contract there may be occasions when a contractual provision is required. The FIDIC suggested wording is as follows: The Engineer or the Contractor's Representative may require the other to attend a management meeting in order to review the arrangements for future work. The Engineer shall record the business of management meetings and supply copies of the record to those attending the meeting and to the Employer. In the record, responsibilities for any actions to be taken shall be in accordance with the Contract.

The purpose of the Sub-Clause is presumably to encourage good management procedures and enable the Contractor to demand a meeting to discuss an important problem or proposal. Management meetings would be particularly useful in a claim situation or to prevent a claim developing into a serious conflict. When the Contractor gives an initial notice of a potential claim situation, a management meeting could serve as an early warning meeting at which the Engineer and the Contractor could discuss alternative ways to avoid or overcome a problem.

If the Engineer wants the Contractor to attend a meeting, for any purpose, then he has always been able simply to tell the Contractor to do so. The significance of this provision is that it enables the Contractor to require the Engineer to attend a meeting. The right for the Contractor to demand a meeting is an extremely useful provision and could help to solve potential problems. For a management meeting to serve its purpose, it will need to be held immediately the need arises so the Engineer should delegate the duty of attending any such meeting to his Resident Engineer.

The most likely reason for the Contractor to wish to discuss the arrangements for future work is that he is aware of some potential problem and wants to discuss the options available to avoid or minimize delay or additional cost. For example, if the Contractor gives notice under Sub-Clause 8.3 of specific probable future events or circumstances which may adversely affect the work, increase the Contract Price or delay the execution of the Works, then it is likely that to avoid or reduce the effect of the problem will require action from the Engineer as well as from the Contractor. Similarly, many of the situations which lead to a reference to the Engineer under Sub-Clause 3.5 might be avoided or the consequences reduced by a meeting held when the problem was first reported.

The final sentence of this additional FIDIC Sub-Clause, referring to responsibilities for any actions to be taken, is confusing and difficult to understand, and could be omitted. Sub-Clause 3.1 is clear that the Engineer has no authority to amend the Contract, so it is difficult to see how the minutes of a meeting could impose responsibilities that are not in accordance with the Contract.

☞ 疑难词汇 ☜

1. discretion 自由裁量权

2. impartially 公平地，无私地

3. competence 能力，胜任

4. discrepancies and noncompliances 差异与不服从

5. additional expenditure 附加费用，追加支出

6. designated figure 指定的（协议中约定的）成本

7. revoke 撤回

8. revocation 废除，取消

9. take effect 生效，起作用

10. prejudice 损害，侵害

11. changeover period 转换期间

12. give effect to 实行，使生效

13. mediator 调停者，调解人

14. regardless of the preferences of either Party 不必考虑（合同）任一方的喜好

15. shall not be unreasonably withheld 不能无原因的审而不决

16. to call a management meeting 召开管理会议

☞ 疑难语句 ☜

1. The Engineer has an extremely important role in the administration of the Contract and the way in which he carries out his duties will have a major impact on the work of the Contractor and the success of the project.

工程师在合同管理过程中有很重要的作用，它履行职责的方式直接影响承包商的工作和项目的进展。

2. When writing the Particular Conditions it is important that the Employer considers the implications on the whole sequence of project management events and does not just consider isolated Sub-Clauses.

当书写特殊条款时，雇主必须在全盘考虑项目管理细节基础上确认条款的含义，而不仅仅是个别条款的含义。

3. The approvals that are required will vary dependent on whether the Engineer is an independent consultant or a member of the Employer's own staff. An Engineer who is a member of the Employer's staff may have limits on his authority such that additional expenditure, or certifying payment, requires approval from a senior person or a different department.

这种批准将根据工程师是独立的咨询师还是雇主的雇员有所不同。作为雇主雇员的工程师，他的权利将受到限制，例如额外的费用、验证付款、需要雇主的高级雇员或不同的部门批准。

4. A problem will arise if the Employer persuades the Engineer to take some action which is clearly against the provisions of the Contract. This situation would be exposed if a dispute is referred to the DAB and their decision so clearly contradicts the action of the Engineer that no reasonable Engineer could have been expected to act in that way.

如果雇主劝说工程师做一些与合同约定相违背的行为将会产生一定的问题。这种情况在纠纷提交争端裁决委员会解决时将会暴露，这种与工程师行为相矛盾的决定是没有工程师愿意做的。

5. FIDIC procedures rely on the exchange of notices and written information whereas from a practical project management point of view a meeting to discuss a problem is far more effective than an exchange of paperwork.

FIDIC 工作程序是通知和书面文件的交换，然而从项目管理实践的角度出发，对问题以会议形式进行讨论的效率要远远高于文字工作的交换。

☞ 中文综述 ☜
一、工程师的含义

工程师（the Engineer），又称监理工程师或咨询工程师，是指由雇主聘任代表雇主对承包商实施的工程项目进行质量、进度、工艺和成本等监督管理的，具有一定资质和专业技术的公司或个人。同时根据 FIDIC "新红皮书" 的规定，工程师也是工程项目的设计者，受雇主委托，负责工程项目的规划和设计。FIDIC "新红皮书" 第 1.1.2.4 款规定工程师的定义是："工程师指雇主为合同目的而指定作为工程师并在招标附录中保持这一称谓的人员；或者雇主根据第 3.4 款随时指定的并通知承包商的任何其他人员。" 在 AIA、NEC 等合同文本中，工程师也被称为建筑师（Architect），其职能与 FIDIC 中的 Engineer 基本一致。

二、工程师的地位

在 FIDIC 合同条款中，工程师的角色十分重要，工程师是 FIDIC 工程项目管理的核心，工程师代表雇主在施工现场工作，对承包商的工作行使决定、指示、监督等权力。因此，工程师的地位是多重的，主要表现在：

1. 工程师是中间人

工程师可以是独立个人，或咨询公司，或是雇主机构中任命的有关职员，但其地位和作用均相同，都是根据合同条款的有关规定，对项目进行具体的合同管理、费用控制、进度跟踪和组织协调。FIDIC 合同的框架关系是基于雇主、工程师与承包商之间的 "三位一体"。工程师虽然在 FIDIC 合同条款上签字，但在法律上并不是施工合同的当事人，处于雇主与承包商之间的中间人地位。尽管工程师受雇于雇主，但是，根据 FIDIC 精神，为了项目实施，工程师更多以中间人的角色，根据合同条款作出自己的客观判断，行使法律中准仲裁员的权利。当然，如果合同双方中有一方不受工程师决定的约束，则可以根据合同条款规定，将争端的解决付诸 DAB。

2. 工程师是设计者

FIDIC "新红皮书" 属于单价合同，前提是工程师负责为雇主做好全部永久工程的设计并列出有关的工程数量清单，而承包商只是进行一些临时工程和施工详图的设计。雇主根据自己的建设意图及资金筹措情况，在决定实施项目后提出设计任务书，一般通过招标选择设计者。设计阶段的工作优劣对于控制整个项目的投资规模及经济性影响很大。工程师应该在充分满足工程需求的条件下，认真进行技术经济比较，优化设计。这时，设计者的唯一任务是为雇主服务，因为此时尚无第三方的介入。

3. 工程师是施工监理

"新红皮书"的主要特点之一就是确定了工程师对施工项目的管理和监理的权力。这里工程师的施工监理作用是指监督管理承包商，控制承包商在施工过程中履行合同的情况，以及在可能的条件下对雇主与承包商进行必要的调解工作。如果承包商对于工程师的指示不能作出有效反应，则工程师有权根据合同提出警告、强迫执行，甚至对承包商违约进行制裁。

4. 工程师是准仲裁员

1987 年第四版 FIDIC 合同条款第 67 条［争端的解决］的仲裁过程分为四步：记录争端、准仲裁、友好解决、正式仲裁即最终裁决。当雇主与承包商意见不一时，首先是异议一方根据［争端的解决］的规定向工程师书面记录争端，并要求其作出准仲裁决定。工程师一般是在听取其法律顾问的建议后，对有关争端其作出准仲裁决定。在 1999 年"新红皮书"中，工程师的仲裁权利受到了限制，其仲裁权被 DAB 争端裁决委员会所取代，但是，工程师的作用和地位仍然是十分重要的。

5. 工程师是雇主的代理人

雇主支付报酬给工程师，工程师为雇主监督管理工程的施工。从这个意义上说，工程师在施工监理的过程中类似雇主的代理人，是为雇主具体管理项目的"项目经理"。此外，工程师管理合同的权利也受到一定的限制。

三、工程师发布指示的权力

在建筑和土木工程施工合同中，工程师在工程项目中处于核心地位。他必须时时或每天发布指示，监督参与工程项目的众多人员，完成工程项目的实施任务。

所有的施工合同以及标准合同文本都对工程师发布指示的权力作了明示规定。在"新红皮书"中，许多条款都规定了工程师发布指示的明示权力。除了这些明示权力外，按照合同的规定，工程师还需要在遇到各种情况时向承包商发出指示，以便承包商按照指示继续进行施工。

FIDIC "新红皮书"中工程师的指示权力主要包括：

（1）在通信交流方面采用书面形式。

（2）在文件优先次序出现问题时，或文件出现歧义、不一致时，发出必要的澄清或指示。

（3）提供图纸或指示。

（4）合作。指示承包商为现场或附近从事工作的人员提供适当的条件。

（5）放线。主要包括①通知承包商原始基准点、基准线、基准标高；②同意或决定工期延长和增加合同价格；③决定错误是否不能被合理发现。

（6）承包商的设备。同意或否决承包商运走设备。

（7）电、水和燃气。根据第 2.5 款和第 3.5 款同意或决定电、水和燃气费用。

（8）雇主设备和免费供应的材料。根据第 2.5 款和第 3.5 款同意或决定雇主设备的数量和应付金额。

(9) 指定分包商付款证据。发出包含应付指定分包商金额的付款证书前，可要求承包商提供合理的证据，证明承包商已支付了指定分包商的款项。

(10) 工作时间。同意承包商在休息日之外工作。

(11) 开工、延误和暂停。除非工程师在收到进度计划后 21 天内向承包商发出通知，指出其中不符合合同要求的部分，承包商即应按照该进度计划，并遵守合同规定的其他义务，进行工作。雇主人员应有权依照该进度计划安排他们的活动。

(12) 竣工试验。①指示承包商进行竣工试验的时间；②在考虑竣工试验结果时，应考虑到雇主对工程的使用，对工程性能和其他特性的影响；③要求重新进行竣工试验；④对未能通过竣工试验的，有权下令重复进行竣工试验。

(13) 雇主的接收（工程和区段工程的接收）。在收到承包商申请通知后的 28 天内：①颁发接收证书；②拒绝申请，说明理由。

(14) 雇主的接收（部分工程的接收）。①颁发永久工程任何部分的接收证书；②根据第 3.5 款的规定，同意或决定增加费用。

(15) 缺陷责任（进一步试验）。要求重新进行任何试验。

(16) 缺陷责任（承包商调查）。①可要求承包商调查任何缺陷原因；②决定调查费用加合理利润。

(17) 测量和估价（需测量的工程）。①测量工程的任何部分；②准备测量记录；③审查记录，进行确认或更改。

(18) 测量和估价（估价）。①根据确定的测量结果和适当的费率和价格，进行估价，再根据第 3.5 款同意或决定合同价格；②在确定适当费率和价格前，应确定临时费率和价格。

(19) 变更和调整（变更权）。①可通过指示或要求承包商递交建议书的方式，提出变更；②取消、确认或改变原指示。

(20) 变更和调整（变更程序）。①尽快对承包商提出的建议进行批准、不批准或提出意见；②向承包商发出执行每项变更的指示。

(21) 变更和调整（暂定金额）。①指示承包商全部或部分地使用暂定金额；②要求承包商出示报价单、发票、凭证或收据。

(22) 合同价格和付款（临时付款证书的签发）。①在收到有关报表和证明文件后的 28 天内，向雇主发出临时付款证书；②在临时付款证书金额低于最低付款金额时，不予签发临时付款证书，并通知承包商；③可对任何一次付款证书金额进行改正或修改。

(23) 合同价格和付款（保留金的支付）。在颁发接收证书和缺陷责任证书时，确认将保留金支付给承包商。

(24) 承包商的索赔。①在收到索赔通知后，可检查记录保持情况，指示承包商保存进一步的同期记录；②在收到索赔报告或进一步的证明资料后的 42 天内，作出回应，表示同意或不批准并附上具体意见，还可要求承包商提供进一步的资料；③根据第 3.5 款的规定，决定工期延长和（或）增加合同价格。

四、工程师的更换

在 FIDIC 合同条款下，不经承包商同意，雇主不得更换工程师。因为在 FIDIC 合同中，工程师有很大的权力，具有特殊的作用，所以工程师的信誉、工作能力、公正性等，已是承包商投标时必须考虑的重要因素之一。雇主和承包商之间的合同文件规定，凡根据合同在工程师有酌情处理权的时候，工程师在雇主和承包商之间应行为公正，以没有偏见的方式使用合同。当然，承包商应衡量，是否相信雇主的工程师具有独立作出决定的能力。如果工程师不能公正地作出决定，承包商可以通过仲裁和诉讼方式取得合理解决，这时工程师也会处于被动地位。FIDIC"新红皮书"第 3.4 款规定：如果雇主准备撤换工程师，则必须在期望撤换日期 42 天以前向承包商发出通知说明拟替换的工程师的名称、地址及相关经历。如果承包商对替换人选向雇主发出了拒绝通知，并附具体的证明资料，则雇主不能撤换工程师。

五、工程师权力的限制

工程师权力过大，不利于工程师客观公正地开展工作，这也是 FIDIC"新红皮书"设立 DAB，限制工程师权力的真正原因。"新红皮书"有很多条款对工程师的权力作了限制性规定，主要表现为："工程师无权修改合同。工程师可行使合同中规定的或必然默示的属于工程师的权力。如果要求工程师在行使规定的权力之前须取得雇主批准，则应在专用条款中规定这些要求。除非获得承包商的同意，雇主保证不对工程师的权力作出进一步的限制。但是，无论何时，当工程师行使需由雇主批准的规定权力时，则（为合同之目的）应视为雇主已予批准。除本条款另有规定外：

（1）无论何时，当工程师履行或行使合同规定的或默示的任务或权力时，应视为代表雇主执行；

（2）工程师无权解除合同规定的任何职责、义务或责任；

（3）工程师的任何批准、校核、证明、同意、检查、检验、指示、通知、建议、要求、试验或类似行动（包括未表示不批准），不应解除承包商在合同项下应承担的任何责任，包括对错误、遗漏、误差和未能遵守的责任。"根据第 3.1 款的描述，工程师作为雇主代表，他的权力会受到一定的限制，在批准延期、额外费用、签认付款时需要得到雇主的同意。

六、工程师与承包商的法律关系

承包商与工程师之间没有合同，因而不存在合同上的法律关系。但在工程实施中，承包商要时时与工程师打交道，因为雇主是通过工程师来管理工程的。承包商必须接受和遵从工程师的指示，工程师在行使权力时，须经雇主事先批准。承包商无权核实工程师是否已获得此类批准。根据"新红皮书"第 2.1 款可以作如下理解：如果承包商按工程师指示施工增加了费用，那么即使工程师无权对该项工作下达命令，承包商也有权得到该项工作的付款；尽管承包商可能不同意工程师颁发的某项指示，但根据"新红皮书"第 13.1 款规定，他必须执行该指示。由工程师完全承担责任的错误一般是导致了承包商的索赔，如拖延给出图纸、拖延决定时间、错误指令等。

Questions

1. Discuss the instruction right of the Engineer.
2. In what situations the engineer can be replaced?
3. How to define the relationship between the Engineer and Contractor?

Chapter 4　The Contractor

4.1　Introduction

In the Red Book the Contract Agreement confirms that the Contractor will execute and complete the Works and remedy any defects therein, in conformity with the provisions of the Contract. In the Yellow Book the Contract Agreement includes that the Contractor will also design the Works. In order to meet this primary obligation the Contractor accepts a large number of secondary obligations. Clause 4 defines and confirms details of many of these obligations. However, this is not the only Clause which imposes detailed obligations on the Contractor and it must be read in conjunction with the other Clauses in the Conditions of Contract. When unexpected problems and costs occur during the construction of a project the Contractor may submit claims in order to recover Costs. The detailed requirements in Clause 4 are often used to support or respond to these claims.

Clause 4 is the longest and one of the most important clauses in the Contract. Clause 4 Sub-Clauses cover a wide range of subjects and frequently include topics which would not be anticipated from the headings.

4.2　Contractor's General Obligations

The Contractor shall design (to the extent specified in the Contract), execute and complete the Works in accordance with the Contract and with the Engineer's instructions, and shall remedy any defects in the Works.

The Contractor shall provide the Plant and Contractor's Documents specified in the Contract, and all contractor's personnel, goods, consumables and other things and services, whether of a temporary or permanent nature, required in and for this design, execution, completion and remedying of defects.

The Contractor shall be responsible for the adequacy, stability and safety of all Site operations and of all methods of construction. Except to the extent specified in the Contract, the Contractor (i) shall be responsible for all Contractor's Documents, Temporary Works, and such design of each item of Plant and Materials as is required for the item to be in accordance with the Contract, and (ii) shall not otherwise be responsible for the design or specification of the Permanent Works.

The Contractor shall, whenever required by the Engineer, submit details of the arrangements and methods which the Contractor proposes to adopt for the execution of the Works. No significant alteration to these arrangements and methods shall be made without this having previously been notified to the Engineer.

　　The FIDIC Conditions of Contract for Construction are intended to be used for projects with the design provided by the Employer. The Contractor's obligation is to execute and complete the Works and remedy any defects. These overall obligations must be read in conjunction with the requirements of other Clauses, such as to proceed with the Works with due expedition and without delay at Sub-Clause 8.1 and take full responsibility for the care of the Works at Sub-Clause 17.2.

　　The phrase "execute and complete" may seem to be repetitive, but it draws attention to the importance of the procedures at Completion, such as those given at Clauses 8, 9 and 10. The requirement to execute and complete can also give an obligation to complete any item of work which is necessary for total completion of the Works, but which may not have been shown in detail on the Drawings. However, this is an obligation to carry out and complete the Works and the question of whether payment is included in the Accepted Contract Amount is a separate issue.

　　If the Employer requires the Contractor to carry out the design of part of the Permanent Works then the requirement must be specified in the Contract. The obligations and procedures given at subparagraphs (a) to (d) will apply and must be read in conjunction with other Clauses which refer to the same subjects.

　　Care must be taken to co-ordinate the various documents that make up the Contract. Problems often arise when different documents are prepared by different consultants and information on the requirements for the Contractor's design is scattered throughout different technical specifications and other documents.

4. 3　Contractor's Representative

　　The Contractor shall appoint the Contractor's Representative and shall give him all authority necessary to act on the Contractor's behalf under the Contract.

　　Unless the Contractor's Representative is named in the Contract, the Contractor shall, prior to the Commencement Date, submit to the Engineer for consent the name and particulars of the person the Contractor proposes to appoint as Contractor's Representative. If consent is withheld or subsequently revoked, or if the appointed person fails to act as Contractor's Representative, the Contractor shall similarly submit the name and particulars of another suitable person for such appointment. The Contractor shall not, without the prior consent of the Engineer, revoke the appointment of the Contractor's Representative or appoint a replacement.

　　The whole time of the Contractor's Representative shall be given to directing the Contractor's performance of the Contract. If the Contractor's Representative is to be temporarily absent from the Site during the execution of the Works, a suitable replacement person shall be appointed, subject to the Engineer's prior consent, and the Engineer shall be notified accordingly.

The Contractor's Representative shall, on behalf of the Contractor, receive instructions under Sub-Clause 3.3 [Instructions of the Engineer] . The Contractor's Representative may delegate any powers, functions and authority to any competent person, and may at any time revoke the delegation. Any delegation or revocation shall not take effect until the Engineer has received prior notice signed by the Contractor's Representative, naming the person and specifying the powers, functions and authority being delegated or revoked. The Contractor's Representative and all these persons shall be fluent in the language for communications defined in Sub-Clause 1.4 [Law and language] .

The Contract gives onerous requirements for the Contractor's Representative. He must have either been named in the Contract or had his name and particulars submitted to the Engineer before the Commencement date; have received the consent of the Engineer, which can subsequently be revoked; not be removed or replaced without the prior consent of the Engineer; have the authority to act on the Contractor's behalf under the Contract; spend the whole of his time directing the Contractor's performance of the Contract; be on the Site whenever work is in progress, or be replaced by an approved substitute; be fluent in the language for communications stated in the Appendix to Tender; ensure that any delegation is to a competent person, fluent in the language for communications and that the Engineer is notified of any delegation.

The FIDIC Guidance for the Preparation of Particular Conditions includes additional paragraphs for the situation when the Contractor's Representative is required to be fluent in more than one language, or when it would be acceptable to use an interpreter.

The Contractor's Representative is, in effect, the Contractor's equivalent to the Engineer. Some Tender documents specify the required qualifications and experience and that the Contractor's Representative must be named in the Tender. This causes problems when the named person is no longer available at the Commencement Date. However, Sub-Clause 4.3 allows for a named person to be replaced, subject to the Engineer's consent to the replacement.

4.4   Progress Reports

Unless otherwise stated in the Particular Conditions, monthly progress reports shall be prepared by the Contractor and submitted to the Engineer in six copies. The first report shall cover the period up to the end of the first calendar month following the Commencement Date. Reports shall be submitted monthly thereafter, each within 7 days after the last day of the period to which it relates.

Reporting shall continue until the Contractor has completed all work which is known to be outstanding of the completion date stated in the Taking-Over Certificate for the Works.

Each report shall include:

(a) charts and detailed descriptions of progress, including each stage of design (if any), Contractor's Documents, procurement, manufacture, delivery to Site, construction, erection and testing; and including these stages for work by each nominated Subcontractor (as defined in Clause 5 [Nominated Subcontractors]);

(b) photographs showing the status of manufacture and of progress on the Site;

(c) for the manufacture of each main item of Plant and Materials, the name of the manufacturer, manufacture location, percentage progress, and the actual or expected dates of: (i) commencement of manufacture, (ii) Contractor's inspections, (iii) tests, and (iv) shipment and arrival at the Site;

(d) the details described in Sub-Clause 6. 10 [Records of Contractor's Personnel and Equipment];

(e) copies of quality assurance documents, test results and certificates of Materials;

(f) list of notices given under Sub-Clause 2. 5 [Employer's Claims] and notices given under Sub-Clause 20. 1 [Contractor's Claims];

(g) safety statistics, including details of any hazardous incidents and activities relating to environmental aspects and public relations.

The requirement for the Contractor to provide monthly progress reports is a new requirement in the New Red Book, although it has sometimes been included by Employers in the Particular Conditions or Specification. The detailed requirements are onerous and are not just a matter of reporting progress on the Site and elsewhere but include safety statistics, lists of claims and other matters. The Particular Conditions may include further requirements, such as submitting the progress report for discussion at a meeting or replacing the six copies by an electronic submission. However, some of the requirements may not be relevant to a particular project and the format of the report should be agreed at the start of the project.

The report will be a substantial document and must be submitted within seven days from the last day of the relevant month, which means five working days. To meet this requirement the Contractor must record and collect the information during the month, including information from Subcontractors. Most of the information will probably have been recorded by the Contractor as part of his own internal procedures and records to monitor the project so the aim must be to keep records in a form that will meet the requirements of Sub-Clause 4. 21 as well as to satisfy the Contractor's internal procedures. The collection and collation of information from Subcontractors may cause problems for the Contractor.

Some Employers and the building laws of some countries also require Contractors to keep progress and other records; these records should be combined wherever possible. The format of the monthly progress report does not have to be agreed with the Engineer, but some discussion is desirable in order to minimize the work and co-ordinate the format and avoid duplication with other submissions such as the Clause 20. 1 claims records.

The progress report is submitted to the Engineer, but does not have to be approved or agreed by the Engineer. However, the information in the progress reports will undoubtedly be used in support of claims. For example, if figures have not been disputed at the time it may be difficult for the Employer to reject them at a later date. A regular progress meeting to discuss the report would enable the Engineer to raise any points which he wishes to query.

4. 5 Safety Procedures

The Contractor shall:

(a) comply with all applicable safety regulations;

(b) take care for the safety of all persons entitled to be on the Site;

(c) use reasonable efforts to keep the Site and Works clear of unnecessary obstruction so as to avoid danger to these persons;

(d) provide fencing, lighting, guarding and watching of the Works until completion and taking over under Clause 10 [Employer's Taking Over]; and

(e) provide any Temporary Works (including roadways, footways, guards and fences) which may be necessary, because of the execution of the Works, for the use and protection of the public and of owners and occupiers of adjacent land.

Most countries have their own health and safety regulations although the details vary considerably. Paragraph (a) of Sub-Clause 4. 8 requires the Contractor to comply with the local regulations. The Sub-Clause includes safety requirements which may be less onerous, or more onerous, than the local regulations. The requirements for safety may be expanded in the Particular Conditions.

If the Contractor does not have exclusive possession of the Site, as permitted by Sub-Clause 2. 1, then the Particular Conditions should clarify the responsibility for site safety.

4. 6 Sufficiency of the Accepted Contract Amount

The Contractor shall be deemed to:

(a) have satisfied himself as to the correctness and sufficiency of the Accepted Contract Amount; and

(b) have based the Accepted Contract Amount on the data, interpretations, necessary information, inspections, examinations and satisfaction as to all relevant matters referred to in Sub-Clause 4. 10 [Site Data].

Unless otherwise stated in the Contract, the Accepted Contract Amount covers all the Contractor's obligations under the Contract (including those under Provisional Sums, if any) and all things necessary for the proper execution and completion of the Works and the remedying of any defects.

4.7　Unforeseeable Physical Conditions

In this Sub-Clause, conditions means natural physical conditions and man-made and other physical obstructions and pollutants, which the Contractor encounters at the Site when executing the Works, including sub-surface and hydrological conditions but excluding climatic conditions.

If the Contractor encounters adverse physical conditions which he considers to have been Unforeseeable, the Contractor shall give notice to the Engineer as soon as practicable.

This notice shall describe the physical conditions, so that they can be inspected by the Engineer, and shall set out the reasons why the Contractor considers them to be Unforeseeable. The Contractor shall continue executing the Works, using such proper and reasonable measures as are appropriate for the physical conditions, and shall comply with any instructions which the Engineer may give. If an instruction constitutes a Variation, Clause 13 [Variations and Adjustments] shall apply.

If and to the extent that the Contractor encounters physical conditions which are Unforeseeable, gives such a notice, and suffers delay and/or incurs Cost due to these conditions, the Contractor shall be entitled subject to Sub-Clause 20.1 [Contractor's Claims] to:

(a) on extension of time for any such delay, if completion is or will be delayed, under Sub-Clause 8.4 [Extension of Time for Completion]; and

(b) payment of any such Cost, which shall be included in the Contract Price.

After receiving such notice and inspecting and/or investigating these physical conditions, the Engineer shall proceed in accordance with Sub-Clause 3.5 [Determinations] to agree or determine (i) whether and (if so) to what extent these physical conditions were Unforeseeable, and (ii) the matters described in subparagraphs (a) and (b) above related to this extent.

However, before additional Cost is finally agreed or determined under subparagraph (ii), the Engineer may also review whether other physical conditions in similar parts of the Works (if any) were more favourable than could reasonably have been foreseen when the Contractor submitted the Tender. If and to the extent that these more favourable conditions were encountered, the Engineer may proceed in accordance with Sub-Clause 3.5 [Determinations] to agree or determine the reductions in Cost which were due to these conditions, which may be included (as deductions) in the Contract Price and Payment Certificates. However, the net effect of all adjustments under sub-paragraph (b) and all these reductions, for all the physical conditions encountered in similar parts of the Works, shall not result in net reduction in the Contract Price.

Unforeseeable physical conditions are probably the most common source of claims and disputes in construction projects. The definition of physical conditions is wider than might be expected and will include many of the unexpected situations which the Contractor encounters at the Site when executing the Works. It was the Employer who decided to construct the project on this particular Site and designed the project to suit the Site; in principle, the Employer should take responsibility for the consequences of any problem present on his Site. The difficult question is whether a particular problem should have been anticipated and allowed for in the Accepted Contract Amount, or whether the situation could not have been foreseen by an experienced Contractor. The restraints of cost and time referred to at Sub-Clause 14. 10 must be considered in making this assessment.

When a problem arises the Contractor must give a notice as soon as practicable describing the physical conditions. This initial notice may result in the Engineer deciding to issue an instruction for a variation under Clause 13 so the delay and additional costs would be covered by the variation procedures. However, the Contractor may also need to consider notices under other clauses, such as the final two paragraphs of Sub-Clause 8. 3, Sub-Clause 8. 4 for an extension of time, Sub-Clause 13. 2 if he has a Value Engineering proposal, Sub-Clause 19. 2 for Force Majeure, and the notice under Sub-Clause 20. 1 which is essential for any claims.

Under the New Red Book the Contractor is obliged to continue the Works, so an immediate notice followed by prompt action from the Engineer is essential. The Contractor can take such proper and reasonable measures as are appropriate for the physical conditions but, if these measures constitute a Variation, an instruction is required from the Engineer. Clearly there is a potential for misunderstanding and claims, particularly if the Engineer fails to give instructions and the Contractor feels obliged to make decisions as to what action to take.

Having received the Contractor's notices the Engineer will investigate the situation and proceed in accordance with the usual claims procedures at Sub-Clauses 20. 1, 8. 4 and 3. 5.

The FDIC Particular Conditions include a suggested provision for the risk of sub-surface conditions being shared between the Parties. The percentage of the cost which is to be borne by the Contractor would be stated in the Particular Conditions. For this provision to be both fair and workable in practice the Contractor must be given the time and opportunity to carry out investigations at Tender stage.

The potential for technical problems, claims and disputes due to unforeseeable physical conditions, enhanced by any uncertainty at Tender stage, demonstrates the importance of the Employer carrying out a proper investigation before calling Tenders. The value of Site investigation is not just in order to prepare the design, but also to enable the Contractor to prepare a realistic Tender.

☞ **疑难词汇** ☜

1. consumables 消耗品，耗材
2. draws attention to 吸引注意
3. collation 校对
4. quality assurance 质量保证
5. safety statistics 安全统计
6. hazardous incidents 危险事件
7. wherever possible 只要有可能，在任何情况下
8. encounter 遭遇
9. query 询问，表示怀疑
10. sub-surface 地下，次表面
11. hydrological conditions 水文条件，水文状况
12. set out 陈述
13. to the extent that 大意是说，在……意义上说

☞ **疑难语句** ☜

1. The Contractor shall, whenever required by the Engineer, submit details of the arrangements and methods which the Contractor proposes to adopt for the execution of the Works. No significant alteration to these arrangements and methods shall be made without this having previously been notified to the Engineer.

应工程师要求，承包商随时提供其计划完成工作任务的详细安排与方法。在没有事先通知工程师的情况下，任何对于上述安排与方法的重大改变都是被禁止的。

2. Reporting shall continue until the Contractor has completed all work which is known to be outstanding of the completion date stated in the Taking-Over Certificate for the Works.

直到承包商完成所有在完工日没有完成的，并在接收证书里提到的没有完成的工作，承包商将继续向工程师提交（月度工作进展）报告。

3. Some Employers and the building laws of some countries also require Contractors to keep progress and other records; these records should be combined wherever possible. The format of the monthly progress report does not have to be agreed with the Engineer, but some discussion is desirable in order to minimize the work and co-ordinate the format and avoid duplication with other submissions such as the Clause 20.1 claims records.

一些国家的雇主和建筑法律要求承包商持续（提交月度报告）和其他记录，这些记录在可能的范围内应进行结合。月进度报告的格式不一定得到工程师的认可，但是为了减少工作量，协调报告格式和避免与其他文件的重叠，例如 20.1 条规定的索赔记录，一些讨论是必要的。

4. Use reasonable efforts to keep the Site and Works clear of unnecessary obstruction so as to avoid danger to these persons.

通过合理的努力确保现场和工程无障碍，以避免（现场工作人员）的风险。

5. However，before additional Cost is finally agreed or determined under subparagraph (ii)，the Engineer may also review whether other physical conditions in similar parts of the Works (if any) were more favourable than could reasonably have been foreseen when the Contractor submitted the Tender. 然而，根据段落（ii）的规定，在额外费用最终同意和决定前，工程师将检查是否其他现场条件的相似工程部分（如果有）比承包商提交标书时可以合理预测的情况更加顺畅。

☞ 中文综述 ☜

一、承包商概述

FIDIC "新红皮书" 第 1.1.2.3 款对承包商的定义是："承包商是指已为雇主接受的投标信中指明作为承包商的当事人及其财产的合法继承人。"也就是说承包商是指与雇主签订工程合同，负责实施、完成和维护工程项目的当事人。该定义有助于区别分包商和工程师，特别是分包商、供货商的含义。承包商的主要义务就是在合同规定的时间内实施和完成他所签约的工程，如工程有缺陷，有义务在缺陷责任期内修补任何缺陷。

在一些大工程中，分包商还可能将自己承包的工程或工作的一部分再分包出去。此外，分包商也需要材料和设备的供应，也可能租赁设备或委托加工，需要材料和设备的运输，以及劳务。所以分包商本身又有复杂的合同关系。这样就有不同层次、不同种类的合同，这些合同之间存在着复杂的内部联系，它们共同构成了该工程的合同体系。其中工程施工承包合同是最有代表性、最普遍，也是最复杂的合同类型。它在国际工程项目的合同体系中处于主导地位，是整个工程项目合同管理的重点。无论是雇主、监理工程师或承包商都将它作为合同管理的主要对象。所以，为了顺利实现合同中约定的承包商义务，承包商需要建立分包合同、供应合同、运输合同、安装合同、装修合同、租赁合同、劳务合同和保险合同等各种合同法律关系。

二、承包商的主要权利义务

承包商的主要权利是对应雇主的主要义务而设定的，承包商权利的实现需要雇主义务和工程师义务履行的支撑。根据 FIDIC 合同条款规定，承包商的权利有：现场工作时对现场的占有和支配权；要求雇主按照合同约定给予工作协助协调的权利；索赔权；指定分包商不接受权；终止合同权；对义务的例外情况不承担责任权；特定情况下的单独验收和竣工检验权；要求支付的权利。

在施工合同中，承包商的主要义务是按照合同的规定，在特定的时间内完成合同规定的工程项目。所有的标准合同格式都对承包商的主要义务作了十分类似的规定，如 "新红皮书" 第 4.1 款规定的 "承包商应按照合同及工程师的指示，设计（在合同规定的范围内）、实施和完成工程，并修补工程中的任何缺陷。" 承包商违反主要义务即构成违约，雇主可根据合同的规定和有关法律的规定采取终止合同、要求赔偿损失等补救措施。

在建筑和土木工程施工领域，承包商承担了许多合同规定的次要义务，如通知义务、警告义务等。在国际司法实践中，违反次要义务的一方当事人应向另一方当事人支付因其违约而造成他人损失的金钱赔偿。例如，许多标准合同格式规定的误期损害赔偿费的内容，即是违约赔偿的表现。如果合同明确规定了承包商违反次要义务时雇主有权终止合同，则雇主可以在承包商违反次要义务时终止合同。一般来说，承包商的义务可以概括为：实施和完成工程项目的义务；质量义务；进度义务；合作义务；设计义务；警告义务；提供保证、保障和保险义务。

三、承包商代表

承包商应任命承包商代表，并授予他代表承包商根据合同采取行动所需要的全部权力。除非合同中已写明承包商代表的姓名，承包商应在开工日期前，将其拟任命为承包商代表的人员姓名和详细资料提交给雇主，以取得同意。如果未获同意，或随后撤销了同意，或任命的人不能担任承包商代表，承包商应同样地提交另外适合人选的姓名、详细资料，以取得该项任命。未经雇主事先同意，承包商不应撤销承包商代表的任命，或任命任何替代人员。

承包商代表可向任何胜任的人员付托任何职权、任务和权力，并可随时撤销付托。任何付托或撤销，应在雇主收到承包商代表签发的指明人员姓名、并说明付托或撤销的职权、任务和权力的事先通知后生效。承包商代表和所有这些人员应能流利地使用第1.4款［法律和语言］规定的交流语言。

在我国，承包商代表主要是以项目经理部的形式出现，项目经理则是承包商在工地现场的总代表。

四、工程进度计划

"新红皮书"第8.3款规定，承包商在接到开工通知后28天内，应向工程师提交详细的进度计划。当原进度计划与实际进度或承包商的义务不符时，承包商还应提交一份修改的进度计划。每份进度计划应包括以下主要内容：

（1）承包商计划实施工程的次序和顺序，包括设计（如有时）、采购、永久设备的制造、现场运送、施工、安装和试验检测的各个阶段的预期时间节点。

（2）在项目运行的各个阶段需要上报批准的分包商。

（3）合同中规定的现场检查巡视和试验检验的次序和时间。

（4）对实施工程中承包商准备采用的方法和主要阶段的总体描述；各主要阶段现场所需的各等级的承包商人员和各类承包商设备的数量的合理估算的详细说明。

五、放线

工程放线，一般的程序是承包商进场之后由工程师向承包商移交正式的"市政控制点"，此后双方签字确认点位移交。承包商以后所有的工程定位依据都是来自移交的"市政控制点"。"新红皮书"第4.7款规定，承包商应根据合同中规定的或工程师通知的原始基准点、基准线和参照标高对工程进行放线。承包商应对工程各部分的正确定位负责，并且矫正工程的位置、标高、尺寸或准线中出现的任何差错。雇主应对此类给定的或通知的参照项目的任何差错负责，但承包商在使用这些参照项目前应付出合理的努力去证实其准确性。

但是如果因放线差错造成工程差错和费用发生，承包商和雇主应根据第4.7款的规定分担责任：如果由于这些参照项目的差错而不可避免地对实施工程造成了延误和（或）导致了费用发生，而且一个有经验的承包商无法合理发现这种差错并避免此类延误和（或）费用发生，承包商应向工程师发出通知并有权依据第20.1款［承包商的索赔］提出索赔。

六、质量保证

工程是承包商实施完成的，质量的好坏与承包商有着直接的关系。工程质量达到或符合双方约定的质量标准，雇主和承包商都相安无恙。如果质量出现了问题，就必须找到解决问题的办法。为了避免质量问题的发生，"新红皮书"第4.9款作出了约束承包商行为的规定："承包商应按照合同的要求建立一套质量保证体系，以保证符合合同要求。该体系应符合合同中规定的细节。工程师有权审查质量保证体系的任何方面。在每一设计和实施阶段开始之前均应将所有程序的细节和执行文件提交工程师，供其参考。任何具有技术特性的文件颁发给工程师时，必须有明显的证据表明承包商已获得该文件的事先批准。遵守该质量保证体系不应解除承包商依据合同具有的任何职责、义务和责任。"

七、承包商安全保障义务

承包商应保障和保持使雇主、雇主人员以及他们各自的代理人免受以下所有索赔、损害赔偿费，损失和开支（包括法律费用和开支）带来的损害：

（1）任何人员的人身伤害、患病、疾病或死亡，不论是由于承包商设计（如果有）、施工和竣工以及修补任何缺陷引起，或在其过程中，或因其原因产生的，除非是由于雇主、雇主人员或他们各自的任何代理人的任何疏忽、故意行为或违反合同造成的；

（2）由下列情况造成的对任何财产、不动产或动产（工程除外）的损害或损失：

1）由于承包商的设计（如果有）、施工和竣工以及修补任何缺陷引起，或在其过程中，或因其原因产生的；

2）由承包商、承包商人员、他们各自的代理人，或由他们中任何人员直接或间接雇用的任何人员的疏忽、故意行为或违反合同造成的。

雇主应保障和保持承包商、承包商人员以及他们各自的代理人，免受以下所有索赔、损害赔偿费、损失和开支（包括法律费用和开支）带来的损害：①由雇主、雇主人员或他们各自的代理人的任何疏忽、故意行为或违反合同造成的人身伤害、患病、疾病或死亡；以及②第18.3款［人身伤害和财产损害险］（d）项（i）、（ii）和（iii）目中所述的其责任可以不包括在保险范围的各类事项。

八、不可预见的物质条件

FIDIC"新红皮书"规定一个有经验的承包商在提交投标书日期前不能合理预见的风险由雇主承担，该原则是基于招标阶段信息不对称的假设条件。所谓"不可预见"要满足三个条件：一是承包商是"有经验的"；二是以"提交投标书日期"为时限；三是要不能"合理预见"。不可预见性的风险分配方式使投标者在投标时将风险限制在"可预见的"范围内，雇主获得的是仅包括了可预见风险费用的合理的低价标。但产生的问题是，"不可预见"的三个条件中除"提交投标书日期"可以准确界定外，其他两个条件存在着很大程度上的主观性，易使雇主和承包商之间产生争议。

九、现场数据

本条体现了"新红皮书"单价包干合同的特性，在一定程度上只要可行（考虑到费用和时间），承包商应被认为已取得了可能对投标文件或工程产生影响或作用的有关风险、意外事故及其他情况的全部必要的资料。在同一程度上，承包商也被认为在提交投标文件之前已对现场及其周围环境、上述数据及提供的其他资料进行了检查与审核，并对所有相关事宜感到满意，包括（但不限定）：①现场的形状和性质，包括地表以下的条件；②水文及气候条件；③为实施和完成工程以及修补任何缺陷所需工作和货物的范围和性质；④工程所在国的法律、程序和雇佣劳务的习惯做法；以及⑤承包商要求的通行道路、食宿、设施、人员、电力、交通、水及其他服务。

十、承包商设备

承包商设备进场，视为专用于工程。正常情况下，机械设备的进出场地费用要比日常运营费高很多。因此，承包商在安装设备进场时要制订严密的计划，不能随意更换已经进入施工现场的设备。承包商应对所有承包商的设备负责。所有承包商的设备一经运至现场，都应视为专门用于该工程的实施。没有工程师的同意，承包商不得将任何主要的承包商的设备移出现场。但负责将货物或承包商的人员运离现场的运输工具，不必经过同意。

Questions

1. Discuss who is responsible for the cost of unforeseeable physical conditions under the New Red Book?

2. What are the contractor's general responsibilities?

3. How do you define the contractor's representatives?

Chapter 5   The Subcontractors

5. 1   Introduction

Naturally a subcontract is an ancillary contract depending on the existence of a main contract. Both contracts, the Main Contract and the Subcontract, are aimed at achieving the same objective or have a common subset of objectives. Subcontracts may be used for a great variety of services, inter alia: the execution and completion of permanent subcontract works, the design and/or the operation or maintenance of the subcontract works as well as mere supply of goods and materials or combined supply and assembly of equipment and plant. The procurement of subcontracts can be done in parallel to the procurement of the main contract but also much later.

From the point of view of Main Contractors, subcontracts are usually aimed at satisfying two different needs: Firstly, a third person (the Subcontractor) will perform either the whole (if allowed) or parts of the works on behalf of the Main Contractor, being either unable or unwilling to perform the relevant works on its own. In this case, the Main Contractor remains fully liable to the Employer under the main contract for all the actions, inactions or negligence of the Subcontractor. Secondly, the Subcontractor shall not cause detriment to the Main Contractor when performing the works and he should not be allowed or be able to claim more additional money and time under the subcontract than the Main Contractor may recover from the Employer under the main contract. This principle is usually referred to as the back-to-back principle. It may be fleshed out by further elements like pay-when-paid clauses (ensuring that the Main Contractor will be able to finance the Subcontractor from the main contract) and clauses ensuring a coherent and consistent dispute management (related disputes will be dealt with at the same time) .

From the point of view of Subcontractors, subcontracts typically have a limited scope but the subcontract works when completed are required to be fit for purpose under the main contract. Subcontractors are usually paid less than Main Contractors and frequently Subcontractors do not have equal bargaining powers like Main Contractors when entering into the subcontract. Thus, Subcontractors may perceive their engagements being that of a servant of two masters, the Main Contractor and the Employer.

Subcontracts, like all type of contracts, are embedded in the governing law of the contract. Some legal systems provide definitions of subcontracts and dictate (mandatory) statutory terms which must be applied under subcontracts, like French law and Qatar law. It is vitally important that users are aware of such statutory terms, when preparing and/or negotiating subcontracts.

5. 2 Clause 4. 4 Subcontractor (The New Red Book 1999)

The Contractor shall not subcontract the whole of the Works. The Contractor shall be responsible for the acts or defaults of any Subcontractor, his agents or employees, as if they were the acts or defaults of the Contractor. Unless otherwise stated in the Particular Conditions:

(a) the Contractor shall not be required to obtain consent to suppliers of Materials, or to a subcontract for which the Subcontractor is named in the Contract;

(b) the prior consent of the Engineer shall be obtained to other proposed Subcontractors;

(c) the Contractor shall give the Engineer not less than 28 days' notice of the intended date of the commencement of each Subcontractor's work, and of the commencement of such work on the Site; and

(d) each subcontract shall include provisions which would entitle the Employer to require the subcontract to be assigned to the Employer under Sub-Clause 4. 5 [Assignment of Benefit of Subcontract] (if or when applicable) or in the event of termination under Sub-Clause 15. 2 [Termination by Employer].

5. 3 FIDIC Subcontract 2011

In 2011 FIDIC has published the FIDIC Subcontract for Works which goes back-to-back with the FIDIC New Red Book. This new format shall help Contractors being involved in the construction of a project and subcontract parts of the Works to a Subcontractor in a way which avoids unnecessary gaps in the chain of liabilities. The Subcontractor accepts to execute the Subcontract Works as if the Main Contractor would carry out the Works. If he fails to provide his services properly and this results in liability of the Main Contractor the Subcontractor shall hold harmless the Contractor from such liability. Additionally the Subcontractor shall enable the Main Contractor to proceed properly under the Main Contract. Sub-Clause 20. 1 of the Conditions of Subcontract requires the Subcontractor to give all notices and to keep all records which are necessary in order to allow the Main Contractor to comply with the claims clauses under the Main Contract.

The Subcontract is not easy to read. Users should start to study the Subcontract together with the Main Contract. A typical feature of the Subcontract is that it merely refers to a clause under the Main Contract rather than to provide the reader with a full set of information. The parties to the Subcontract shall then read the Main Contract as if it had been changed for the purposes of the Subcontract, for example whenever the Main Contract uses the term "Contractor" then for the purposes of the Subcontract the "Subcontractor" is meant. Words under the Subcontract are used as defined in the Main Contract.

However, there is never a rule without exception. Thus, users should be very careful in reading the Subcontract.

Once the parties to the Subcontract have acquainted themselves with the concepts and the wording they will understand that the General Conditions of Subcontract reflect the Main Contract (Red Book) in terms of the number of Clauses and the numbering of clauses. Thus, the Subcontract incorporates 20 Clauses. The clause headings are similar or the same than under the Main Contract.

The FIDIC Subcontract is intended for use with the FIDIC "Red Book" 1999 edition. The Subcontract is intended to be used when the Red Book is the main contract on a project. The Subcontract is drafted in a way which assumes that all the obligations of the Contractor under the Main Contract are passed down to the Subcontractor via the Subcontract and that the numbering of both the Main Contract and Subcontract are unchanged.

5.4　Main Features of the FIDIC Subcontract

5.4.1　Risk Pass Down

The Subcontract works on the basis that the risks assumed by the Contractor under the Main Contract are passed down to the Subcontractor and the Subcontractor is deemed to have "full knowledge of the relevant provisions of the Main Contract". The Subcontract is therefore drafted on a "back to back" basis with the Main Contract, with the Subcontractor obliged to perform "all the obligations and liabilities of the Contractor under the Main Contract" insofar as relevant to the Subcontract works - albeit with some modifications. For example in relation to the time limits for giving notice in Sub-Clause 20.1, the Subcontractor has a shorter time limit than the corresponding time limit in the Main Contract. This is in order to ensure that the Contractor has sufficient time to receive and process the information from the Subcontractor and still meet the deadline for giving notice to the Employer. There are also stated exceptions to the risk pass down approach. These are listed at Sub-Clause 2.2 of the Subcontract and include the Contractor's obligations in relation to setting out and obtaining permits, licenses and approvals.

5.4.2　Payment

The Subcontractor must submit his draft final statement 28 days after the end of the Subcontractor Defects Notification Period (which is tied into the Defects Notification Period under the Main Contract). The Contractor may require additional information if he is unable to verify any part of the final statement. The Contractor must pay the balance of the Subcontract Price within 56 days after the end of the Subcontractor Defects Notification Period.

The Contractor can defer payments to the Subcontractor if the amount has not been certified by the Engineer or the amount has been certified by the Engineer but not paid by the Employer. He may not do so if the non-certification or non-payment is due to Contractor default or Employer insolvency. FIDIC recognizes that this pay when paid approach may not be consistent with the local law (e. g. the UK HGCRA regime**❶**) and so includes alternative provisions in the Guidance Notes to the Subcontract.

5. 4. 3　Co-operation with other Subcontractors

The Contractor is responsible for the overall co-ordination and project management of the Works and for the co-ordination of the Subcontract Works with the Main Contract Works and the works of any other Subcontractors.

However, these obligations of the Contractor are subject to Sub-Clause 6. 1 which requires the Subcontractor to co-operate with any other Subcontractors. Sub-Clause 6. 1 also provides that if the Subcontractor is delayed or impeded by another Subcontractor he must give notice of this to the Contractor. In these circumstances the Subcontractor may be entitled to an extension of time and payment of any costs incurred.

5. 4. 4　Loss or damage to Subcontract Works

The Subcontractor is by default obliged to rectify all loss or damage to the Subcontract Works during the period when he is responsible for their care. Clause 17 sets out the circumstances for which the Subcontractor is responsible for the cost of that rectification and contains a mechanism whereby the Subcontractor can recover its costs for rectification of loss or damage caused by something for which he is not responsible.

5. 4. 5　Termination

Sub-Clause 15. 1 entitles the Contractor to terminate the Subcontract if the Main Contract is terminated. Other rights of the Contractor to terminate the Subcontract are set out in Sub-Clause 15. 6 and arise if any one or more of the events or circumstances set out in Sub-Clause 15. 2 (a) - (f) of the Main Contract are applicable to the Subcontractor's performance under the Subcontract.

5. 5　Nominated Subcontractors

5. 5. 1　Definition of nominated Subcontractor

In the Contract, nominated Subcontractor means a Subcontractor:

(a) who is stated in the Contract as being a nominated Subcontractor; or

(b) whom the Engineer, under Clause 13 [Variations and Adjustments], instructs

---

❶　UK HGCRA regime : Housing Grants, Construction and Regeneration Act 1996 (HGCRA 1996) which is commonly known as the 'Construction Act', and which is the key piece of legislation in the construction industry. The HGCRA 1996 came into force in 1998, and was amended by the Local Democracy, Economic Development and Construction Act 2009 (LDEDCA 2009) which came into force on 1 October 2011. The HGCRA 1996 applies to all contracts which fall under the statutory definition of a 'construction contract' for 'construction operations' . The HGCRA 1996 provides a statutory framework for making interim payments in the construction industry and also enables parties to refer disputes to adjudication. This Practice Note includes a summary of the payment provisions and the process for determining a dispute by way of adjudication. See
https: //www. lexisnexis. com/uk/lexispsl/construction/synopsis/93690: 135597/Construction-contracts/HGCRA-1996.

the Contractor to employ as a Subcontractor.

Previous FIDIC Contracts had a definition of nominated Subcontractors which included anyone who supplied Goods for which a Provisional Sum had been included in the Contract, as well as those who executed work. Sub-Clause 5. 1 now refers only to Subcontractors who are either named in the Contract or are the subject of a Variation under Clause 13. Subcontractors are defined at Sub-Clause 1. 1. 2. 8 to include a person who is appointed as a Subcontractor for a part of the Works and Materials are defined at Sub-Clause 1. 1. 5. 3 as forming part of the Permanent Works. Hence, under FIDIC, a material supplier who is nominated would appear to be a nominated Subcontractor and be covered by the provisions of Clause 5.

Instructions for the purchase of plant, materials or services are also covered at Sub-Clause 13. 5 concerning Provisional Sums. Paragraph (b) refers to plant, materials or services to be purchased from a nominated Subcontractor or otherwise.

5. 5. 2   Objection to Nomination

The Contractor shall not be under any obligation to employ a nominated Subcontractor against whom the Contractor raises reasonable objection by notice to the Engineer as soon as practicable, with supporting particulars. An objection shall be deemed reasonable if it arises from (among other things) any of the following matters, unless the Employer agrees to indemnify the Contractor against and from the consequences of the matter:

(a) there are reasons to believe that the Subcontractor does not have sufficient competence, resources or financial strength;

(b) the subcontract does not specify that the nominated Subcontractor shall indemnify the Contractor against and from any negligence or misuse of Goods by the nominated Subcontractor, his agents and employees; or

(c) the subcontract does not specify that, for the subcontracted work (including design, if any), the nominated Subcontractor shall:

(i) undertake to the Contractor such obligations and liabilities as will enable the Contractor to discharge his obligations and liabilities under the Contract, and

(ii) indemnify the Contractor against and from all obligations and liabilities arising under or in connection with the Contract and from the consequences of any failure by the Subcontractor to perform these obligations or to fulfill these liabilities.

If the Contractor does not wish to employ a particular nominated Subcontractor he must raise an objection as soon as practicable. If the nominated Subcontractor was named in the Tender documents then the Contractor had the opportunity to object before signing the Contract. The causes for an objection are not limited to the matters stated at paragraphs (a) to (c), but must be reasonable. Any dispute about whether an objection is reasonable could result in considerable problems and delays. If the Contractor does not wish to employ a particular Subcontractor then for the Employer to insist could result in problems later if there is a query, concerning the Subcontractor's performance. Some queries as to whether a Subcontractor should be imposed on a Contractor might be overcome by an indemnity from the Employer as provided for at Sub-Clause 5.2.

5.5.3 Payments to nominated Subcontractors

The Contractor shall pay to the nominated Subcontractor the amounts which the Engineer certifies to be due in accordance with the subcontract. These amounts plus other charges shall be included in the Contract Price in accordance with sub-paragraph (b) of Sub-Clause 13.5 [Provisional Sums], except as stated in Sub-Clause 5.4 [Evidence of Payments].

Payments to a nominated Subcontractor are certified by the Engineer as being due under the particular subcontract. These payments are certified by the Engineer in the Clause 14 Payment Certificates and are included in the Contract Price as Provisional Sums under Sub-Clause 13.5 (b). The Contractor is also paid for overheads and profit at the percentage stated either in an appropriate Schedule or in the Appendix to Tender.

5.5.4 Evidence of Payments

Before issuing a Payment Certificate which includes amount payable to a nominated Subcontractor, the Engineer may request the Contractor to supply reasonable evidence that the nominated Subcontractor has received all amounts due in accordance with previous Payment Certificates, less applicable deductions for retention or otherwise. Unless the Contractor:

(a) submits this reasonable evidence to the Engineer; or

(b) (i) satisfies the Engineer in writing that the Contractor is reasonably entitled to withhold or refuse to pay these amounts, and (ii) submits to the Engineer reasonable evidence that the nominated Subcontractor has been notified of the Contractor's entitlement; then the Employer may (at his sole discretion) pay, direct to the nominated Subcontractor, part or all of such amounts previously certified (less applicable deductions) as are due to the nominated Subcontractor and for which the Contractor has failed to submit the evidence described in sub-paragraphs (a) or (b) above. The Contractor shall then repay, to the Employer, the amount which the nominated Subcontractor was directly paid by the Employer.

The Engineer is entitled to check that the Contractor has passed on the payments to the nominated Subcontractor and, in certain circumstances, to make payments direct to the Subcontractor. Any payment that has been made to the nominated Subcontractor, after having been paid to the Contractor, will be recovered from the Contractor.

Before making any direct payment the Engineer will need to check why the money has not been paid to the nominated Subcontractor, following the procedure of paragraph (b) (i). Any subsequent deduction from the Contractor will need to follow the procedures of Sub-Clause 2.5. Any action for direct payments to a Subcontractor must also be considered in conjunction with any relevant provisions in the governing law.

☞ **疑难词汇** ☜

1. ancillary contract 辅助（从属性）合同
2. inter alia 尤其
3. in parallel to 并行的，平行的
4. detriment 损害，伤害
5. fleshed out 充实，具体化
6. coherent and consistent 连贯的，一致的，始终如一的
7. perceive 认识到
8. engagements 承诺，工作
9. dictate 要求，指示
10. Qatar law 卡塔尔法律
11. acquainted with 熟悉，了解
12. passed down 传递给，转移给
13. numbering 编号方式，合同编号
14. risk pass down 风险转移
15. setting out 启程，开工
16. specific exclusions 特殊除外事项
17. timeframe for payment 付款时间表
18. take precedence over 优先于，地位高于
19. defects notification period 缺陷通知期
20. impeded 阻碍
21. catch-all 全方位的，所有的
22. disbar 剥夺，剥夺律师资格
23. overriding 主要的，高于一切的
24. a full appreciation of the potential problems 潜在问题的全面爆发
25. underlying risk allocation 潜在的风险分配
26. with due expedition 以应有的速度
27. eventuality 可能发生的事，不测之事
28. provisional sums 暂定金额，临时款项
29. as soon as practicable 尽快，尽快可行的
30. overheads and profit 经常性开支和利润
31. applicable deductions 适当的抵扣
32. for retention 以供存照，以供存档

☞ **疑难语句** ☜

1. Subcontracts may be used for a great variety of services，inter alia：the execution and completion of permanent subcontract works，the design and/or the operation or maintenance of the subcontract works as well as mere supply of goods and materials or combined supply and assembly of equipment and plant.

分包可以用来做各种服务工作，尤其是永久性分包工程的履行与完成，分包工程的设计、操作或维护，以及商品和材料供应，设备的安装与调试。

2. The Contractor shall not be required to obtain consent to suppliers of Materials, or to a subcontract for which the Subcontractor is named in the Contract.

承包商在选择材料供应商或向合同中已注明的分包商进行分包时，无需征得（雇主或工程师的）同意。

3. The Subcontractor must submit his draft final statement 28 days after the end of the Subcontractor Defects Notification Period (which is tied into the Defects Notification Period under the Main Contract). The Contractor may require additional information if he is unable to verify any part of the final statement. The Contractor must pay the balance of the Subcontract Price within 56 days after the end of the Subcontractor Defects Notification Period.

分包商应该在分包商缺陷通知期限届满 28 之内将工程最终决算书交给承包商。承包商如果不能验证或证明分包商的文件，可能会要求分包商提交额外的信息。承包商将在收到缺陷通知期限届满 56 天之内向分包商支付款项。

4. The Contractor is responsible for the overall co-ordination and project management of the Works and for the co-ordination of the Subcontract Works with the Main Contract Works and the works of any other Subcontractors.

承包商负责项目所有的协调和管理工作，协调主合同与分包合同的工作关系，协调分包商之间的工作关系。

☞ 中文综述 ☜

一、概述

分包（subcontract）是指（主）承包商将部分工程交由他人实施和完成的行为。在分包合同关系中，分包商只是承揽、实施和完成主包商交给他的部分工程，而主合同中对雇主的全部责任和义务仍由主包商承担。分包合同的成立是以雇主与主包商签订的主合同为前提条件。没有主合同为前提，分包合同就不能成立，即使分包商已经向主包商报价或主包商已将其列入分包商的名单中。

各国法律均对分包法律行为进行了不同程度的规定，大陆法系国家多体现在民法典中，如德国、法国、日本等国的民法典或合同法中有关分包商的规定。以英美为代表的普通法系国家，多在成文的合同法或判例中予以规定。另外，雇主还会在招标文件中明确分包的原则，主包商在投标和实施中应遵守这些原则和合同规定。

根据工程合同管理管理实践，工程分包有以下几个法律特征：

（1）分包是主包商为实现主合同之目的，将工程的一部分以合同形式分担给其他承包商，并与之签订分包合同的行为。国际工程合同关系中的参与者包括雇主、工程师、主包商、分包商、施工经理、供应商、设计咨询公司、专业设计咨询公司等，这些参与者之间的关系以不同的合同相互联系，形成了不同参与者之间的权利义务关系，构成了国际承包工程的合同关系和合同链。在分包合同链中，雇主雇用承包商、雇用工程师或建筑师，而主包商雇用分包商，并与分包商签订分包合同。

（2）分包是分包商承揽一部分工程的行为。如果某个分包商从主包商那里将整个工程承包下来，就不是 FIDIC 合同条件下的分包，而是转包。根据我国法律规定，转包行为是违法的，"新红皮书"第 4.4 款规定，承包商不得将整个工程分包出去。

（3）分包商与主包商共同对雇主承担连带责任。

（4）分包商的选择应通知工程师。这主要表现在：除了承包商在选择材料供应商或向合同中已注明的分包商进行分包，无需征得工程师同意外，其他承包商拟雇用的分包商须得到工程师的事先同意。并且承包商应至少提前 28 天将每位分包商的工程预期开工日期以及现场开工日期通知工程师。

（5）分包并没有改变主包商与雇主的权利义务关系，分包商向主包商负责，主包商对雇主负责。

二、分包的法律性质

关于分包的法律性质，英国约翰·尤夫教授在《建筑法律》一书中曾明确指出："分包商的履约属于分包商代表承包商的受托履约，除非主合同另有约定，承包商仍要对工程承担全部责任。"分包的法律性质如下：

1. 分包是第三人代为履行，是指合同之外的第三人依照合同当事人约定由其向债权人履行债务。第三人不履行债务或者履行债务不符合约定的，债务人应当向债权人承担违约责任。我国《合同法》第六十五条规定："当事人约定由第三人向债权人履行债务的，第三人不履行债务或者履行债务不符合约定，债务人应当向债权人承担违约责任。"

2. 分包是附条件的民事法律行为

当事人在民事法律行为中约定一定的条件，并将条件的成就与否作为民事法律行为效力发生或者消灭的根据，这种法律行为称为附条件的法律行为。民事法律行为所附加的条件对民事法律行为的效力有直接的限制作用。条件的成就与否，可以决定民事法律行为效力的发生或者消灭。在一般分包合同中，由于分包商是从总承包商处获得分包工程，与雇主并无实质上的直接合同关系，没有雇主和承包商签订的合同为前提，分包就不能成立。

三、分包合同的几个主要条款

1. 责任传递条款

责任传递条款（Conduit Clause）是指主合同中有关分包合同工程的规定适用于分包合同，分包商就分包合同工程承担与主包商在主合同中向雇主承担的同样的责任和义务。从主包商的立场而言，他会自然地考虑像雇主对待主包商一样对待分包商，也希望他对雇主有什么样的权利、义务、赔偿和补救措施，分包商也要对主包商有同样的权利、义务、补偿和补救措施。

2. 附条件支付条款

附条件支付条款是指分包合同的支付条款写明在主包商从雇主那里收到分包款后，主包商才向分包商支付的规定。典型的附条件支付条款（Pay-When-Paid）内容如下："承包商同意在分包商完成其工程、经工程师确认并在雇主向承包商支付分包工程款后的第 30 天内向分包商支付其分包工程款项。"

在分包实务中，又出现了一种新的附条件支付条款，即如果雇主支付后承包商才能支付分包商的条款，称为"Pay-if-Paid Clause"，内容如下："在雇主或雇主代表预付或支付了主包商时，主包商负有责任和义务向分包商支付除保留金之外的，雇主代表承认和批准的款项和比例。只有雇主或雇主代表向主包商预付或支付工程款项，主包商才有责任或被要求向分包商预付和支付工程款项。"

3. 留置权条款

留置权是指债权人按照合同约定占有债务人财产，在与该物有牵连关系的债权未受清偿前，有留置该财产，并就该财产优先受偿的权利。各国法律对留置权的规定不尽相同，形成了包括留置标的物、行使留置权时间、程序等不同内容的复杂的法律制度。在工程建设领域，为规范建筑业发展，平衡雇主、承包商、分包商、供应商以及劳务人员等各参与主体之间的利益，杜绝相互拖欠工程款现象的发生，某些国家就施工留置权作了法律规定，如美国各州均对施工留置权，包括雇主和承包商之间、承包商与分包商之间如何实现留置权等作了繁复的法律规定，形成了约束建筑业的法律机制和体系，有效地保护了雇主、承包商、分包商、劳务人员等主体的利益。

4. 保障和保证不受损害条款

保障和保证不受损害条款（Indemnity and Hold Harmless Clause）或称免责条款，是指当事人双方在合同中事先约定的，旨在限制或者免除其未来责任的条款。在国际工程承包实务中，承包商或分包商也会经常遇到保障和保证不受损害条款，如 FIDIC 合同 1987 年第四版第 22 条、FIDIC 分包合同 1994 年第一版第 13 条、ICE 合同第 22 条、AIA 分包合同格式以及 AGC 分包合同格式等都有类似的规定。

分包合同中的保障和保证不受损害条款应严格限于因分包工程以及分包商、其代理人或其雇员引起的伤害和损失。如果分包商接受了广义条款内容，就等于他承担了应由主包商或者雇主承担的责任，承担了他不应承担的义务。

保障和保证不受损害条款构成了主包商和分包商之间对明示的约定风险的分担和转移。对于主包商和分包商而言，应尽量采用普遍使用的分包合同中的保障和保证不受损害条款的内容，理解这种条款的实质含义和法律意义。

四、指定分包商

指定分包商是指雇主指定分包主包商一部分工程或工作的分包商。在工程实践中，指定分包商的存在会引发责任分担问题，既然不是主包商自己选择的分包商，甚至主包商并不同意该分包商的加入，那么，如果指定分包商没有按约定履行合同，对主承包商和（或者）雇主产生违约责任，主包商是否要与指定分包商一起承担连带责任。FIDIC 合同条款规定，在指定分包的情形下，雇主、主包商和指定分包商之间也形成了相互制约的合同链。根据一般法律原则，除非指定分包合同有除外规定或雇主直接负责的情形外，主包商应对指定分包商所做的工程、材料和提供的服务对雇主承担责任。

为了解决这一问题，FIDIC 赋予了主包商对指定分包商反对的权利。承包商没有义务雇用一名他已通知工程师并提交具体证明资料说明其有理由反对的指定分包商。如果因为（但不限于）下述任何事宜而反对，则该反对应被认为是合理的，除非雇主同意保障承包商免于承担下述事宜的后果：

（1）有理由相信分包商没有足够的能力、资源或资金实力；

（2）分包合同未规定指定分包商应保障承包商免于承担由分包商、其代理人、雇员的任何疏忽或对货物的错误操作的责任；

（3）分包合同未规定指定分包商对所分包工程（包括设计，如有时），应该：①向承包商承担该项义务和责任以使承包商可以依照合同免除他的义务和责任，以及②保障承包商免于按照合同或与合同有关的以及由于分包商未能履行这些义务或完成这些责任而导致的后果所具有的所有义务和责任。

英国 ICE 合同第七版第 59（3）条有关主包商对指定分包的责任明确规定："除非本条款和第 58（3）条另有规定，主包商应对他雇用的指定分包商所做的工程、提供的货物材料或服务负责，如同主包商自己实施这些工程，提供这些货物材料、服务一样。"

五、FIDIC 2011 分包合同第一版

2009 年 12 月 2～3 日，FIDIC 在伦敦召开的研讨会上正式对外公布了用于由雇主设计的建筑和工程的新版《施工分包合同（测试版）》（Conditions of Subcontract for Construction，Test Edition），该版分包合同将与 1999 版"新红皮书"和 2005 年版多边发展银行《协调版施工合同》配套使用。2009 年新版 FIDIC 分包合同将取代 1994 年第一版 FIDIC《土木工程施工分包合同》。该分包合同正式版于 2011 年出版使用，称为分包合同第一版（First Edition）。

Questions

1. What are the Main Features of the FIDIC Subcontract?

2. Please discuss the clause of "Pay when paid ".

3. What is the difference between nominated subcontractors and domestic subcontractors?

Chapter 6   Staff and Labour

6. 1   Introduction

Under Sub-Clause 4. 1 the Contractor is required to provide all Contractor's Personnel. Clause 6 covers requirements for the recruitment, employment and behaviour of the Contractor's staff and labour, together with specific requirements for superintendence and records.

The description of staff and labour appears to refer to personnel who are employed by the Contractor, whereas Contractor's Personnel, as defined at Sub-Clause 1. 1. 2. 7, includes the employees of Subcontractors and any other personnel assisting the Contractor in the execution of the Works. Many of the requirements of Clause 6 include Subcontractors and the conditions of Subcontracts should include similar provisions.

Additional requirements to suit local conditions may be included in the Particular Conditions. Example clauses are included in the FIDIC Guidance for the Preparation of Particular Conditions for Foreign Staff and Labour; Measures against Insect and Pest Nuisance; Alcohol Liquor or Drugs; Arms and Ammunition; Festivals and Religious Customs. When it is considered necessary to include these matters they are likely to be the subject of local Laws or regulations.

6. 2   Engagement of Staff and Labour

Except as otherwise stated in the Specification, the Contractor shall make arrangements for the engagement of all staff and labour, local or otherwise, and for their payment, housing, feeding and transport.

In the Yellow Book the reference to Specification is replaced by Employer's Requirements. Sub-Clause 6. 1 requires the Contractor to make all the necessary arrangements for his staff and labour, but allows for this to be overruled by the Specification or Employer's Requirements. The Specification or Employer's Requirements could state that some aspect of recruitment, payment, housing, feeding or transport would be provided by the Employer, either direct or through some other agency. This exception is important because, without a specific exception, if there is any difference between the Contract Clause and the Specification or Employer's Requirements, the requirement of the Contract Clause would take priority under Sub-Clause 1. 5.

6.3   Rates of Wages and Conditions of Labour

The Contractor shall pay rates of wages, and observe conditions of labour, which are not lower than those established for the trade or industry where the work is carried out. If no established rates or conditions are applicable, the Contractor shall pay rates of wages and observe conditions which are not lower than the general level of wages and conditions observed locally by Employers whose trade or industry is similar to that of the Contractor.

The Particular Conditions may include additional requirements to conform to local requirements. The Contractor will also need to comply with any local Laws and regulations that apply to wages and working conditions, in accordance with Sub-Clauses 1.13 and 6.4.

6.4   Persons in the Service of Employer

The Contractor shall not recruit, or attempt to recruit, staff and labour from amongst the Employer's Personnel.

Employees of the Employer will have knowledge of local conditions which may be valuable for the Contractor. However, the Employer will not want to lose the services of valuable staff. At pre-qualification stage the Contractor may have been asked how he proposes to recruit staff for the project, either by local recruitment or by bringing in expatriate staff and labour.

Sub-Clause 6.3 attempts to prevent the Contractor from recruiting, or attempting to recruit, staff and labour from amongst the Employer's Personnel. The subtitle refers to "Persons in the Service of the Employer's Personnel" and the Sub-Clause, by referring to Employer's Personnel, covers a wider range than people who are directly employed by the Employer, as defined at Sub-Clause 1.1.2.6.

Whilst the intention of this Sub-Clause is clear, experience of similar Clauses in practice suggests its application may be more difficult. If the person concerned decided that he wanted to change his employment then it is difficult for the Employer to prevent his departure. If he has already left the employment of the Employer before he is recruited by the Contractor, then the requirement may not be applicable. However, it would be a breach of Contract for the Contractor, or a Subcontractor, to take the initiative and persuade someone to leave the employment of the Employer.

6.5   Labour Laws

The Contractor shall comply with all the relevant Labour Laws applicable to the Contractor's Personnel, including Laws relating to their employment, health, safety, welfare, immigration and emigration, and shall allow them all their legal rights.

The Contractor shall require his employees to obey all applicable Laws, including those concerning safety at work.

6. 6   Working Hours

No work shall be carried out on the Site on locally recognized days of rest, or outside the normal working hours stated in the Appendix to Tender, unless:

(1) otherwise stated in the Contract;

(2) the Engineer gives consent; or

(3) the work is unavoidable, or necessary for the protection of life or property or for the safety of the Works, in which case the Contractor shall immediately advise the Engineer.

The normal working hours may be restricted by the Employer, due to security or other local requirements, or may be left open for the Appendix to Tender to be completed by the Contractor.

The Contractor's normal working hours will also depend on whether he is bringing workers from outside the Country. Expatriate workers will often expect to work long hours, with fewer than normal days for weekends. Workers from the Country, or nearby countries, may have a tradition of long weekends after pay day. The Contractor will be deemed to have made enquiries and taken local custom into account when preparing his Tender, as required by Sub-Clauses 4. 10 and 4. 11.

Work outside the normal working hours requires the consent of the Engineer. The additional work will presumably benefit the project so consent should not normally be refused. Exceptions to the normal working hours may be necessary for particular operations, when the Contractor wishes to overcome delays, or when the Engineer has invoked the procedures of Sub-Clause 8. 6 and required the Contractor to adopt measures to expedite progress. Sub-Clause 8. 6 enables the Employer to claim from the Contractor any additional supervision Costs and similar provisions may be instructed as a condition of the Engineer's consent to work out of normal hours.

6. 7   Facilities for Staff and Labour

Except as otherwise stated in the Specification, the Contractor shall provide and maintain all necessary accommodation and welfare facilities for the Contractor's Personnel. The Contractor shall also provide facilities for the Employer's Personnel as stated in the Specification.

The Contractor shall not permit any of the Contractor's Personnel to maintain any temporary or permanent living quarters within the structures forming part of the Permanent Works.

In the Yellow Book the reference to Specification is replaced by Employer's Requirements. Sub-Clause 6.6 repeats the same requirement and exclusion as Sub-Clause 6.1, specifically for the provision of accommodation and welfare facilities. The Contractor is also required to provide the facilities for the Employer's Personnel, including the Engineer's Site staff as stated at Sub-Clause 1.1.2.6, which are stated in the Specification or Employer's Requirements.

6.8   Health and Safety

The Contractor shall at all times take all reasonable precautions to maintain the health and safety of the Contractor's Personnel. In collaboration with local health authorities, the Contractor shall ensure that medical staff, first aid facilities, sick bay and ambulance service are available at all times at the Site and at any accommodation for Contractor's and Employer's Personnel, and that suitable arrangements are made for all necessary welfare and hygiene requirements and for the prevention of epidemics.

The Contractor shall appoint an accident prevention officer at the Site, responsible for maintaining safety and protection against accidents. This person shall be qualified for this responsibility, and shall have the authority to issue instructions and take protective measures to prevent accidents. Throughout the execution of the Works, the Contractor shall provide whatever is required by this person to exercise this responsibility and authority.

The Contractor shall send, to the Engineer, details of any accident as soon as practicable after its occurrence. The Contractor shall maintain records and make reports concerning health, safety and welfare of persons, and damage to property, as the Engineer may reasonably require.

This Sub-Clause must be considered together with the health and safety regulations which apply under the applicable Laws. The Contractor is also required to appoint an accident prevention officer, who is suitably qualified and is responsible for ensuring that these requirements are followed. The requirement to ensure that medical facilities are available at the Site could be an onerous requirement for a project that is located a long way away from any centre of population. If the project is intended to encourage further development in the area, the Employer should consider including the provision of a permanent medical facility as a part of the project.

The Contractor must keep records of safety matters as required by the Engineer and these records will form a basis for the safety statistics which are necessary for the monthly progress reports under Sub-Clause 4.21(g).

6.9   Contractor's Superintendence

Throughout the execution of the Works, and as long thereafter as is necessary to fulfill the Contractor's obligations, the Contractor shall provide all necessary superintendence to plan, arrange, direct, manage, inspect and test the work.

Superintendence shall be given by a sufficient number of persons having adequate knowledge of the language for communications (defined in Sub-Clause 1.4 [Law and Language]) and of the operations to be carried out (including the methods and techniques required, the hazards likely to be encountered and methods of preventing accidents), for the satisfactory and safe execution of the Works.

In the Yellow Book Sub-Clause 6.8 imposes an all-embracing obligation on the Contractor to provide all necessary superintendence, which is described as the people who will plan, arrange, direct, manage, inspect and test the work and to comply with the detailed requirements. This requirement may seem to be obvious, but it gives the Engineer the opportunity to raise the matter, as a breach of this Sub-Clause, if he considers that the progress or quality of the work has suffered due to the lack of a suitable person to fulfill one of these functions.

6.10 Contractor's Personnel

The Contractor's Personnel shall be appropriately qualified, skilled and experienced in their respective trades or occupations. The Engineer may require the Contractor to remove (or cause to be removed) any person employed on the Site or Works, including the Contractor's Representative if applicable, who:

(1) persists in any misconduct or lack of care;

(2) carries out duties incompetently or negligently;

(3) fails to conform with any provisions of the Contract; or

(4) persists in any conduct which is prejudicial to safety, health, or the protection of the environment.

If appropriate, the Contractor shall then appoint (or cause to be appointed) a suitable replacement person.

This provision applies, by the definition at Sub-Clause 1.1.2.7, to personnel employed by Subcontractors as well the Contractor's own personnel. If the person concerned is in a supervisory position then Sub-Clause 6.8 could also be relevant.

6.11 Records of Contractor's Personnel and Equipment

The Contractor shall submit, to the Engineer, details showing the number of each class of Contractor's Personnel and of each type of Contractor's Equipment on the Site. Details shall be submitted each calendar month, in a form approved by the Engineer, until the Contractor has completed all work which is known to be outstanding at the completion date stated in the Taking-Over Certificate for the Works.

The records and monthly reports under Sub-Clause 6.10 must include Contractor's Equipment and Personnel, as well as staff and labour. The Contractor's Equipment and Personnel includes those provided by Subcontractors. The report is included in the monthly progress report under Sub-Clause 4. 21 (d). For a large or complex project it may be useful for the Particular Conditions to require that the numbers are allocated to particular parts of the project. It is also essential that any contemporary records, which are submitted under Sub-Clause 20. 1, are consistent with these records.

6. 12 Disorderly Conduct

The Contractor shall at any time take all reasonable precautions to prevent any unlawful, riotous or disorderly conduct by or amongst the Contractor's Personnel, and to preserve peace and protection of persons and property on and near the Site.

Failure to comply with these requirements could result in a claim under the insurance provided to Sub-Clause 18. 3 or the indemnity under Sub-Clause 17. 1, as well as under the provisions of Sub-Clause 4. 14. It could also affect any liability of the Employer under other clauses, exclude Force Majeure under Sub-Clause 19. 1 (iii) and liability as an Employer's risk under Sub-Clause 17. 3 (c).

☞ 疑难词汇 ☜

1. insect and pest nuisance 不良行为者
2. arms and ammunition 武装力量（军火；武器弹药）
3. rates of wages 工资标准
4. expatriate staff 外籍员工
5. take the initiative 积极主动；带头
6. first aid facilities 急救设施
7. sick bay 病房，医务室
8. disorderly conduct 不良行为，违纪行为

☞ 疑难语句 ☜

1. Except as otherwise stated in the Specification, the Contractor shall make arrangements for the engagement of all staff and labour, local or otherwise, and for their payment, housing, feeding and transport.

除非规范中另有规定，承包商应安排从当地或其他地方雇用所有的职员和劳工，并负责他们的报酬、住房、膳食和交通。

2. No work shall be carried out on the Site on locally recognized days of rest, or outside the normal working hours stated in the Appendix to Tender.

在当地公认的休息日，或在投标函附录中规定的正常工作时间以外，不得在现场进行任何工作。

☞ 中文综述 ☜

一、概述

在完成工程所需要的资源中，人力资源无疑是最活跃的因素。工程管理领域的一些研究发现，项目人力资源水平的高低，对项目执行的情况有很大的影响。在国际工程合同中，雇主方主要从保证项目顺利进行的角度出发，对承包商在雇用和管理其项目的职员和劳工方面提出了要求。

承包商员工的来源渠道主要有三个：本国员工、当地员工和第三国雇用的员工。对于自己从本国带来的人员，承包商一般在现场或附近建立自己的营地或租赁当地人的住房为他们提供食宿；对于当地的雇员，如果施工现场距离当地的居民区不太远，一般承包商只提供上下班交通，不提供住房，也可以不提供三餐，但需要在现场提供饮用水。无论对人员怎么安排，均须在雇用合同中明示，且不违反当地劳动法的有关规定。

许多国际工程承包合同均规定承包商必须雇用一定数量和比例的当地员工，以缓解当地的就业压力。特别是劳务输出国，雇用当地员工的比例会更高。甚至，合同会要求外国承包商在中标后必须将一定比例的合同额分包给当地公司实施。

二、工资标准和劳动条件

每个国家和地区都有自己的工资标准和劳动环境。FIDIC 合同条款规定了承包商人员的工资标准及劳动条件，并且指出了在没有固定标准的情况下，工资标准及遵守的劳动条件应不低于工程所在地商业或工业的其他雇主在与工程相似的环境下所付的一般工资标准和遵守的劳动条件。"新红皮书"第 6.2 款规定，承包商所付的工资标准及遵守的劳动条件应不低于其从事工作的地区同类工商业现行的标准和条件。如果没有现成的标准或条件可适用，承包商所付的工资标准及遵守的劳动条件应不低于从事类似于此承包商工作的当地工商业雇主所付的一般工资标准及遵守的劳动条件。

三、为他人提供服务的人员

承包商从雇主人员中招收人员或试图招收人员，有贿赂嫌疑，是被禁止的。无论是否存在贿赂事实，只要雇主人员从承包商处获得金钱，问题就出现了甚至难以解释清楚。因此，如果合同的一方需要招聘另一方的人员，必须征得对方的同意。这一点对于双方能否友好合作至关重要。"新红皮书"第 6.3 款规定，承包商不应从雇主的人员中招收或试图招收职员或劳工。

四、劳动法

劳动法是保护劳工之法，确保劳动者在劳动关系中的权利与人格的实现，是现代劳动法的神圣使命。我国《劳动法》第一条清楚地表明该法的宗旨是：为了保护劳动者的合法权益，调整劳动关系，促进社会进步与经济发展。在国际工程承包实践中，由于劳动者来自不同国家，对劳动和劳动文化有不同的理解，因此，遵守 FIDIC 合同条款中关于劳动法律的约定和遵守项目所在国地方劳动法律显得十分重要。

本款主要强调了承包商应当保障其雇员的合法权益。承包商应当遵守这些法律法规，并为此支付应有费用。如果承包商未遵守这些法律法规而遭到索赔，雇主概不负责。因此，承包商在投标前，应当对于工程所在国的法律法规了解透彻。

五、工作时间限制

工作时间是指法律规定的或者单位要求职工工作的时间。如根据法律规定，在通常情况下，劳动者每日工作时间不超过 8 小时，平均每周工作时间不超过 40 小时。如果职工所在单位对工作时间没有新的要求，只是规定了上下班的具体时间，那么这段时间就属于职工的工作时间。但是，如果单位在合法的前提下对其职工的工作时间有特殊要求，比如对那些实行不定时工作制的职工来说，单位确定的工作时间，就应该属于工作时间。

"新红皮书"第 6.5 款规定，在当地公认的休息日，或在投标函附录中规定的正常工作时间以外，不得在现场进行任何工作，除非：①合同另有规定；②工程师同意；③为了抢救生命或财产，或为了工程的安全，该工作是无法避免的或必须进行的，在此情况下，承包商应立即通知工程师。

六、为员工提供的设施

为了更好地履行合同，承包商应当为其与合同有关的人员提供必需的膳食条件和生活环境，包括生活用的通道、供电、供水、卫生设施、炊事用具、空调、冰箱、家具、防火及消防设施、商店、电话等。

"新红皮书"第 6.6 款规定，除非规范中另有规定，承包商应为其人员提供并维护所有必需的膳宿及福利设施。承包商还应为雇主的人员提供规范中规定的设施。承包商不得允许任何承包商的人员在构成永久工程部分的构筑物内保留任何临时或永久的居住场所。

七、健康和安全

健康和安全是承包商应当给予高度关注的主要问题之一，即使合同中没有严格规定，也应慎重对待此问题，以免违反当地的法律规定。"新红皮书"第 6.7 款规定，承包商应采取合理的预防措施以维护其人员的健康和安全。承包商应与当地卫生部门合作，自始至终在现场以及承包商和雇主的人员住地确保配备医务人员、急救设施、病房以及救护服务，并应作出适当安排提供所有必要的福利和卫生条件，并防止传染病的发生。承包商应在现场指派一名事故预防官员负责维持安全并防止事故发生。该人员应能胜任此责任，并有权发布指示及采取预防事故发生的保护措施。在工程的整个实施过程中，承包商应提供该人员为执行职责和权力所必需的任何物品。一旦发生事故，承包商应及时向工程师通报事故详情。承包商应按工程师的合理要求，就有关人员的健康、安全和福利以及财产损坏情况进行记录并撰写报告。

如果现场较小，员工集中，则提供医疗服务会很容易，但对于公路、铁路、管线等类型的工程，现场很长，交通不便，员工分散，提供医疗服务的难度就会很大。为确保员工的健康与安全，并在事故发生后尽快到达事故发生地进行医疗救护，需要提供一笔不小的专用经费进行仔细筹划和实施，承包商应在报价中考虑相应的费用。当承包商进行现场考察时，应关注工程项目所在地的传染病情况。在传染病的多发季节，要采取措施保证员工的健康。

八、承包商的监督

在建筑工程承包合同签订后，承包商有义务对承包商人员的全部活动进行监督。监督的主要内容如下：

1. 承包商具有对工程进行管理和监督的责任。承包商应提供数量足够的，具有相应知识和语言能力的监督人员。由于对监督人员的素质要求较高，因此，对于承包商选择的监督人员，工程师具有否决的权力。但是，否决权的行使是比较严肃的，因此，此权力只能由工程师行使而不能委托给他人。

2. 承包商应根据合同规定对计划、安排、管理、检验、试验等活动提供必要的监督，为工程的设计、实施及运营服务提供监督。

九、承包商人员

"新红皮书"第 6.9 款规定：承包商的人员应是在他们各自行业或职业内具有技术和经验的合格人员。工程师可以要求承包商撤换（或使他人撤换）雇用于现场或工程中他认为有下列行为的任何人员，包括承包商的代表（如果适用）：①经常行为不轨或不认真；②履行职责时不能胜任或玩忽职守；③不遵守合同的规定；④经常出现有损健康与安全或有损环境保护的行为。如果适当的话，承包商应随后指定（或使他人指定）合适的替代人员。

本款规定体现了合同对承包商人员的素质要求，具体分为两个方面：技术水平和职业道德。

（1）在技术水平方面，为了保质保量地完成合同规定的责任和义务，承包商的人员应该是在本行业或本专业中熟悉而又具有经验的熟练工、半熟练工、普通工人、技术代表和称职而出色的管理人员。

（2）在职业道德方面，"新红皮书"做了一些限制性规定。主要包括：①经常行为不当或工作漫不经心；②无能力履行义务或玩忽职守；③不遵守合同的任何规定；④坚持有损安全、健康或有损环境保护的行为。本款赋予了雇主代表撤换承包商中不称职的任何人员的权力，这样的规定有利于保证项目拥有高素质的人员。同时，为了避免雇主代表滥用这一职权，规定了行使这一权力的前提必须是出现上述四种行为之一，雇主代表在行使此权力时，必须指出人员的不当行为。因此，对雇主代表不恰当的要求撤换人员的指示，承包商也可根据本款提出反对意见。

同时为了保障承包商人员的素质，"新红皮书"赋予了工程师撤换承包商雇员的权力。工程师有权否定由承包商雇用的他认为不合适的雇员，尤其是工程师认为那些行为不端、不称职或玩忽职守或因其他原因工程师认为不宜留在工地的任何人员，并要求承包商从工地把这些人员撤走。凡被撤走的人员，未经工程师允许，不得在本工程中重新雇用，被撤走的任何人员应尽早由他人替代。

十、承包商人员和设备的记录

"新红皮书"第 6.10 款规定，承包商应向工程师提交记录详细说明现场各等级的承包商人员及各类承包商设备的数量。该记录应以工程师批准的格式在每个日历月提交，直至承包商完成了在工程接收证书中注明的竣工日期时尚未完成的所有工程。

人员和设备是保证工程进度的基本要素，因此承包商在投标时，其标书中会列入计划投入的人员和设备数量及其动迁时间安排。如果承包商实际的设备与人员投入量与原计划有偏差，在出现进度延误时，将很难索赔到全部延误的时间，甚至被雇主代表完全拒绝。

本款并未说明承包商人员和设备记录的详细程度及格式以及提交的时间间隔。关于记录的内容和格式，需要承包商和雇主代表在开工前协商确定，通常包括设备名称、型号、数量、工作状态等。关于提交的时间间隔，按我国承包商的习惯做法，每天需记录施工日志，记录的内容就包括了现场施工设备的信息，而且每日要将这些信息发送给雇主代表。另外，施工周报和月报也会记录相关信息并发送给雇主代表。

在工程实践中，承包商往往更希望自己提交的这些日报、周报和月报，能得到雇主人员的签字确认，对此，双方可在合同中约定。但雇主往往担心自己签字的这些记录，会成为承包商日后索赔的证据，从而拒绝签字。那么这些签字应该作何理解呢？本款规定要求承包商提交这些记录，只是合同规定的收发文件的程序，雇主人员自然有义务签收这些记录，但雇主人员的签字不应被视为是对这些记录内容的认可。

十一、无序行为

工程中常见一些纠纷矛盾，因此"新红皮书"规定了无序行为，旨在承包商能始终采取各种合理的预防措施，以防止其人员发生任何非法的、制造事端以及妨碍治安的行为，并保持其人员安定，以及保证现场及邻近地区人员和财产的安全。

Questions

1. Are there any specific requirements for workers in construction field in China?
2. Discuss the main features of labour and staff section of Red Book 1999.

Chapter 7　Plant, Materials and Workmanship

7.1　Introduction

New Red Book Sub-Clause 7.1 expressly introduces an additional standard in respect of workmanship by requiring that the works not only must be carried out in accordance with the contract, but also, in a proper workmanlike and careful manner, in accordance with recognized good practice and with properly equipped facilities and non-hazardous Materials, except as otherwise specified in the Contract.

The requirement that the works be undertaken as above is of a more objective standard, and significantly different, from that of the Fourth Edition of the Red Book, where workmanship was subject to the engineer's instructions.

Sub-Clause 7.7 of the New Red Book states that every item of plant and material will become the property of the employer when it is delivered to the site or when the contractor is entitled to payment for the plant and materials under Sub-Clause 8.10 of these conditions. It is important, from a legal point of view, to establish ownership of any plant or materials at the very outset of the works, or at the least upon delivery to the site. This means that, should the contractor run into financial difficulties during the course of the contract, such plant and materials cannot be repossessed by creditors. It also means, of course, that should the employer terminate the contract pursuant to Sub-Clause 15.2 of the contract, all plant and material is retained by him for a future contractor to use in completing the works.

7.2　Manner of Execution

The Contractor shall carry out the manufacture of Plant, the production and manufacture of Materials, and all other execution of the Works:

　(a) in the manner (if any) specified in the Contract;

　(b) in a proper workmanlike and careful manner, in accordance with recognized good practice; and

　(c) with properly equipped facilities and non-hazardous Materials, except as otherwise specified in the Contract.

The quality of Materials and standard of workmanship will be specified elsewhere in the Contract documents, and will normally refer to the national standard specifications of the Country of the project. Phrases such as "proper workmanlike and careful manner", "recognized good practice" and "properly equipped facilities", which are used in this Sub-Clause are not precise. These requirements will be interpreted by the Engineer in relation to the actual Goods supplied and the work that is executed by the Contractor.

7.3 Samples

The Contractor shall submit the following samples of Materials, and relevant information, to the Engineer for consent prior to using the Materials in or for the Works:

(a) manufacturer's standard samples of materials and samples specified in the Contract, all at the Contractor's cost; and

(b) additional samples instructed by the Engineer as a Variation.

Each sample shall be labelled as to origin and intended use in the Works.

When samples are specified or instructed then the requirement and details should be clear. The requirement for manufacturer's standard samples is not always clear. However, the Sub-Clause refers only to samples of Materials which, by definition, excludes Plant. The samples are provided to the Engineer for consent which, under Sub-Clause 1.3, shall not be unreasonably withheld or delayed.

7.4 Inspection

The Employer's Personnel shall at all reasonable times:

(a) have full access to all parts of the Site and to all places from which natural Materials are being obtained; and

(b) during production, manufacture and construction (at the Site and elsewhere), be entitled to examine, inspect, measure and test the materials and workmanship, and to check the progress of manufacture of Plant and production and manufacture of Materials.

The Contractor shall give the Employer's Personnel full opportunity to carry out these activities, including providing access, facilities, permissions and safety equipment. No such activity shall relieve the Contractor from any obligation or responsibility.

The Contractor shall give notice to the Engineer whenever any work is ready and before it is covered up, put out of sight, or packaged for storage or transport. The Engineer shall then either carry out the examination, inspection, measurement or testing without unreasonable delay, or promptly give notice to the Contractor that the Engineer does not require to do so. If the Contractor fails to give the notice, he shall, if and when required by the Engineer, uncover the work and thereafter reinstate and make good, all at the Contractor's cost. Sub-Clause 7.3 requires the Contractor to allow the Employer's Personnel to enter the Site and any factories, quarries or other places where work is being carried out for the Works. The Contractor must provide access, facilities, permissions and safety equipment to enable the person concerned to inspect and check the materials, workmanship and progress.

Clearly, the Contractor can insist that anyone carrying out an inspection shall have proper authority to enter the Site and inspect the work. This is covered by the definition of Employer's Personnel at Sub-Clause 1. 1. 2. 6, which requires that all Employer's Personnel have been notified to the Contractor by the Employer or Engineer. The person concerned can inspect, but cannot give any instructions unless they have been given delegated authority under Sub-Clause 3. 3. The Contractor will also insist that anyone entering the Site or other premises shall follow the appropriate safety regulations.

The Contractor is required to give notice when any work is ready for inspection and before it is concealed in any way. The Specification or Employer's Requirements will often include a more detailed procedure and standard notice for inspection, or the Contractor may introduce his own standard form. The notice should also state when the Contractor wishes to proceed with the work in order to comply with his programme. Standard notice forms often have space for the Inspector to sign that the work has passed or failed the inspection. Any such signature must have been authorized in accordance with Sub-Clause 3. 3 and the Engineer may decide only to authorize an "I have inspected" signature.

The Engineer will either inspect without unreasonable delay or indicate that he does not need to do so. If the Contractor fails to give notice that work is ready then he can be required to uncover the work and reinstate at his own cost. This will be at the Contractor's cost, regardlessof whether the work is found to be faulty.

If the Contractor gives notice but then, for whatever reason, the work is covered before it is inspected then the Contractor would appear to be in breach of Sub-Clause 7. 3, unless the Engineer failed to inspect within a reasonable time.

The provisions of this Sub-Clause are typical of the provisions for the supervision of civil engineering work. If the Works include mechanical and electrical work then the application of the provisions may be difficult. Items of Plant may include items of standard manufacture which the Subcontractor purchases when they are required. The extent of detail which is required for compliance with paragraph (b) and with paragraph (c) of the monthly progress report under Sub-Clause 4. 21, will need to be agreed to suit the actual procedures that are normally adopted. Items which are specified by performance and subject to Tests on, or after, Completion would not normally be subject to the same detailed inspection during manufacture as is required for civil engineering work.

7. 5　Testing

This Sub-Clause shall apply to all tests specified in the Contract, other than the Tests after Completion (if any).

The Contractor shall provide all apparatus, assistance, documents and other information, electricity, equipment, fuel, consumables, instruments, labour, materials, and suitably qualified and experienced staff, as are necessary to carry out the specified tests efficiently. The Contractor shall agree, with the Engineer, the time and place for the specified testing of any Plant, Materials and other parts of the Works.

The Engineer may, under Clause 13 [Variations and Adjustments], vary the location or details of specified tests, or instruct the Contractor to carry out additional tests. If these varied or additional tests show that the tested Plant, Materials or Workmanship is not in accordance with the Contract, the cost of carrying out this Variation shall be borne by the Contractor, notwithstanding other provisions of the Contract.

The Engineer shall give the Contractor not bess than 24 hours' notice of the Engineer's intention to attend the tests. If the Engineer does not attend at the time and place agreed, the Contractor may proceed with the tests, unless otherwise instructed by the Engineer, and the tests shall then be deemed to have been made in the Engineer's presence.

If the Contractor suffers delay and/or incurs cost from complying with these instructions or as a result of delay for which the Employer is responsible, the Contractor shall give notice to the Engineer and shall be entitled subject to Sub-Clause 20. 1 [Contractor's Claims] to:

(a) on extension of time for any such delay, if completion is or will be delayed, under Sub-Clause 8. 4 [Extension of Time for Completion]; and

(b) payment of any such cost plus reasonable profit, which shall be included in the Contract Price.

After receiving this notice, the Engineer shall proceed in accordance with Sub-Clause 3. 5 [Determinations] to agree or determine these matters.

The Contractor shall promptly forward to the Engineer duly certified reports of the tests. When the specified tests have been passed, the Engineer shall endorse the Contractor's test certificate, or issue a certificate to him. If the Engineer has not attended the tests, he shall be deemed to have accepted the readings as accurate. Sub-Clause 7. 4 gives the procedures for tests specified in the Contract and additional tests instructed under Clause 13. Tests on Completion are covered at Clause 9, which refers back to Sub-Clause 7. 4. Tests after Completion, as Yellow Book Clause 12, require different procedures because, after completion, the project is occupied and controlled by the Employer. For a New Red Book Contract, Tests after Completion must be required in the Particular Conditions, as referred to at Sub-Clause 1. 1. 3. 6 (RB).

The Contractor will have given notice under Sub-Clause 7. 3 that the item is ready to be tested. The Engineer will then give the Contractor not less than 24 hours' notice of his intention to attend the tests and the time and place will be agreed between Engineer and Contractor. The Contractor will provide all the facilities necessary for the test. If the Engineer wants to change any of the specified details then he must issue a Variation under Clause 13. If the Engineer fails to attend the test, without issuing an appropriate instruction, then the Contractor can proceed. The tests are deemed to have been made in the Engineer's presence and he will be deemed to have accepted the readings as accurate. After the tests, the Contractor will send to the Engineer a certified report and, when the test has been successful, the Engineer will issue a Certificate.

7. 6　Rejection

If, as a result of on examination, inspection, measurement or testing, any Plant, Materials or Workmanship is found to be defective or otherwise not in accordance with the Contract, the Engineer may reject the Plant, Materials or Workmanship by giving notice to the Contractor, with reasons. The Contractor shall then promptly make good the defect and ensure that the rejected item complies with the Contract.

If the Engineer requires this Plant, Materials or Workmanship to be retested, the tests shall be repeated under the same terms and conditions. If the rejection and retesting cause the Employer to incur additional costs, the Contractor shall subject to Sub-Clause 2. 5 [Employer's Claims] pay these costs to the Employer. The cost of tests is dealt with at Sub-Clauses 7. 4 and 7. 5.

7. 7　Remedial Work

Notwithstanding any previous test or certification, the Engineer may instruct the Contractor to:

(a) remove from the Site and replace any Plant or Materials which is not in accordance with the Contract;

(b) remove and re-execute any other work which is not in accordance with the Contract; and

(c) execute any work which is urgently required for the safety of the Works, whether because of on accident, unforeseeable event or otherwise.

The Contractor shall comply with the instruction within a reasonable time, which shall be the time (if any) specified in the instruction, or immediately if urgency is specified under sub-paragraph (c) .

If the Contractor fails to comply with the instruction, the Employer shall be entitled to employ and pay other persons to carry out the work. Except to the extent that the Contractor would have been entitled to payment for the work, the Contractor shall subject to Sub-Clause 2. 5 [Employer's Claims] pay to the Employer all costs arising from this failure.

Sub-Clause 7. 6 gives powers to the Engineer to deal with items which, in his opinion, are not in accordance with the Contract. The Engineer may instruct that Plant, Materials or any other work is removed from the Site and the item replaced. The Contractor must comply with the instruction within a reasonable time, which may be stated in the instruction.

Under Sub-Clause 7.6 (c) the Engineer may also issue instructions for any work which is required for the safety of the Works, which must be carried out immediately. If the Contractor fails, or is unable, to comply with this instruction then the Employer may employ others to carry out the work and claim the Costs arising from the failure to the Contractor under Sub-Clause 2.5.

7.8 Ownership of Plant and Materials

Each item of Plant and Materials shall, to the extent consistent with the Laws of the Country, become the property of the Employer at whichever is the earlier of the following times, free from liens and other encumbrances:

(a) when it is delivered to the Site;

(b) when the Contractor is entitled to payment of the value of the Plant and Materials under Sub-Clause 8.10 [Payment for Plant and Materials in Event of Suspension].

Sub-Clause 7.7 states that any item of Plant and Materials which has been delivered to the Site becomes the property of the Employer. The definition of Site at Sub-Clause 1.1.6.7 includes places specified in the Contract as forming part of the Site. The Plant and Materials which become the property of the Employer should have been included in Interim Payment Certificates under Sub-Clause 14.5, if the Contractor has provided all the paperwork required by this Sub-Clause. This provision could be unfair on the Contractor in the event that the Employer went into liquidation before the payment had actually been made.

The reference to the Laws of the Country is extremely important and should also refer to the governing law as stated in the Appendix to Tender. Any conflict between the law and Sub-Clause 7.7 should have been checked by the Employer and clarified in the Particular Conditions.

☞ 疑难词汇 ☞

1. plant, materials and workmanship 设备，材料和工艺

2. workmanlike 技术熟练的

3. non-hazardous materials 无害材料

4. reinstate 使恢复，使复原

5. make good 补偿，赔偿

6. quarries 采石场

7. delegated authority 代理权

8. premises 楼宇，住所

9. uncover 发现，揭开，揭露

10. endorse 背书，认可

11. as accurate 精确的，真实的

☞ 疑难语句 ☜

1. Liens and other encumbrances.

留置权及其他权利负担。

2. Each sample shall be labelled as to origin and intended use in the Works.

每种样品应标记原产地或在工程中的预期用途。

3. The Contractor shall give notice to the Engineer whenever any work is ready and before it is covered up, put out of sight, or packaged for storage or transport.

承包商应在工作准备就绪，并且这些工作在被覆盖、掩蔽或包装用于储存和运输之前通知工程师。

4. The Engineer shall give the Contractor not less than 24 hours' notice of the Engineer's intention to attend the tests. If the Engineer does not attend at the time and place agreed, the Contractor may proceed with the tests, unless otherwise instructed by the Engineer, and the tests shall then be deemed to have been made in the Engineer's presence.

工程师需要提前 24 小时通知承包商其参加试验的意愿。如果工程师没有按照约定的时间和地点参加试验，除非得到工程师的其他指示，承包商可继续试验，而且这种试验应被视为工程师到场监督了试验的过程。

5. Promptly forward to the Engineer duly certified reports of the tests.

尽快将验证的试验报告交给工程师。

6. The Contractor shall then promptly make good the defect and ensure that the rejected item complies with the Contract.

承包商应迅速修复缺陷，并确保修复的缺陷符合合同的要求。

7. Notwithstanding any previous test or certification, the Engineer may instruct the Contractor.

不论以前是否进行了任何检验或颁发了证书，工程师仍可以指示承包商。

8. Each item of Plant and Materials shall, to the extent consistent with the Laws of the Country, become the property of the Employer at whichever is the earlier of the following times, free from liens and other encumbrances.

在下述较早时间内，符合工程所在国法律规定范围内的每项永久设备和材料均应成为雇主的财产，无任何留置权和其他限制。

☞ 中文综述 ☜

本章规定了合同双方在生产设备、材料和工艺的检验和试验过程中的权利和义务，是雇主和承包商在履行合同过程中进行质量管理的依据，其中提交样品、检验、试验都是质量控制的手段。本条的质量管理内容基本上与黄皮书的规定相同，区别只是一些原则上的规定和操作程序。而具体的技术性操作标准通常不在合同条件中予以规定，而放入附件或雇主要求部分。

一、实施方法

在 FIDIC 合同条款中，承包商应按以下方法进行生产设备的制造、材料的生产加工，以及工程的所有其他实施作业，这些方法主要包括：按照合同规定的方法（如果有）；按照公认的良好惯例，使用恰当、精巧和仔细的方法；以及除合同另有规定外，使用适当配备的设施和无危险的材料。

合同中使用的所有材料、设备和工艺等的质量都必须符合上述三点要求。无论哪一方建议、指示或双方协商使用不符合样品的材料，都必须在合同或补充合同中写明，双方签字确认，否则承包商无法免除其根据本款应承担的责任。

另外，这里的无危险材料，包括三种情况：其一，生产过程有危险，但产出的材料无危险，就是说要求使用无危险的材料；其二，在材料形成永久工程的过程中，不得使用有危险的现场程序；其三，这种材料必须在未来也不会有任何危险，如在其寿命期内或随后的拆除与弃置过程中。

二、样品

材料的质量直接关系到工程的质量，提交材料样品和相关参数是雇主控制工程质量的重要手段之一。承包商在采购使用材料前，应将样品和相关资料提交给雇主代表确认。

承包商提供样品或工料小样实质上是确立工程标准，既是材质标准，也是价格标准，材料材质达到小样标准才能用于工程。伴随着材料标准的确立，工料的合同价格也就按小样标准确立下来。FIDIC 合同条款在招标投标时有"工料规范"文件，其已相当精确地确立了相关工料标准，施工过程中要求承包商提供小样，只是进一步明确精细的外观等较小的细节标准。这些工料新标准的确立，并不构成对投标报价的实质性影响，相关分项综合单价也不会因为这样的小样申报而调整。

三、检查

"新红皮书"第 7.3 款规定，雇主的人员在一切合理的时间内应完全能进入现场及进入获得自然材料的所有场所，以及有权在生产、制造和施工期间（在现场或其他地方）对材料和工艺进行审核、检查、测量与检验，并对永久设备的制造进度和材料的生产及制造进度进行审查。承包商应向雇主的人员提供一切机会执行该任务，包括提供通道、设施、许可及安全装备。但此类活动并不免除承包商的任何义务和责任。

此条规定了雇主人员检查检验工程的权利。但是本条并没有规定承包商应承担雇主人员此类检查检验可能发生的费用，而只是规定了承包商人员应为雇主人员承担此项工作提供便利。在我国，对于常规的检查检验科目，国家有相应的检查检验程序与标准，只要在这些标准范围之内，或者在招标要求范围之内就视为已经包括在合同价格之内。

为了保障检查工作的顺利进行，"新红皮书"规定，承包商应为雇主人员进行检验提供一切机会，包括提供进入条件、设施、许可和安全装备。此类活动不应解除承包商的任何义务或职责。每当工作已经做好，在覆盖、掩蔽、包装以便储存或运输前，承包商应通知工程师。这时，工程师应及时进行检查、检验、测量或试验，不得无故拖延，或立即通知承包商无需进行这些工作。如果承包商没有发出此类通知，而当工程师提出要求时，承包商应除去物件上的覆盖，并在随后恢复完好，全部费用由承包商承担。

关于隐蔽工程，FIDIC 与国内相关监理规范的规定是一样的，即工程师（监理）没有签署的隐蔽工程，视为不合格。在工程师不能证实工程可靠性的情况下，工程师有权要求

中 文 综 述

承包商推倒重来。

四、检验

在很多承揽的大型工程项目中，承包商都会设置自己的实验室。如果按照 ISO 质量管理体系标准运作，承包商自己的实验室就可以对工程进行相当准确的监控性试验。

"新红皮书"第 7.4 款规定，为有效进行规定的试验，承包商应提供所需的所有仪器、帮助、文件和其他资料、电力、装备、燃料、消耗品、工具、劳力、材料，以及具有适当资质和经验的工作人员。对任何生产设备、材料和工程其他部分进行规定的试验，其时间和地点，应由承包商与工程师商定。

根据第 13 条 [变更和调整] 的规定，工程师可以按工程的实际情况改变进行规定试验的位置或细节，或指示承包商进行附加的试验。如果这些改变的或附加的试验表明，经过试验的生产设备、材料或工艺不符合合同要求，不管合同有无其他规定，承包商应负担进行本项变更的费用。工程师应至少提前 24 小时将参加试验的意图通知承包商。如果工程师没有在商定的时间和地点参加试验，除非工程师另有指示，承包商可自行进行试验，这些试验应被视为是工程师在场情况下进行的。

如果由于服从这些指示或因雇主应负责的延误的结果，使承包商遭受延误和（或）招致增加费用，承包商应向工程师发出通知，并有权根据第 20.1 款 [承包商的索赔] 的规定要求提出索赔。工程师收到此通知后，应按照第 3.5 款 [确定] 的规定，对这些事项进行商定或确定。承包商应迅速向工程师提交充分证实的试验报告。当规定的试验通过时，工程师应在承包商的试验证书上签字，或向承包商颁发等效的证书。如果工程师未参加试验，他应被视为已经认可试验数据是准确的。

五、拒收

如果检查、检验、测量或试验结果，发现任何生产设备、材料或工艺有缺陷，或不符合合同要求，工程师可向承包商发出通知，并说明理由，拒收该生产设备、材料或工艺。承包商应迅速修复缺陷，并保证上述被拒收的项目符合合同规定。

如果工程师要求对上述生产设备、材料或工艺再次进行试验，这些试验应按相同的条款和条件进行。如果此项拒收和再次试验使雇主增加了费用，承包商应按照第 2.5 款 [雇主的索赔] 的规定，向雇主支付这笔费用。

六、修补工作

在验收过程中，如果发现了不合格的工程部分和设备，工程师可以指示承包商进行修补，承包商也有义务进行修补。主要表现在：①将不符合合同要求的任何生产设备或材料移出现场，并进行更换；②去除不符合合同的任何其他工作，并重新实施；③实施因意外、不可预见的事件或其他原因引起的、为工程的安全迫切需要的任何工作。

承包商应在指示规定的合理时间（如果有）内执行该指示，如果承包商未能遵从指示，雇主有权雇用并付款给他人从事该工作。除承包商有权从该工作所得付款的范围外，承包商应按照第 2.5 款 [雇主的索赔] 的规定，向雇主支付因其未履行指示而使雇主支付的所有费用。

七、生产设备和材料的所有权

"新红皮书"第 7.7 款对实施工程过程中的生产设备和材料所有权归属进行了界定，具体规定如下：从下列二者中较早的时间起，在符合工程所在国法律规定的范围内，每项生产设备和材料都应无抵押权和其他阻碍地成为雇主的财产：①当上述生产设备和材料运至现场时；②当根据第 8.10 款［暂停时对生产设备和材料的付款］的规定，承包商有权得到按生产设备和材料价值的付款时。

雇主在付款之后具有生产设备和材料的完全所有权是非常重要的，即使承包商在后续履行合同过程中陷入资金困难，其相关债务人也无权收回这些生产设备和材料，有效地保障了雇主的权益。

Questions

1. Who is responsible for specified testing of Plant，Materials the Works?

2. How does New Red Book define the ownership of plant and materials?

Chapter 8　Commencement, Delays and Suspension

8. 1　Introduction

FIDIC New Red Book Clause 8 covers three very important subjects, all of which are related to the period during which the Contractor will construct the Works:

(1) the start and duration of the construction period, at Sub-Clauses 8. 1-8. 3;

(2) programme, delays and extension of time, at Sub-Clauses 8. 4-8. 7;

(3) suspension of work by the Engineer, at Sub-Clauses 8. 8-8. 12. The procedures for the completion of the Works are given at Clause 10.

Under Clause 8 of the New Red Book, the commencement delays and suspensions of the works under the contract are set out in full. Sub-Clause 8. 3 deals with the programme for the works which is to be submitted by the contractor to the engineer. It further states that whenever the programme is inconsistent with actual progress, a revised programme should be submitted that is in line with the actual progress of the works. Unless any other intention is expressed by the engineer, the contractor shall proceed with the works in accordance with the timetable set out in the programme. Of course, it is obvious that the programme should be in accordance with the terms of the contract.

Under Sub-Clause 8. 4, the contractor becomes entitled to an extension of the time for completion of the works, subject to the claims procedure to be followed under Sub-Clause 20. 1, if completion of the works is delayed as a result of:

(a) a Variation (unless an adjustment to the Time for Completion has been agreed under Sub-Clause 13. 3 [Variation Procedure]) or other substantial change in the quantity of any item of work included in the Contract,

(b) a cause of delay giving an entitlement to extension of time under a Sub-Clause of these Conditions,

(c) exceptionally adverse climatic conditions,

(d) unforeseeable shortages in the availability of personnel or Goods caused by epidemic or governmental actions, or

(e) any delay, impediment or prevention caused by or attributable to the Employer, the Employer's Personnel, or the Employer's other contractors on the Site.

8. 2　Commencement of Work

The Engineer shall give the Contractor not less than 7 days' notice of the Commencement Date. Unless otherwise stated in the Particular Conditions, the Commencement Date shall be within 42 days after the Contractor receives the Letter of Acceptance. The Contractor shall commence the execution of the Works as soon as is reasonably practicable after the Commencement Date, and shall then proceed with the Works with due expedition and without delay.

The "Commencement Date" is the start of the "Time for Completion" which is the period within which the Contractor has agreed to construct the Works. When the Commencement Date has been determined the Engineer should calculate the calendar date for completion. Potential arguments can be avoided by agreeing the calendar date at the start of the construction period. The number of days in the Time for Completion is given in the Appendix to Tender and may refer to the whole of the Works, or a designated Section of the Works. Day is defined as a calendar day and not a working day and so the number of days includes weekends and holidays.

The Commencement Date is fixed by the Engineer, subject to the requirements of Sub-Clause 8.1. The Commencement Date shall be within 42 days after the Contractor receives the Letter of Acceptance, unless a different period is stated in the Particular Conditions, the Engineer shall give the Contractor not less than 7 days notice of the Commencement Date.

The 7 day notice period is short, particularly for a Design-Build Contract which extends over a period of several years, and the Contractor must commence his preparation immediately he receives the Letter of Acceptance. Sub-Clause 2.1 then requires the Employer to give the Contractor access to and possession of the Site within the number of days from the Commencement Date stated in the Appendix to Tender.

If, for any reason, it is not possible for the Engineer to meet these dates, or for the Employer to give possession of the Site, then a change to the Conditions of Contract must be agreed between the Contractor and the Employer. The Engineer does not have the authority to issue an instruction to change these requirements.

The Contractor is then required to start the execution of the Works as soon as is reasonably practicable and proceed with due expedition and without delay. The precise interpretation of due expedition and without delay will depend on the circumstances but the general requirement imposes an overall obligation on the Contractor to continue working, even when some problem has arisen.

8.3   Time for Completion

The Contractor shall complete the whole of the Works, and each Section (if any), within the Time for Completion for the Works or Section (as the case may be), including: (a) achieving the passing of the Tests on Completion; and (b) completing all work which is stated in the Contract as being required for the Works or Section to be considered to be completed for the purposes of taking-over under Sub-Clause 10. 1 [Taking Over of the Works and Sections] .

Under Sub-Clause 8. 2 the Contractor is obliged to complete all the work which is required for taking over under Sub-Clause 10. 1, including passing the Tests on Completion as Clause 9, before expiry of the Time for Completion.

If Sections of the Works are required to be completed before the overall Time for Completion then the Sections must be described in the Appendix to Tender, together with the Time for Completion and delay damages for each Section.

Sub-Clause 10. 1 [Taking Over of the Works and Sections] just refers back to Sub-Clause 8. 2, which is not very helpful. The Particular Conditions could include a more detailed list of the work which must be completed, in addition to the actual construction and tests. Under the Yellow Book this includes training, commissioning and trial operation.

8. 4   Extension of Time for Completion

The Contractor shall be entitled subject to Sub-Clause 20. 1 [Contractor's Claims] to an extension of the Time for Completion if and to the extent that completion for the purposes of Sub-Clause 10. 1 [Taking Over of the Works and Sections] is or will be delayed by any of the following causes: (a) a Variation (unless an adjustment to the Time for Completion has been agreed under Sub-Clause 13. 3 [Variation Procedure]) or other substantial change in the quantity of an item of work included in the Contract; (b) a cause of delay giving an entitlement to extension of time under a Sub-Clause of these Conditions; (c) exceptionally adverse climatic conditions; (d) Unforeseeable shortages in the availability of personnel or Goods caused by epidemic or governmental actions; or (e) any delay, impediment or prevention caused by or attributable to the Employer, the Employer's Personnel, or the Employer's other contractors on the Site.

If the Contractor considers himself to be entitled to on extension of the Time for Completion, the Contractor shall give notice to the Engineer in accordance with Sub-Clause 20. 1 [Contractor's Claims] . When determining each extension of time under Sub-Clause 20. 1, the Engineer shall review previous determinations and may increase, but shall not decrease, the total extension of time.

The matters in relation to extension of time listed are as follows.

(a) Variation. Clause 13 gives the Engineer the power to issue instructions to vary the Works and the Engineer may ask for a proposal from the Contractor before issuing the instruction. If the Engineer has not asked for such a proposal then the Contractor must give notices promptly under Sub-Clause 8. 3 and within 28 days under Sub-Clause 20. 1 if he considers that the Variation may delay completion. The Contractor may also claim an extension of time if there is a substantial change in the quantity of an item of work, which would presumably occur as a consequence of the measurement procedure under Clause 12.

(b) Other Sub-Clauses. The other Sub-Clauses which entitle the Contractor to an extension of time are discussed under the relevant Sub-Clause: such as clause 1.9 Delayed Drawings or Instructions; clause 2.1 Right of Access to the Site; clause 4.7 Setting Out; clause 4.12 Unforeseeable Physical Conditions; clause 4.24 Fossils; clause 7.4 Testing; clause 10.3 Interference with Tests on Completion; clause 13.7 Adjustments for Changes in Legislation; clause 19.4 Consequences of Force Majeure.

(c) Climatic conditions. To justify an extension of time the Contractor must demonstrate that the climatic conditions were exceptionally adverse and actually delayed completion. It will be necessary to submit records for the normal weather over a period of, say, five years. The Employer may already have such records and made them available at Tender stage under Sub-Clause 4.10 or the Contractor should have obtained all available information under Sub-Clause 4.10 (b). In order to record the actual conditions, it will be necessary for the Contractor to have the necessary equipment in place from the start of the project, such that rainfall or other conditions are recorded automatically when they occur, even though such conditions may occur outside normal working hours. Claims for climatic conditions will only result in additional time, but not money, and they are specifically excluded from the unforeseeable physical conditions situations under Sub-Clause 4.12.

(d) Shortages of personnel or Goods. The shortage must have been unforeseeable by an experienced Contractor, as defined at Sub-Clause 1.1.6.8, and caused by epidemic or governmental action. Governmental action is not restricted to the government of the Country of the project.

8.5   Delay Damages

If the Contractor fails to comply with Sub-Clause 8.2 [Time for Completion], the Contractor shall subject to Sub-Clause 2.5 [Employer's Claims] pay delay damages to the Employer for this default. These delay damages shall be the sum stated in the Appendix to Tender, which shall be paid for every day which shall elapse between the relevant Time for Completion and the date stated in the Taking-Over Certificate. However, the total amount due under this Sub-Clause shall not exceed the maximum amount of delay damages (if any) stated in the Appendix to Tender.

These delay damages shall be the only damages due from the Contractor for such default, other than in the event of termination under Sub-Clause 15.2 [Termination by Employer] prior to completion of the Works. These damages shall not relieve the Contractor from his obligation to complete the Works, or from any other duties, obligations or responsibilities which he may have under the Contract.

The Appendix to Tender must state the daily sum and the maximum total amount of the damages due from the Contractor to the Employer if the Works are not completed by the due date. These figures are required to be given as percentages of the final Contract

Price. That is the final sum, as Sub-Clause 14. 1, after taking into account all adjustments for remeasurement, Variations and otherwise under the Contract. Hence the sum for delay damages cannot be determined finally until after agreement of the Final Statement.

By the normal definition of the word damages, the figures for delay damages should be a reasonable estimate of the actual losses which will be incurred by the Employer. If the governing law entitles the Employer to deduct penalties then the Sub-Clause and the Appendix to Tender should be amended by the Particular Conditions.

The FIDIC Guidance for the Preparation of Particular Conditions includes an example Sub-Clause if the Employer decides to include an incentive for early completion. The principle of a bonus for early completion will appeal to many tenderers and act as an incentive to acceleration or to maintaining progress when the work proceeds ahead of the programme. However, it would only be applicable when the Employer is in a position to occupy and use the Works as soon as they are complete. This principle is recognized in the provision for accelerated completion in the value engineering provision at Sub-Clause 13. 2.

8. 6　Suspension

8. 6. 1　Suspension of Work

The Engineer may at any time instruct the Contractor to suspend progress of part or all of the Works. During such suspension, the Contractor shall protect, store and secure such part or the Works against any deterioration, loss or damage.

The Engineer may also notify the cause for the suspension. If and to the extent that the cause is notified and is the responsibility of the Contractor, the following Sub-Clauses 8. 9, 8. 10 and 8. 11 shall not apply.

Sub-Clause 8. 8 entitles the Engineer to instruct the Contractor to suspend progress of part or all of the Works. Surprisingly, the Engineer is not obliged to give the reason for the suspension but may notify the cause. Clearly the reasonable Engineer should tell the Contractor the reason and likely extent of the suspension in order that the Contractor can decide how to meet his obligation to protect, store and secure that part of the Works.

8. 6. 2　Consequences of Suspension

If the Contractor suffers delay and/or incurs Cost from complying with the Engineer' s instructions under Sub-Clause 8. 8 [Suspension of Work] and/or from resuming the work, the Contractor shall give notice to the Engineer and shall be entitled subject to Sub-Clause 20. 1 [Contractor's Claims] to: (a) an extension of time for any such delay, if completion is or will be delayed, under Sub-Clause 8. 4 [Extension of Time for Completion]; and (b) payment of any such Cost, which shall be included in the Contract Price. After receiving this notice, the Engineer shall proceed in accordance with Sub-Clause 3. 5 [Determinations] to agree or determine these matters.

The Contractor shall not be entitled toon extension of time for, or to payment of the

Cost incurred in, making good the consequences of the Contractor's faulty design, workmanship or materials, or of the Contractor's failure to protect, store or secure in accordance with Sub-Clause 8. 8 [Suspension of Work] .

The Contractor must give the usual notices under Clause 20. 1 in order to claim any Costs and extension of time. This Sub-Clause also covers the Costs of resuming work, such as any remobilization Costs.

8. 6. 3   Payment for Plant and Materials in Event of Suspension

The Contractor shall be entitled to payment of the value (as at the date of suspension) of Plant and/or Materials which have not been delivered to Site, if: (a) the work on Plant or delivery of Plant and/or Materials has been suspended for more than 28 days; and (b) the Contractor has marked the Plant and/or Materials as the Employer's property in accordance with the Engineer's instructions.

Any request for payment for Plant and/or Materials which have not been delivered to Site would presumably require notice from the Contractor and confirmation from the Engineer, either as an item in the monthly Statement under Sub-Clause 14. 3 or as a claim under Sub-Clause 20. 1.

8. 6. 4   Prolonged Suspension

If the suspension under Sub-Clause 8. 8 [Suspension of Work] has continued for more than 84 days, the Contractor may request the Engineer's permission to proceed. If the Engineer does not give permission within 28 days after being requested to do so, the Contractor may, by giving notice to the Engineer, treat the suspension as on omission under Clause 13 [Variations and Adjustments] of the affected part of the Works. If the suspension affects the whole of the Works, the Contractor may give notice of termination under Sub-Clause 16. 2 [Termination by Contractor] .

If the Engineer waits for the full 28 days before replying to the request, then the suspension will have lasted 106 days, by which time the Contractor may have incurred substantial costs and disruption to planning his allocation of recourses to different projects. This would presumably be the tie to cancel the suspended work.

If the suspension is not lifted and the Contractor chooses to treat suspension of part of the Works as an omission under Sub-Clause 13. 1 (d) then the omitted work will either be valued by agreement, or under Sub-Clause 12. 4. Following omission under Sub-Clause 13. 1 (d) the omitted work cannot be carried out by others. If the whole of the Works was suspended and the Contractor decides to give notice of termination under Sub-Clause 16. 2 (f) then the payment will be made under the provisions of Sub-Clause 19. 6, as for Force Majeure termination, plus loss of profit and other losses or damage under Sub-Clause 16. 4 (c) . Clearly this would be expensive for the Employer, so sustained suspension should be avoided and should not be used for ulterior motives or as a weapon against the Contractor.

规定的开工日期起计算承包商的施工时间。如果在施工过程中承包商没有遭受可原谅的延误，则承包商应在合同规定的工期内完成工程项目。

"新红皮书"第8.1款只是规定了开工日期的时间要求，但并未涉及承包商开工需具备的前提条件，例如雇主应向承包商提供现场占有权、雇主应向承包商支付预付款（如有）等。在雇主不能交付现场占有权时，承包商将无法遵守工程师发布的开工指示，更无法开始施工。如果开工需具备一定的物质条件，雇主应在专用条款中予以明确规定，或者，在工程师签发开工令之前，承包商应与雇主和工程师协商，确定开工需具备的前提条件，并声明只有在开工的前提条件具备的情况下才能开始施工，起算工期。

一般来说，开工日期最好是在中标通知书中直接写明，否则工程师有可能由于进场时的混乱遗漏了这个重要的时间确认。通常情况下，中标通知书中的开工日期就定在比发布中标通知书晚7天的日期。由于中标通知书都会先行以电话类的形式提前通知，所以一般不会影响工程的进程。

三、竣工时间

竣工时间也可以理解为完工时间，是指一个时间段，相当于国内通常所称的工期。承包商需要在竣工时间内完成全部施工合同要求完成的工作。开工日期一旦确定，根据竣工时间就可以准确计算出竣工日期。"新红皮书"第8.2款【竣工时间】中列明了在竣工时间内所要完成工作的具体内容，该条款规定，承包商应在工程或区段（如有时）的竣工时间内完成整个工程以及每一区段的工作，并使这些工作能够通过竣工检验，以及完成合同中规定的所有工作。

四、进度计划

进度计划是承包商向工程师呈交的工程计划安排。"新红皮书"要求，承包商在接到工程开工通知后28天内向工程师提交详细的进度计划。当原进度计划与实际进度或承包商的义务不符时，承包商还应提交一份修改的进度计划。每份进度计划应包括：

（1）承包商计划实施工程的次序，包括设计（如有时）、承包商的文件、采购、永久设备的制造、运达现场、施工、安装和检验的各个阶段的预期时间；

（2）每个指定分包商的工程的各个阶段；

（3）合同中规定的检查和检验的次序和时间；

（4）一份证明文件，内容为：

1）对实施工程中承包商准备采用的方法和主要阶段的总体描述，以及；

2）各主要阶段现场所需的各等级的承包商的人员和各类承包商的设备数量的合理估算的详细说明。

（5）除非工程师在接到进度计划后21天内通知承包商该计划不符合合同规定，否则承包商应按照此进度计划履行义务，但不应影响合同中规定的其他义务。雇主的人员应有权在计划他们的活动时依据该进度计划；

（6）承包商应及时通知工程师，具体说明可能发生将对工程造成不利影响、使合同价格增加或延误工程施工的事件或情况。工程师可能要求承包商提交一份对将来事件或情况的预期影响的估计，和（或）按第13.3款【变更程序】提交一份建议书；

（7）如果在任何时候工程师通知承包商该进度计划（规定范围内）不符合合同规定，

或与实际进度及承包商说明的计划不一致，承包商应按本款规定向工程师提交一份修改的进度计划。

五、进展速度

进展速度是检验承包商工作的重要标准。如果实际进度比照进度计划过于缓慢以致无法按竣工时间完工，和进度已经（或将要）落后于进度计划中规定的现行进度计划，工程师要引起注意。除了雇主原因以外，工程师可以指示承包商按照进度计划的规定提交一份修改的进度计划以及证明文件，详细说明承包商为加快施工并在竣工时间内完工拟采取的修正方法。

除非工程师另有通知，承包商应自担风险和自付费用采取这些修正方法，这些方法可能需要增加工作时间和（或）增加承包商人员和（或）货物。如果这些修正方法导致雇主产生了附加费用，则除第 8.7 款中所述的误期损害赔偿费（如有时）外，承包商还应按第 2.5 款【雇主的索赔】的规定向雇主支付该笔附加费用。

六、工期延误

1. 工期延误的含义

工期延误是指在不影响合同竣工日期的前提下，仅对承包商进度造成的延误。工期延误可分为雇主原因引起的和承包商原因引起的延误。按照责任划分，延误通常可分为可原谅的延误、不可原谅的延误，而可原谅的延误又可分为可补偿的延误和不可补偿的延误。

可原谅的延误（excusable delay）是指由于雇主或其代理的行为或疏忽所导致的承包商可被原谅的延误。例如，工程师未能及时向承包商提供设计图纸、雇主未能按照合同规定的时间提供现场占有权等。不可原谅的延误（non-excusable delay）是指由于承包商自身行为或不作为所导致的延误。例如，承包商未能提供使工程按期完工的足够的施工人员、承包商未能提供足够的施工设备、承包商因自身的原因拖延工期等。

可原谅的延误又可以分为可补偿的延误（compensable delay）和不可补偿的延误（non-compensable delay）。前者使得受到延误的一方，通常为承包商，以雇主或其代理的行为或疏忽为由，有权对其所遭受的延误要求金钱补偿。另一方面，不可补偿的延误是指因中立事件（例如极端恶劣的气候条件）、第三方等导致的延误。

2. 工期延误的原因

工期延误的原因主要有工程变更、不可预见事件发生、投标文件与合同矛盾、设计延误等，不同的工程项目性质不同、所在地点不同、技术要求不同、外部环境不同，造成工期延长的原因以及发生的概率高低也会不尽相同。

(1) 工程变更

"新红皮书"第 13 条赋予了工程师签发变更工程指示的权力，工程师也可以在签发指示前要求承包商递交建议书。如果承包商认为变更可能延误竣工时间，并增加工程费用，承包商也可就工期和费用提出索赔。

(2) 不可预见的物质条件或事件

不可预见的物质条件或事件是指一个有经验的承包商在提交投标书之前不能合理预见的。由于建筑和土木工程项目易受外界条件的影响和干扰，因此，不可预见的物质条件或事件成为延误的一项主要原因。"新红皮书"第 4.12 款将"物质条件"定义为："指承包商在现场施工时遇到的自然物质条件、人为的及其他物质障碍和污染物，包括地下和水文条件，但气候条件除外。"

承包商在施工过程中遇到的"物质条件"必须是不可预见的。根据"新红皮书"的定义，不可预见的物质条件的范围十分广泛，主要包括：

1）自然物质条件，包括地下和水文条件；

2）人为的物质障碍，包括罢工、雇主行为等；

3）其他的物质障碍和污染物，如不可抗力事件等。

承包商在施工过程中遇到其不可预见的物质条件时，应根据第 4.12 款的规定及时通知工程师，并遵守该款的其他有关规定，同时承包商有权根据该款规定索赔工期和费用。一般而言，物质条件的改变会导致设计的变更以及施工方法的改变。

（3）雇主原因

如果雇主造成了延误，作为合同另一方的承包商可以有权要求补偿。"新红皮书"第 8.4 款赋予了承包商就工期延长提出索赔的所有权利，并且第 17.3 款和第 17.4 款雇主风险条款中也规定了承包商索赔的权利。

（4）人员或货物的短缺

根据"新红皮书"第 1.1.6.8 款规定，短缺是一个有经验的承包商无法预见的，并且是由于流行病或政府行为造成的。在出现人员或货物的短缺时，承包商应及时通知工程师，提出人员或货物短缺的证据，并采取相应的措施克服短缺现象。

（5）其他原因

工期延误的原因还包括：第 2.1 款现场进入权、第 4.7 款放线、第 4.24 款化石、第 7.4 款试验、第 10.3 款对竣工验收的干扰、第 13.7 款因法律改变的调整、第 16.1 款承包商暂停工作的权利、第 17.4 款雇主风险的后果以及第 19.4 款不可抗力的后果。

七、工期暂停

"新红皮书"规定，工程师可随时指示承包商暂停进行部分或全部工程。暂停期间，承包商应保护、保管以及保障该部分或全部工程免遭任何侵蚀、损失或损害。

工程师应通知停工原因，如果工程师已通知了原因并认为是承包商的责任所致，承包商将对此承担一定的责任。但是，如果是雇主的原因引起工期暂停，使承包商在遵守工程师所发出的指示以及/或在复工时遭受了延误和/或导致了费用，则承包商应通知工程师并有权依据第 20.1 款【承包商的索赔】要求：延长工期，如果竣工已经或将被延误；以及支付任何有关费用，并将之加入合同价格。同时，承包商有权获得未被运至现场的永久设备以及/或材料的支付，付款应为该永久设备以及/或材料在停工开始日期时的价值，如果：

（1）有关永久设备的工作或永久设备以及/或材料的运送被暂停超过 28 天；

（2）承包商根据工程师的指示已将这些永久设备和/或材料标记为雇主的财产。

如果上述工程暂停已持续 84 天以上，承包商可要求工程师同意继续施工。若在接到上述请求后 28 天内工程师未给予许可，则承包商可以通知工程师将把暂停影响到的工程视为第 13 款【变更和调整】所述的删减。如果此类暂停影响到整个工程，承包商可根据第 16.2 款【承包商提出终止】发出通知，提出终止合同。

Questions

1. Please discuss the matters in relation to extension of time.

2. Who is responsible for delay damages? Employer or Contractor?

Chapter 9   Tests on Completion

9.1   Introduction

Tests on Completion are the tests that are carried out after the Works have been completed and before the Engineer will issue the Taking-Over Certificate. The responsibilities and procedures for the "Tests on Completion" are given at Clause 9, which also requires compliance with the testing procedures at Sub-Clause 7.4 and the submission of Contractor 's Documents as Sub-Clause 4.1 (d). The technical details of the required tests will be given in the Specification.

Under the "New Red Book", the Materials and other aspects of the Works are normally tested during construction and further tests before the issue of the Taking-Over Certificate should only be specified if testing at an earlier stage was not possible. If the Contract includes items of Plant, or other work which is designed by the Contractor to a performance specification, then the Yellow Book procedures will be appropriate.

The Yellow Book includes additional requirements for commissioning and trial operation. The tests before taking-over are inevitably more extensive, and the criteria for acceptance are more complex, under a Yellow Book Contract.

9.2   Contractor's Obligations

The Contractor shall carry out the Tests on Completion in accordance with this Clause and Sub-Clause 7.4 [Testing], after providing the documents in accordance with sub-paragraph (d) of Sub-Clause 4.1 [Contractor's General Obligations]. The Contractor shall give to the Engineer not less than 21 days' notice of the date after which the Contractor will be ready to carry out each of the Tests on Completion. Unless otherwise agreed, Tests on Completion shall be carried out within 14 days after this date, on such day or days as the Engineer shall instruct.

In considering the results of the Tests on Completion, the Engineer shall make allowances for the effect of any use of the Works by the Employer on the performance or other characteristics of the Works. As soon as the Works, or a Section, have passed any Tests on Completion, the Contractor shall submit a certified report of the results of these Tests to the Engineer.

During trial operation, when the Works are operating under stable conditions, the Contractor shall give notice to the Engineer that the Works are ready for any other Tests on Completion, including performance tests to demonstrate whether the Works conform with criteria specified in the Employer's Requirements and with the Schedule of Guarantees.

Trial operation shall not constitute a taking-over under Clause 10 [Employer's Taking Over]. Unless otherwise stated in the Particular Conditions, any product produced by the Works during trial operation shall be the property of the Employer.

In considering the results of the Tests on Completion, the Engineer shall make allowances for the effect of any use of the Works by the Employer on the performance or other characteristics of the Works. As soon as the Works, or Section, have passed each of the Tests on Completion described in sub-paragraph (a), (b) or (c), the Contractor shall submit a certified report of the results of these Tests to the Engineer.

Sub-Clause 8. 2 requires that the Works have passed any Tests on Completion before issue of the Taking-Over Certificate under Clause 10. It is not stated whether the Tests on Completion can be carried out immediately the particular item is complete, or whether all Tests on Completion must be carried out immediately prior to the issue of the Taking-Over Certificate. In practice this will depend on the circumstances and any requirements should be detailed in the Specification.

Sub-Clause 9. 1 states that the Tests on Completion cannot be carried out until the Contractor has provided the Engineer with the documents listed at Sub-Clause 4. 1 (d). This refers to the as-built drawings and the operation and maintenance manuals for any part of the Permanent Works which had been designed by the Contractor. The items required to be tested after they are complete will often be items of Plant which have been designed by the Contractor to meet a performance specification.

The Contract requires the documents to have been submitted to the Engineer, but does not require them to have been approved by the Engineer. However, Sub-Clause 4. 1 (d) requires these documents to be in accordance with the Specification and in sufficient detail for the Employer to operate, maintain, dismantle, reassemble, adjust and repair this part of the Works'. Hence the Employer will expect the Engineer to confirm that the submitted documents are acceptable.

The Contractor must give 21 days' notice of the date when he will be ready to carry out the Tests on Completion, which gives time for the Engineer to arrange for any specialist engineers to attend and for the Employer to make any necessary arrangements, particularly in parts of the Works which may already have been taken over by the Employer. The Employer may require that his staff who will maintain the Works should observe the tests. The tests must be carried out within 14 days after this date, on a date instructed by the Engineer.

9. 3　Delayed Tests

If the Tests on Completion are being unduly delayed by the Employer, Sub-Clause 7. 4 [Testing] (fifth paragraph) and/or Sub-Clause 10. 3 [Interference with Tests on Completion] shall be applicable.

If the Tests on Completion are being unduly delayed by the Contractor, the Engineer may by notice require the Contractor to carry out the Tests within 21 days after receiving the notice. The Contractor shall carry out the Tests on such day or days within that period as the Contractor may fix and of which he shall give notice to the Engineer.

If the Contractor fails to carry out the Tests on Completion within the period of 21 days, the Employer's Personnel may proceed with the Tests at the risk and cost of the Contractor. The Tests on Completion shall then be deemed to have been carried out in the presence of the Contractor and the results of the Tests shall be accepted as accurate.

If the Tests on Completion are delayed then the provisions of Sub-Clause 9.2 will apply. If the tests are delayed by the Employer then the Contractor can give notice to the Engineer under Sub-Clause 7.4 and follow the Sub-Clause 20.1 procedure to claim for an extension of time and additional payment. If the delay lasts for more than 14 days then, under Sub-Clause 10.3, the Employer is deemed to have taken over the Works or Section on the date when the Tests on Completion would otherwise have been completed. The tests must then be carried out as soon as practicable before the expiry date of the Defects Notification Period. The procedures for the Engineer to issue a Taking-Over Certificate and for any claims are given at Sub-Clause 10.3.

9.4 Retesting

If the Works, or a Section, fail to pass the Tests on Completion, Sub-Clause 7.5 [Rejection] shall apply, and the Engineer or the contractor may require the failed Tests, and Tests on Completion on any related work, to be repeated under the same terms and conditions.

Sub-Clause 9.3 requires that Sub-Clause 7.5 shall apply to the Works, or a Section, which has failed to pass the Tests on Completion. Sub-Clause 7.5 provides that the Engineer may reject the "Plant, Materials or Workmanship" and the Contractor must promptly make good the defect. The Engineer can require a repeat test.

9.5 Failure to Pass Tests on Completion

If the Works, or a Section, fail to pass the Tests on Completion repeated under Sub-Clouse 9.3 [Retesting], the Engineer shall be entitled to:

(a) order further repetition of Tests on Completion under Sub-Clause 9.3;

(b) if the failure deprives the Employer of substantially the whole benefit of the Works or Section, reject the Works or Section (as the case maybe), in which event the Employer shall have the some remedies as are provided in subparagraph (c) of Sub-Clause 11.4 [Failure to Remedy Defects]; or

(c) issue a Taking-Over Certificate, if the Employer so requests.

In the event of subparagraph (c), the Contractor shall proceed in accordance with all other obligations under the Contract, and the Contract Price shall be reduced by such a-mount as shall be appropriate to cover the reduced value to the Employer as a result of this failure. Unless the relevant reduction for this failure is stated (or its method of calculation is defined) in the Contract, the Employer may require the reduction to be (i) agreed by both Parties (in full satisfaction of this failure only) and paid before this Taking-Over Certificate is issued, or (ii) determined and paid under Sub-Clause 2.5 [Employer's Claims] and Sub-Clause 3.5 [Determinations].

Sub-Clause 9.4 refers to failure by the Works, or a Section. If a particular part of the Works, or a single item of Plant fails a test then the whole of the Works or Section has failed. If the Engineer then decides to order a repetition of the tests, as option (a), then his decision is a technical matter and may, or may not, resolve the problem. If the item being tested again fails the test, despite the making good as Sub-Clause 7.5, then the Engineer will consider other technical alternatives before going to options (b) or (c).

Sub-Clause 7.6 enables the Engineer to instruct the Contractor to remove and replace Plant or Materials or remove and re-execute other work. If the Contractor fails to carry out this instruction then the Employer is entitled to arrange for other persons to carry out the work and claim the Costs under Sub-Clause 2.5.

Option (b) refers to the procedure at sub-paragraph (c) of Sub-Clause 11.4. The Employer can terminate the Contract, in whole or in part, and recover all his Costs as defined at sub-paragraph (c). It is difficult to envisage circumstances where this could be appropriate under a Red Book Contract and before invoking this procedure the Engineer should also consider alternative actions available under Sub-Clause 11.4.

Any acceptance of work that has failed a test must be agreed by the Employer and Contractor in which must be confirmed as a Variation, signed by both Parties, stating the terms and conditions under which the work has been accepted.

☞ 疑难词汇 ☜

1. performance specification 性能说明，性能规格

2. commissioning 试车，试运转

3. unless otherwise agreed 除非另有约定

4. make allowances for 体谅，考虑到

5. as-built drawings 竣工图

6. unduly 过度地，不适当地

7. envisage 面对，想象

☞ 疑难语句 ☜

1. Under a New Red Book the Materials and other aspects of the Works are normally

tested during construction and further tests before the issue of the Taking-Over Certificate should only be specified if testing at an earlier stage was not possible.

根据"新红皮书"的规定，工程的材料和其他方面检验通常在施工阶段进行，颁发接收证书的进一步检验，如果不能在施工阶段进行的话，必须加以注明。

2. In considering the results of the Tests on Completion, the Engineer shall make allowances for the effect of any use of the Works by the Employer on the performance or other characteristics of the Works.

在确定完工验收结果时，工程师应考虑雇主在工程性能和其他特性方面的使用效果。

3. If the Tests on Completion are being unduly delayed by the Contractor, the Engineer may by notice require the Contractor to carry out the Tests within 21 days after receiving the notice. The Contractor shall carry out the Tests on such day or days within that period as the Contractor may fix and of which he shall give notice to the Engineer.

如果承包商无故延误竣工检验，工程师可通知承包商要求他在收到该通知后21天内进行此类检验。承包商应在该期限内他可能确定的某日或数日内进行检验，并将此日期通知工程师。

☞ 中文综述 ☜

一、概述

对于国内的工程竣工试验，国家有很多规范性的要求，承包商与雇主完成相关的工作一般都比较顺利。"新红皮书"的竣工试验要求提供竣工文件并提供"操作和维护手册"，这是FIDIC合同的一项特殊要求，国内合同提到的则比较少。

在国内竣工试验中，若雇主先行使用工程的部分或全部，则试验过程就会较复杂。如果雇主先使用工程的某个部分，则竣工试验可能就无法体现整个试验系统的状况，最终的竣工试验就会出现问题。解决此问题最常见的方法是个别评定，即对于能够分割的竣工试验，则对先交付的工程部分以竣工试验标准进行试验，达标后单独评定此部分，到最后总验收时与总体工程同时确认其结果。对于不能分割的整个系统需竣工试验的情况，一般的处理方法是完成部分单独可保证质量的先期试验。到竣工试验时，不论先期系统现状如何，一律并入总系统内试验，由雇主负责保证在使用状态下的试验核查条件。一般总试验时都会拆开一些装饰工程，以保证试验能够顺利进行，但尽量还是少拆为宜。

二、承包商在完工验收中的义务

在"新红皮书"中，承包商应按照第5.6款［竣工文件］和第5.7款［操作和维修手册］的要求，提供各种文件后，按照第7.4款［试验］的要求进行竣工试验。承包商应提前21天将他可以进行每项竣工试验的日期通知雇主，除非另有商定，竣工试验应在此通知日期后的14天内，在雇主指示的某日或某几日内进行。进行竣工试验时，除非专用条件中另有说明，竣工试验应按照以下顺序进行：

（1）启动前试验，应包括适当的检验和性能试验，以证明每项生产设备能够安全地承受下一阶段试验；

（2）启动试验，应包括规定地操作试验，以证明工程或分项工程能够在所有可利用的操作条件下安全地操作；

（3）试运行应证明工程或分项工程运行可靠，符合合同要求。

试运行期间，当工程正在稳定条件下运行时，承包商应通知雇主，告知工程已可以做任何其他竣工试验，包括各种性能试验，以证明工程是否符合雇主规定的标准和履约保证的要求。工程在试运行期间生产的任何产品应属于雇主的财产。在考虑竣工试验结果时，雇主应适当考虑到因雇主对工程的任何使用，对工程的性能或其他特性产生的影响。一旦工程或某分项工程通过了竣工试验，承包商应向雇主提供一份经证实的这些试验结果的报告。

三、竣工验收的程序

"新红皮书"第9.1款规定，如果承包商要求对工程进行竣工检验，他应至少提前21天将可以进行某项竣工检验的日期通知工程师。除非另有商定，检验应在该日期后14天内于工程师指示的某日或数日内进行。关于工程的接收，第10.1款规定，工程经工程师进行竣工检验后，承包商可以在他认为工程将完工并准备移交前14天内，向工程师发出通知，申请接收证书。工程师在收到申请后28天内决定是否出具接收证书。

如果雇主不当地延误竣工试验，雇主可通知承包商，要求在接到通知后21天内进行竣工试验，承包商应在上述期限内的某日或某几日内进行竣工试验，并将该日期通知雇主。如果承包商未在规定的21天内进行竣工试验，雇主人员可自行进行这些试验，试验的风险和费用应由承包商承担。这些竣工试验应被视为是承包商在场时进行的，试验结果应认为准确，予以认可。

四、重新试验

如果工程或分项工程未能通过竣工试验，应适用第7.5款［拒收］的规定，工程师或承包商可要求按相同的条款和条件，重新进行此项未通过的试验和相关工程的竣工试验。

五、未能通过竣工试验

如果竣工试验失败，就应重新试验。进行重新试验工程师将有权：

（1）下令根据第9.3款再次重复竣工试验；

（2）如果此项试验未通过，使雇主实质上丧失了工程或分项工程的全部利益时，拒收工程或分项工程（视情况而定）；

（3）颁发接收证书。

在进行重新试验的情况下，承包商应继续履行合同规定的所有其他义务。但合同价格应予降低，减少的金额应足以弥补此项试验未通过的后果给雇主带来的价值损失。

在国内，若未通过竣工试验，产品就不合格，无法通过质监审批，也就无法获得相关的证书，工程就不能正常使用，所以国内工程是一定要通过竣工试验的。

Questions

1. What is the procedure of tests on completion?

2. Discuss the situations in case failure to pass tests on completion.

Chapter 10　Employer's Taking Over

10. 1　Introduction

The most important part of a project is handing over the Works to the Client. And when it comes to the Taking Over process, the Contractor should carefully study the Conditions of Contract to ensure that the correct notices are given in writing to the Engineer. Also make sure to understand if any milestones are applicable as these require separate taking over requests and certificates.

The next task is to ascertain from the Engineer at what stage he is prepared to issue a Taking Over Certificate - for example the Client may be prepared to Take Over the works before landscaping is completed, provided the company gives a written undertaking to complete the outstanding work during the maintenance period.

Once the client's requirements are known, the Contractor should satisfy himself that the works are complete as required. He must make regular inspections of the Works, with or without attendance of the Engineer, produce punch lists (snag lists) of outstanding items and ensure that all outstanding items are completed. He must make every effort to obtain the Taking Over certificate as soon as possible.

Once ready for hand over, the Contractor should submit his notice in writing, to the Engineer with a copy to the Employer, that a Section or the Whole of the Works are ready for Takeing Over. The Contractor must then agree a date and time for the Take Over inspection with the Engineer. If the inspection is satisfactory, the Engineer should issue a Taking Over Certificate (Practical Completion Certificate in some cases) within 21 days for the Contract. This certificate is an important legal document and the original must be sent to your Head Office immediately as apart from the release of retention, it transfers ownership of the works to the client and affects insurance of the works, sureties and bonds and liability for liquidated damages.

If the Engineer issues a Taking Over Certificate or Completion Certificate with exceptions, the Contractor should assess the seriousness of the exceptions and endeavour to clear all items before the Company leave site. There can be practical difficulties when returning to site to complete or repair work and the costs will normally be much greater. In addition the contractual implications of exceptions, if not speedily and satisfactorily resolved can be very expensive.

Occasionally the Client will require Beneficial Occupation of a section of the works before the contract is complete. The Contractor must study the provisions of the contract carefully as some conditions of contract permit only one completion certificate for the whole contract and do not allow for a reduction of retention, for example, on the portion taken over or for which beneficial occupation has been given.

The Contractor must carefully inspect with the Engineer any portions for which Beneficial Occupation is sought and will produce a list of omissions, defects, etc. which must be included in the Partial Taking Over Certificate. If necessary this list should be supported with photographs as, under Beneficial Occupation, all risks remain with the company who may be called upon to repair damage at its own cost, unless it can be proved that the damage resulted during beneficial occupation by the client.

In view of the legal implications of Take Over, it is essential that all Site Management is aware of the contractual obligations and associated penalties in order to ensure that the Taking Over certificate is received timeously.

10.2 Taking-Over of the Works and Sections

According to the Sub-Clause 10.1 [Taking Over of the Works and Sections], in the Taking Over Certificate is to be stated the date on which the Works or Section were completed in accordance with the Contract, except for any minor outstanding work and defects which will not substantially affect the use of the Works or Section for their intended purpose.

According to Sub-Clause 8.2 [Time for Completion]: "The Contractor shall complete the whole of the Works, and each Section (if any), within the Time for Completion for the Works or Section (as the case may be), including:

(a) achieving the passing of the Tests on Completion, and

(b) completing all work which is stated in the Contract as being required for the Works or Section to be considered to be completed for the purposes of Taking-Over under Sub-Clause 10.1 [Taking Over of the Works and Sections]"

According to the New Red Book, Sub-Clause 10.1 [Taking Over of the Works and Sections]: The Contractor may apply by notice to the Engineer for a Taking-Over Certificate not earlier than 14 days before the Works will, in the Contractor's opinion, be complete and ready for taking over. ...

The Engineer shall, within 28 days after receiving the Contractor's application:

(1) issue the Taking-Over Certificate to the Contractor, stating the date on which the Works or Section were completed in accordance with the Contract, except for any minor outstanding work and defects which will not substantially affect the use of the Works or Section for their intended purpose (either until or whilst this work is completed and these defects are remedied); or

(2) reject the application, giving reasons and specifying the work required to be done by the Contractor to enable the Taking-Over Certificate to be issued. The Contractor shall

then complete this work before issuing a further notice under this Sub-Clause.

If the Engineer fails either to issue the Taking-Over Certificate or to reject the Contractor's application within the period of 28 days, and if the Works or Section (as the case may be) are substantially in accordance with the Contract, the Taking-Over Certificate shall be deemed to have been issued on the last day of that period.

Sub-Clause 10. 1 requires that the Works will be taken over when completed in accordance with the Contract. This requirement specifically includes the matters described at Sub-Clause 8. 2 specified above. However, Sub-Clause 10. 1 (a) states that it is not necessary to complete any minor outstanding work and defects which will not substantially affect the use of the Works or Section for their intended purpose (either until or whilst this work is completed and these defects are remedied) . This specific exclusion is a considerable improvement on the wording of previous Conditions, which referred to the Works being "substantially completed" . It is now clear that some outstanding work or defects will not delay the issue of the Taking-Over Certificate, provided that they do not substantially affect the use of the Works for their intended purpose. The question of whether a particular item will "substantially affect" such use will be a matter for the Engineer to exercise his judgement, but the emphasis on the use of the Works should help towards a clearer definition of when the Works are ready to be taken over by the Employer.

The minor outstanding work must be completed during the Defects Notification Period as instructed by the Engineer under Sub-Clause 11. 1 (a) .

The procedure for the Employer to take over the Works is given at Sub-Clause 10. 1 as follows.

(1) When the Contractor decides that the Works are within 14 days of being ready to be taken over, he issues a notice to apply to the Engineer for a Taking-Over Certificate.

(2) Within 28 days of receiving the Contractor's application, the Engineer must either:

(a) issue the Taking-Over Certificate stating the date when the Works were completed in accordance with the Contract; or

(b) reject the application.

If the Engineer rejects the application he must give his reasons and specify the work that must be done by the Contractor to enable the Taking-Over Certificate to be issued. The Contractor must then complete this work and issue another notice.

If the Engineer fails either to issue the Taking-Over Certificate or to reject the application within the 28 day period then the Contract states that the Taking-Over Certificate shall be deemed to have been issued on the last day of the 28 day period, provided that the Works are substantially completed in accordance with the Contract.

10. 3 Taking-Over of Parts of the Works

The Engineer may, at the sole discretion of the Employer, issue a Taking-Over Certificate for any part of the Permanent Works.

The Employer shall not use any part of the Works unless and until the Engineer has issued a Taking-Over Certificate for this part. However, if the Employer does use any part of the Works before the Taking-Over Certificate is issued:

(1) the part which is used shall be deemed to have been taken over as from the date on which it is used;

(2) the Contractor shall cease to be liable for the care of such part as from this date; when responsibility shall pass to the Employer, and

(3) if requested by the Contractor, the Engineer shall issue a Taking-Over Certificate for this part.

After the Engineer has issued a Taking-Over Certificate for a part of the Works, the Contractor shall be given the earliest opportunity to take such steps as may be necessary to carry out any outstanding Tests on Completion. The Contractor shall carry out these Tests on Completion as soon as practicable before the expiry date of the relevant Defects Notification Period.

If the Contractor incurs Cost as a result of the Employer taking over and/or using a part of the Works, other than such use as is specified in the Contract or agreed by the Contractor, the Contractor shall (i) give notice to the Engineer and (ii) be entitled subject to Sub-Clause 20. 1 [Contractor's Claims] to payment of any such Cost plus reasonable profit, which shall be included in the Contract Price. After receiving this notice, the Engineer shall proceed in accordance with Sub-Clause 3. 5 [Determinations] to agree or determine this Cost and profit.

If a Taking-Over Certificate has been issued for a part of the Works (other than a Section), the delay damages thereafter for completion of the remainder of the Works shall be reduced. Similarly, the delay damages for the remainder of the Section (if any) in which this part is included shall also be reduced.

Only the Employer has the right to decide that a certain part of the Works will be taken over before the remainder of the Works. This discretion may be exercised when the Employer wishes to use a part of the Works before the whole of the Works is complete. The Employer can require the Engineer to issue a Taking-Over Certificate and the Employer would then be responsible for the care of that part.

If the Employer's use of part of the Works is a temporary measure, which is specified in the Contract or agreed by both Parties, then a Taking-Over Certificate is not required. If the Employer uses a part of the Works without a Taking-Over Certificate then Sub-Clause 10. 2 requires that:

(1) the part which is used shall be deemed to have been taken over as from the date on which it is used;

(2) the Contractor shall cease to be liable for the care of such part as from this date, when responsibility shall pass to the Employer; and

(3) if requested by the Contractor, the Engineer shall issue a Taking-Over Certificate for this part.

The taking over of a part of the Works was not envisaged in the Contract and is likely to cause problems for any Tests on Completion. Any such tests must be carried out as soon as practicable, but may have to be coordinated with tests in other parts of the Works.

Sub-Clause 10. 2 provides that if the Contractor incurs Cost as a result of the Employer using and/or taking over a part of the Works then the Contractor will give notice and proceed as Sub-Clauses 20. 1 and 3. 5. The Contractor could then be entitled to his Cost plus reasonable profit.

10. 4   Interference with Tests on Completion

If the Contractor is prevented, for more than 14 days, from carrying out the Tests on Completion by a cause for which the Employer is responsible, the Employer shall be deemed to have taken over the Works or Section (as the case may be) on the date when the Tests on Completion would otherwise have been completed.

The Engineer shall then issue a Taking-Over Certificate accordingly, and the Contractor shall carry out the Tests on Completion as soon as practicable, before the expiry date of the Defects Notification Period. The Engineer shall require the Tests on Completion to be carried out by giving 14 days' notice and in accordance with the relevant provisions of the Contract.

If the Contractor suffers delay and/or incurs Cost as a result of this delay in carrying out the Tests on Completion, the Contractor shall give notice to the Engineer and shall be entitled subject to Sub-Clause 20. 1 [Contractor's Claims] to:

(a) an extension of time for any such delay, if completion is or will be delayed, under Sub-Clause 8. 4 [Extension of Time for Completion]; and

(b) payment of any such Cost plus reasonable profit, which shall be included in the Contract Price.

After receiving this notice, the Engineer shall proceed in accordance with Sub-Clause 3. 5 [Determinations] to agree or determine these matters.

Sub-Clause 10. 3 states that the Works shall be deemed to have been taken over by the Employer if the Contractor is prevented, for more than 14 days, from carrying out the Tests on Completion by a cause for which the Employer is responsible. The Engineer is required to issue a Taking-Over Certificate for the date on which the tests would have been completed if they had not been delayed by this cause.

If the Contractor suffers delay and/or incurs Costs as a result of this delay to the Tests on Completion he can give notice under Sub-Clause 10. 3 and follow the procedures of Sub-Clauses 20. 1 and 3. 5.

The delay to the tests may be due to more than one cause, or the critical cause may be disputed. The Contractor's claim would include a statement that a certain cause was critical and establish the responsibility for the critical cause.

When the cause which prevented the Tests on Completion from being carried out has been removed, the Engineer can require them to be carried out by giving 14 days' notice. The Contractor is then obliged to carry out the tests as soon as practicable and before the expiry date of the Defects Notification Period. In the unlikely event that this cause continues to the end of the Defects Notification Period then the Engineer will need to consider what action to take, by agreement with the Employer and Contractor. The situation would be outside the provisions of the Contract and therefore outside the authority of the Engineer.

10.5 Surfaces Requiring Reinstatement

Except as otherwise stated in a Taking-Over Certificate, a certificate for a Section or part of the Works shall not be deemed to certify completion of any ground or other surfaces requiring reinstatement.

Sub-Clause 10.4 covers the situation when the ground or other surface needs to be reinstated after the Works are complete. Final reinstatement may not be physically possible until after the Contractor has completed the Works, or even until the end of the Defects Notification Period. This Sub-Clause states that a Taking-Over Certificate shall not be deemed to cover such reinstatement unless it is stated in the Certificate. The completion of reinstatement would become 'minor outstanding work' to be carried out during the Defects Notification Period, or as an unfulfilled obligation under Sub-Clause 11.10.

☞ **疑难词汇** ☜

1. punch lists (snag lists) 剩余工作清单
2. Taking-Over Certificate 接收证书
3. minor outstanding work 不影响实质性的未完成工作
4. at the sole discretion of the Employer 根据雇主的自作主张
5. surfaces requiring reinstatement 地表需要恢复原状

☞ **疑难语句** ☜

1. The Engineer shall, within 28 days after receiving the Contractor's application, issue the Taking-Over Certificate to the Contractor, stating the date on which the Works or Section were completed in accordance with the Contract, except for any minor outstanding work and defects which will not substantially affect the use of the Works or Section for their intended purpose (either until or whilst this work is completed and these defects are remedied); or reject the application, giving reasons and specifying the work required to be done by the Contractor to enable the Taking-Over Certificate to be issued. The Contractor

shall then complete this work before issuing a further notice under this Sub-Clause.

工程师在收到承包商的申请后 28 天内，应向承包商颁发接收证书，说明根据合同工程或区段完工的日期，但某些不会实质影响工程或区段按其预定目的使用的扫尾工作以及缺陷除外（直到或当该工程已完成且已修补缺陷时），或驳回申请，提出理由并说明为使接收证书得以颁发承包商尚需完成的工作。随后承包商应在根据本款再一次发出申请通知前，完成此类工作。

2. If the Engineer fails either to issue the Taking-Over Certificate or to reject the Contractor's application within the period of 28 days, and if the Works or Section (as the case may be) are substantially in accordance with the Contract, the Taking-Over Certificate shall be deemed to have been issued on the last day of that period.

若在 28 天期限内工程师既未颁发接收证书也未驳回承包商的申请，而当工程或区段（视情况而定）基本符合合同要求时，应视为在上述期限内的最后一天已经颁发了接收证书。

3. The taking over of a part of the Works was not envisaged in the Contract and is likely to cause problems for any Tests on Completion. Any such tests must be carried out as soon as practicable, but may have to be coordinated with tests in other parts of the Works.

部分工程的接收并不是合同订立时的本意，并且可能引发完工试验的问题。实践中，完工试验需要尽快完成，而且与其他部分工程的完工试验相协调。

☞ 中文综述 ☜

一、概述

建设项目竣工验收是指由发包人、承包人和项目验收委员会，以项目批准的设计任务书和设计文件，以及国家或有关部门颁发的施工验收规范和质量检验标准为依据，按照一定的程序和手续，在项目建成并试生产合格后（工业生产性项目），对工程项目的总体进行检验和认证、综合评价和鉴定的活动。竣工验收是建设工程的最后阶段，是全面检验建设项目是否符合设计要求和工程质量检验标准的重要环节。只有经过竣工验收，建设项目才能实现由承包人管理向发包人管理的过渡。

在 FIDIC 合同条款中，雇主有权对正在施工过程中的任何部分的工程要求优先使用，承包商应无费用、无附加条件地按雇主的安排优先移交相关工程，同时需保证与相邻部分的分隔处理的要求。承包商考虑这种"无费用、无附加条件"风险的时候，就应该综合考虑雇主最可能想接受哪个部分（Part），一般是商业部分或办公部分的先期使用。只有考虑这种风险并体现在报价中，承包商接受部分工程的移交，就不会出现问题。承包商也可以先行与雇主进行沟通，如果能够达成早期交付工程的意向，会非常有利于工程报价。

二、"Part" 与 "Section" 的关系

"新红皮书"第 10 条出现了 "Section" 和 "Part" 两个词语。"Section" 和 "Part" 都有部分的意思，它们都指组成工程内容的一个部分。这个部分是如何划分的？"Section" 和 "Part" 都没有硬性的规定，所以从物理层面说，"Section" 和 "Part" 没有非常严格的区别。但是合同定义上的 "Section" 和 "Part" 却有着很严格的区分。

"Section"是指在投标函附录中指明的雇主在招标文件中要求的必须单独接收的工程部分，而"Part"是指在施工过程中，合同中没有约定的，雇主决定单独提前接收的部分工程。所以正常的"Section"接收是不会给承包商以任何费用和工期的补偿。而"Part"是中标后由雇主方提出的合同中没有约定的额外要求，相当于雇主变更合同，因此雇主应给予承包商一定的补偿。

三、对工程和区段的接收

对工程和区段的接收是在工程根据合同已竣工的情况下进行的。承包商可在他认为工程将完工并准备移交前 14 天内，向工程师发出申请接收证书的通知。如果工程划分为区段，则承包商应同样为每一区段申请接收证书。

工程师在收到承包商的申请后 28 天内，应向承包商颁发接收证书，说明根据合同工程或区段完工的日期，但某些不会实质影响工程或区段按其预定目的使用的扫尾工作以及缺陷除外（直到或当该工程已完成且已修补缺陷时），或者驳回申请，提出理由并说明为使接收证书得以颁发承包商尚需完成的工作。随后承包商应在根据本款再一次发出申请通知前，完成此类工作。

若在 28 天期限内工程师既未颁发接收证书也未驳回承包商的申请，而当工程或区段（视情况而定）基本符合合同要求时，应视为在上述期限内的最后一天已经颁发了接收证书。

四、对部分工程的接收

根据承包商申请，工程师可以为部分永久工程颁发接收证书。只有在工程师颁发接收证书后，雇主才可以使用工程的接收部分。但是，如果在接收证书颁发前雇主确实使用了工程的任何部分：

(1) 该被使用的部分自被使用之日，应视为已被雇主接收；

(2) 承包商应从使用之日起停止对该部分的照管责任，此时，责任应转给雇主；

(3) 当承包商要求时，工程师应为此部分颁发接收证书。

工程师为此部分工程颁发接收证书后，应尽早给予承包商机会以使其采取可能必要的步骤完成任何尚未完成的竣工检验，承包商应在缺陷通知期期满前尽快进行此类竣工检验。

如果由于雇主接收和（或）使用该部分工程（承包商同意的使用除外）而使承包商招致了费用，承包商可以通知工程师并有权依据第 20.1 款【承包商的索赔】获得有关费用以及合理利润的支付，并将之加入合同价格。

五、对竣工检验的干扰

如果由于雇主的原因妨碍承包商进行竣工检验已达 14 天以上，则应认为雇主已在本应完成竣工检验之日接收了工程或区段（视情况而定）。工程师随后应相应地颁发一份接收证书，并且承包商应在缺陷通知期期满前尽快进行竣工检验。工程师应提前 14 天发出通知，要求根据合同的有关规定进行竣工检验。若延误进行竣工检验致使承包商遭受了延误和（或）导致了费用，则承包商应通知工程师并有权依据第 20.1 款【承包商的索赔】获得任何延长的工期，如果竣工已经或将被延误；以及要求雇主支付任何有关费用加上合理的利润，并将之加入合同价格。

六、地表需要恢复原状

除非接收证书中另有规定，区段或部分工程的证书并不认为可以证明任何需要恢复原状的场地或其他地表面的工作已经完成。"Section" 和 "Part" 工程接收了，与 "Section" 和 "Part" 工程相连接的地面工程也同时 "完工" 移交给雇主使用了，但这一块不能以 "已经完成" 为理由在将来整体工程竣工后不重做。通常情况下，"Section" 和 "part" 工程本身在最后竣工时不需要再做什么改动，但与之相连的外场地面通常都是要与整个外场一起重做的，这样做出来的外场才能和谐一致。费用当然发生了两次，但工程不能以 "已经完成" 为理由而不做。此时，费用一般是先交工部分的外场地面按 "先行移交" 计算，后面与大面积场地一块做的部分按清单正常结账。

Questions

1. What is the procedure for the Employer to take over the Works?

2. What will happen if the Employer does use any part of the Works before the Taking-Over Certificate is issued?

3. If the Contractor suffers delay and/or incurs Cost as a result in carrying out the Tests on Completion, is employer responsible for it?

Chapter 11   Defects and Liability

11. 1   Introduction

11. 1. 1   The construction defects

The law of construction defects is largely based on contract. Think about how many contracts might be involved in a single construction project. The Employer of a building enters into a contract with an architect to design plans for a renovation. The architect enters into a contract with an engineer to review drawings to make sure they comply with engineering principles. The Employer then contracts with a general contractor to implement the plans. The general contractor contracts with a dozen subcontractors to assist in implementation.

Every one of those contracts will probably have provisions indicating which party will be responsible for which type of defect. So, when construction contracts are negotiated, it is critical for the parties to pay close attention to the liability provisions. The result of all of this negotiation is usually that liability is passed down the chain. In other words, the Employer will require the general contractor to accept responsibility for defects. The general contractor will then require each of the subcontractors to accept responsibility for defects.

This passing of liability is often done with "indemnification" provisions. If a subcontractor indemnifies a contractor for certain liability, it means that the subcontractor guarantees that if the contractor is later sued, the subcontractor will pay for any judgments that are rendered against the contractor. As a result, subcontractors often carry insurance policies protecting them from liability for defects. So, at the end of the day, many lawsuits resulting from construction defects are paid for by insurance companies.

11. 1. 2   Defects provisions in FIDIC

Clause 11 deals with the procedures during the Defects Notification Period, immediately after the Works have been taken over by the Employer. During this period the Contractor is responsible for correcting any defects. If, for any reason, the Employer does not fully occupy and use the project immediately after taking it over, then the Employer will lose the benefits of the full Defects Notification Period.

The duration of the Defects Notification Period is stated in the Appendix to Tender. Most of the items in the Appendix to Tender have been left blank in the FIDIC form, for details to be inserted by the Employer before calling Tenders, but the figure of 365 days has been printed for the Defects Notification Period. This period may need to be changed by the Employer in the Tender documents. Whilst a period of one year will generally be suitable for civil engineering projects, a longer period may be required for electrical, mechanical or building services work. For example, performance tests on air conditioning plant must be carried out during hot weather, may be specified as Tests after Completion and are often followed by balancing and adjustment of the plant. For the Defects Notification Period to include a full hot-weather season after the completion of the balancing will require a two-year or 730-day period.

The procedures under Clause 11 generally require notifications and actions by the Employer, whereas similar actions before Completion would have been undertaken by the Engineer. This is a logical change because the Employer has occupied the Works, will be aware of any defects or other problems and the Contractor will need to liaise with the Employer in order to carry out repairs. The Employer will need to make the appropriate arrangements to identify any defects and must designate a representative to liaise with the Contractor. In practice, as the Engineer is now defined as Employer's Personnel, it may be convenient for these tasks to be carried out by the Engineer.

During this period the Engineer has certain powers and responsible as stated in the Sub-Clauses, but no longer has the power to issue instructions for Variations. Under Sub-Clause 13. 1 Variations can only be issued prior to the issue of the Taking-Over Certificate.

11. 2   Completion of Outstanding Work and Remedying Defects

In order that the Works and Contractor's Documents, and each Section, shall be in the condition required by the Contract (fair wear and tear excepted) by the expiry date of the relevant Defects Notification Period or as soon as practicable thereafter, the Contractor shall:

(a) complete any work which is outstanding on the date stated in a Taking-Over Certificate, within such reasonable time as is instructed by the Engineer; and

(b) execute all work required to remedy defects or damage, as may be notified by (or on behalf) of the Employer on or before the expiry date of the Defects Notification Period for the Works or Section (as the case may be) .

If a defect appears or damage occurs, the Contractor shall be notified accordingly, by (or on behalf of) the Employer. Sub-Clause 11. 1 gives the overall requirement and procedures for the Defects Notification Period. During the Defects Notification Period, the Works have been occupied and are being used by the Employer. At the end of the period, the Works must be in the condition required by the Contract, with the exception of "fair wear and tear" . Routine maintenance and problems caused by the Employer's use of the Works are the responsibility of the Employer. This means that: any work which was outstanding at the date of the Taking-Over Certificate will have been completed, and any defects or damage which has been notified to the Contractor by the Employer will have been repaired.

Any defect will be notified to the Contractor by (or on behalf of) the Employer. Any such notification should be copied to the Engineer, in order that he can take any necessary action under other Sub-Clauses.

In earlier Conditions of Contracts this period was known as the "Maintenance Period" or the "Defects Liability Period". The change to the name "Defects Notification Period" emphasizes that the Contractor's liability is to repair any defects that have been notified during the period.

11. 3　Extension of Defects Notification Period

The Employer shall be entitled subject to Sub-clause 2. 5 [Employer's Claims] to an extension of the Defects Notification Period for the Works or a Section if and to the extent that the Works, Section or a major item of Plant (as the case may be, and after taking over) cannot be used for the purposes for which they are intended by reason of a defect or damage. However, a Defects Notification Period shall not be extended by more than two years.

If delivery and/or erection of Plant and/or Materials was suspended under Sub-Clause 8. 8 [Suspension of Work] or Sub-Clause 16. 1 [Contractor's Entitlement to Suspend Work], the Contractor's obligations under this clause shall not apply to any defects or damage occurring more than two years after the Defects Notification Period for the Plant and/or Materials would otherwise have expired.

The duration of the Defects Notification Period is stated in the Appendix to Tender but may be extended under Sub-Clause 11. 3. If the Employer considers that he is entitled to an extension of this period, then either the Employer or the Engineer must give notice to the Contractor. The notice must be given, under Sub-Clause 2. 5, as soon as practicable after the Employer became aware of the circumstances and before the expiry of the period. The Engineer will then make a determination under Sub-Clause 3. 5.

To establish an entitlement to an extension, the Employer must prove that the whole or a Section of the Works or a major item of Plant could not be used for the purpose for which it was intended due to a defect or damage. The Defects Notification Period for the whole, or the Section of the Works or the major item of Plant could then be extended for an appropriate period, which must not exceed two years.

11. 4　Failure to Remedy Defects

If the Contractor fails to remedy the defect or damage by this notified date and this remedial work was to be executed at the cost of the Contractor under Sub-Clause 11. 2 [Cost of Remedying Defects], the Employer may (at his option):

(a) carry out the work himself or by others, in a reasonable manner and at the Contractor's cost, but the Contractor shall have no responsibility for this work; and the Contractor shall subject to Sub-Clause 2. 5 [Employer's Claims] pay to the Employer the costs reasonably incurred by the Employer in remedying the defect or damage;

(b) require the Engineer to agree or determine a reasonable reduction in the Contract Price in accordance with Sub-Clause 3. 5 [Determinations]; or

(c) if the defect or damage deprives the Employer of substantially the whole benefit of the Works or any major part of the Works, terminate the Contract as a whole, or in respect of such major part which cannot be put to the intended use. Without prejudice to any other rights, under the Contract or otherwise, the Employer shall then be entitled to recover all sums paid for the Works or for such part (as the case may be), plus financing costs and the cost of dismantling the same, clearing the Site and returning Plant and Materials to the Contractor.

Before taking any action the Employer's preference must be discussed with the Engineer and Contractor, in an attempt to reach agreement on the proposed action, and any appropriate notices given to the Contractor. The Employer may:

(a) make other arrangements to carry out the work and claim the Cost against the Contractor, under Sub-Clause 2. 5, or

(b) accept the work including the defect and reduce the Contract price, under the procedures of Sub-Clause 3. 5 (this is a practical procedure and can be used when the remedial work would cause substantial inconvenience or damage and the Employer would prefer to accept the out of specification work), or

(c) terminate the Contract as a whole or in respect of the relevant part of the Works. This would obviously be a very serious action and would result in the Employer claiming substantial sums of money from the Contractor. The termination procedures at Clause 15 would apply, with the additional requirements of Sub-Clause 11. 4 (c) .

11. 5   Removal of Defective Work and Further Tests

11. 5. 1   Removal of Defective Work

If the defect or damage cannot be remedied expeditiously on the Site and the Employer gives consent, the Contractor may remove from the Site for the purposes of repairing such items of Plant as are defective or damaged.

This consent may require the Contractor to increase the amount of the Performance Security by the full replacement cost of these items, or to provide other appropriate security. The Employer must give his consent before any item of Plant is removed from the Site for repair. Before giving consent the Employer will want to know how long the repair will take and what action is proposed to enable the Works to be used during its absence. The situation envisaged at Sub- Clause 11. 5 could result in an extension to the Defects Notification Period under Sub-Clause 11. 3.

11. 5. 2 Further Tests

If the work of remedying of any defect or damage may affect the performance of the Works, the Engineer may require the repetition of any of the tests described in the Contract. The requirement shall be made by notice within 28 days after the defect or damage is remedied.

These tests shall be carried out in accordance with the terms applicable to the previous tests, except that they shall be carried out at the risk and cost of the Party liable, under Sub-Clause 11. 2 [Cost of Remedying Defects], for the cost of the remedial work.

11. 6 Performance Certificate

Performance of the Contractor's obligations shall not be considered to have been completed until the Engineer has issued the Performance Certificate to the Contractor, stating the date on which the Contractor completed his obligations under the Contract.

The Engineer shall issue the Performance Certificate within 28 days after the latest of the expiry dates of the Defects Notification Periods, or as soon thereafter as the Contractor has supplied all the Contractor's Documents and completed and tested all the Works, including remedying any defects. A copy of the Performance Certificate shall be issued to the Employer. Only the Performance Certificate shall be deemed to constitute acceptance of the Works.

The Performance Certificate is issued when the Engineer is satisfied that the Contractor has fulfilled his obligations during the Defects Notification Period. The delay of 28 days from the end of the Defects Notification Period allows time for a joint inspection of the Works and for the Contractor to complete any outstanding work.

The final sentence of Sub-Clause 11. 9 confirms the Contract requirements, such as Sub-Clause 3. 2 (a), which stipulate that any failure to notice and report, at the time, any item of work that does not comply with the Specifications does not mean that the work has been accepted. The receipt of the Performance Certificate starts the 56 day period for the Contractor to submit a draft final account which includes all outstanding claims.

11. 7 Clearance of Site

Upon receiving the Performance Certificate, the Contractor shall remove any remaining Contract's Equipment, surplus material, wreckage, rubbish and Temporary Works from the Site.

If all these items have not been removed within 28 days after the Employer receives a copy of the Performance Certificate, the Employer may sell or otherwise dispose of any remaining items. The Employer shall be entitled to be paid the costs incurred in connection with, or attributable to, such sale or disposal and restoring the Site. Any balance of the moneys from the sale shall be paid to the Contractor. If these moneys are less than the Employer's costs, the Contractor shall pay the outstanding balance to the Employer.

The time periods for actions under Sub-Clause 11. 11 start from the receipt of the Performance Certificate by the Contractor and Employer. The dates of receipt must be recorded by the Engineer. The requirements for the Contractor's final Site clearance may also be the subject of regulations under the governing law.

☞ 疑难词汇 ☜

1. calling tenders 招标
2. liaise with 与……保持联系，与……沟通
3. fair wear and tear 合理损耗，正常损耗
4. without prejudice to any other rights 在不影响其他权利情况下
5. routine maintenance 日常维护
6. emphasize 强调
7. maintenance period 保修期
8. Defects Liability Period 瑕疵责任期
9. erection 架设，安装
10. remedial work 补救工作
11. dismantle 拆除，废除
12. a pot of the design 设计的一部分
13. out of specification work 规范的工作
14. entitlement 授权
15. final account 最后决算
16. wreckage 残骸，废旧物
17. take precedence over 地位高于，比……重要
18. expeditiously 迅速地，敏捷地

☞ 疑难语句 ☜

1. The Employer shall be entitled subject to Sub-Clause 2. 5 〔Employer's Claims〕 to an extension of the Defects Notification Period for the Works or a Section if and to the extent that the Works, Section or a major item of Plant (as the case may be, and after taking over) cannot be used for the purposes for which they are intended by reason of a defect or damage. However, a Defects Notification Period shall not be extended by more than two years.

如果且在一定程度上工程、区段或主要永久设备（视情况而定，并且在接收以后）由于缺陷或损害而不能按照预定的目的进行使用，则雇主有权依据第 2.5 款【雇主的索赔】要求延长工程或区段的缺陷通知期。但缺陷通知期的延长不得超过 2 年。

2. If delivery and/or erection of Plant and/or Materials was suspended under Sub-Clause 8. 8 [Suspension of Work] or Sub-Clause 16. 1 [Contractor's Entitlement to Suspend Work], the Contractor's obligations under this Clause shall not apply to any defects or damage occurring more thon two years after the Defects Notification Period for the Plant and/or Materials would otherwise have expired.

如果永久设备和（或）材料的运送以及（或）安装根据第 8.8 款【工程暂停】或第 16.1 款【承包商有权暂停工作】发生了暂停，则本款所规定的承包商的义务不适用于永久设备和（或）材料的缺陷通知期期满 2 年后发生的任何缺陷或损害的情况。

3. The Employer shall be entitled to be paid the costs incurred in connection with, or attributable to, such sale or disposal and restoring the Site. Any balance of the moneys from the sale shall be paid to the Contractor. If these moneys are less than the Employer's costs, the Contractor shall pay the outstanding balance to the Employer.

雇主将获得出售、处置和恢复现场所支付的费用。扣除上述（雇主处置、变卖等的）费用的余额将返还给承包商。但是如果上述支付雇主的费用少于雇主的花费，承包商负责支付。

4. If the defect or damage deprives the Employer of substantially the whole benefit of the Works or any major part of the Works, terminate the Contract as a whole, or in respect of such major part which cannot be put to the intended use. Without prejudice to any other rights, under the Contract or otherwise, the Employer shall then be entitled to recover all sums paid for the Works or for such part (as the case may be), plus financing costs and the cost of dismantling the same, clearing the Site and returning Plant and Materials to the Contractor.

在该缺陷或损害致使雇主基本上无法享用全部工程或部分工程所带来的全部利益时，对整个工程或不能按期投入使用的那部分主要工程终止合同。在不影响任何其他权利的前提下，依据合同或其他规定，雇主还应有权收回为整个工程或该部分工程（视情况而定）所支付的全部费用以及融资费用、拆除工程、清理现场和将永久设备和材料退还给承包商所支付的费用。

☞ **中文综述** ☜

一、概述

FIDIC "新红皮书"中工程竣工验收完成后应承包商申请，工程师向承包商颁发《接收证书》。承包商接收到《接收证书》后，工程进入缺陷责任期。

一般要颁发两个证书，一是《移交证书》，二是《缺陷责任证书》，两个证书各有不同的作用。

在工程基本竣工后，承包商可以以书面形式向工程师申请颁发《移交证书》，并同时附上一份在缺陷责任期内未完工程的书面保证。基本竣工指工程通过竣工检验，能够按照合同约定的时间交给雇主占用或使用，工程扫尾、清理、地面等不影响工程使用的某些次要部分缺陷修复工作可以在缺陷责任期内进行，缺陷责任期的长短由承包商在投标时根据雇主的要求确定。工程移交给雇主后，工程进入缺陷责任期。

当工程各部分全部完工，并完成了承包商保证在缺陷责任期应完成的收尾工作和雇主接收工程后在运行过程中发现的除正常磨损以外的任何缺陷等工作，则在缺陷责任期期满后的 28 天内，由工程师颁发《履约证书》，并将副本送给承包商。

《履约证书》的作用体现在：首先，《履约证书》是承包商按合同规定完成全部工作的证明；其次，《履约证书》证明除合同中关于财务和管理方面的内容外，合同其他内容终止；再次，《履约证书》意指工程师无权再指令承包商进行任何施工工作，承包商可按合同约定与雇主办理最终决算；最后，雇主在颁发《履约证书》后，应退还承包商另一半保留金。

需要注意的是，FIDIC 合同条款并未对工程全部竣工后的质量保修问题作出相应规定，究其原因，FIDIC 合同条款虽然具有国际适用性，但在某个具体国家的项目上运用时，还是要根据项目所在国的法律进行调整，各国对工程移交后的保修期限规定不同，故将此空间留给合同双方在特殊条款中约定较为适宜。

二、缺陷通知期

"新红皮书"规定"缺陷通知期"指根据投标函附录中的规定，从工程或区段按照第 10.1 款［工程或区段的接收］被证明完工的日期算起，到按照第 11.1 款［完成扫尾工作和修补缺陷］通知工程或该区段（视情况而定）中的缺陷的期限（包括按照第 11.3 款［缺陷通知期的延长］决定的任何延期）。

这里的缺陷通知期也就是通常所说的 FIDIC 合同条件下的保修期。首先，它是指工程师通知承包商修复工程缺陷的期间；其次，工程是雇主已经接收并颁发给承包商接收证书的工程或区段；第三，该期限的长短在投标函附录中写明；第四，该期限可以根据"新红皮书"第 13 条规定予以延长；第五，该期限从工程或区段的竣工日期开始计算。

三、修补缺陷的费用

如果承包商负有缺陷责任，承包商将承担缺陷的修补费用。根据"新红皮书"第 11.1 款的规定，由承包商自担风险的修补缺陷包括：任何承包商负责的设计；永久设备、材料或工艺不符合合同要求；或承包商未履行任何其他义务。如果且在一定程度上上述工作的必要性是由于任何其他原因引起的，雇主（或雇主授权的他人）应立即通知承包商，此时适用第 13.3 款［变更程序］。

四、缺陷通知期的延长

如果且在一定程度上工程、区段或主要永久设备（视情况而定，并且在接收以后）由于缺陷或损害而不能按照预定的目的进行使用，则雇主有权依据第 2.5 款［雇主的索赔］要求延长工程或区段的缺陷通知期。但缺陷通知期的延长不得超过 2 年。

如果永久设备和（或）材料的运送以及（或）安装根据第 8.8 款［工程暂停］或第 16.1 款［承包商有权暂停工作］发生了暂停，则本款所规定的承包商的义务不适用于永久设备和（或）材料的缺陷通知期期满 2 年后发生的任何缺陷或损害的情况。

五、雇主擅自使用未经竣工验收的工程的后果

"新红皮书"第 10.2 款规定：在雇主完全自主决定的情况下，工程师可颁发永久工程任何部分的接收证书。除非并直到工程师已颁发任何部分工程的接收证书，雇主不得使用该部分工程（除合同规定或经双方同意作为临时措施外）。但是，如果雇主在颁发接收证书前确实使用了任何部分工程，则：

（1）使用的部分应视为从开始使用的日期起已被接收；

（2）承包商应从此日起不再承担该部分的照管责任，应转由雇主负责；

（3）如承包商提出要求，工程师应颁发该部分的接收证书。

在我国，在建筑工程未经竣工验收或者验收未通过的情况下，雇主擅自或强行使用的，即可视为雇主对建设工程质量是认可的，或者虽然工程质量不合格，但其自愿承担质量责任。基于上述理由，《最高人民法院关于审理建设工程施工合同纠纷案件适用法律问题的解释》第13条规定："建设工程未经竣工验收，雇主擅自使用后，又以使用部分质量不符合约定为由主张权利的，不予支持；但是承包商应当在建设工程的合理使用寿命内对地基基础工程和主体结构质量承担民事责任。"

六、缺陷通知期限内承包商的义务

在缺陷责任期限内，承包商的主要义务是完成扫尾工作和修补缺陷。FIDIC "新红皮书" 第11.1款规定，承包商应：

（1）在工程师指示的合理时间内，完成接收证书注明日期时尚未完成的任何工作；

（2）在工程或区段工程（视情况而定）的缺陷通知期限届满日期或以前，根据雇主（或其代表）可能通知的要求，完成修补缺陷或损害所需的所有工作。

如果承包商未能在合理的时间内修复任何缺陷或损害，雇主（或其代表）可确定一个日期，要求到或不迟于该日期修复缺陷和损害，且应将此日期向承包商发出合理的通知。

如果承包商到此通知的日期仍未修复缺陷或损害，并且根据第11.2款［修补缺陷的费用］的规定，此项修复工作应由承包商承担实施的费用，雇主可以（自行选择）：

（1）以合理的方式由他本人或他人进行此项工作，由承包商承担费用，但承包商对此项工作将不再承担责任；根据第2.5款［雇主的索赔］的规定，承包商应向雇主支付由雇主修复缺陷或损害而发生的合理费用；

（2）要求工程师根据第3.5款［决定］的规定，同意或决定合同价格的合理减少额；

（3）如果缺陷或损害使雇主实质上丧失了工程或工程的任何主要部分的整体利益时，雇主可终止整个合同或不能按照预期使用功能使用的该项主要部分。雇主有权在不损害按照合同或其他规定所具有的任何其他权利的情况下，收回对工程或该部分工程（视情况而定）的全部支付总额，加上融资费用和拆除工程、清理现场，以及将生产设备和材料退回给承包商所支付的费用。

Questions

1. How the New Red Book defines the Defects Notification Period? Can Defects Notification Period be extended?

2. If the Contractor fails to remedy the defect or damage in the notified period, what the Employer may do according to Clauses 11. 2 of New Red Book?

3. Please specify the responsibilities of the Contractor during Defects Notification Period.

Chapter 12　Measurement and Evaluation

12. 1　Introduction

Clause 12 in the New Red Book is written for a remeasurement in which the Accepted Contract Amount is based on estimated quantities but the Contractor is obliged to carry out all the work which is required by the Specification and Drawings and is paid for the actual quantities of work which he has executed. The Clause covers the procedures for the measurement and evaluation of the Works that have been executed, or have been omitted by a Variation.

The New Red Book is clear that the quantities in the Bill of Quantities are only estimates. Hence any changes due to remeasurement are not Variations, but are part of the original obligations of both Parties. If the Employer, for his own internal accounting purposes, requires the additional Cost due to changes in quantities to be confirmed by a Variation order then this is just an administrative procedure and does not indicate that the change is a Variation.

12. 2　Works to be Measured

The Works shall be measured, and valued for payment, in accordance with this Clause. Whenever the Engineer requires any part of the Works to be measured, reasonable notice shall be given to the Contractor's Representative, who shall:

(1) promptly either attend or send another qualified representative to assist the Engineer in making the measurement; and

(2) supply any particulars requested by the Engineer.

If the Contractor fails to attend or send a representative, the measurement made by (or on behalf of) the Engineer shall be accepted as accurate.

Except as otherwise stated in the Contract, wherever any Permanent Works are to be measured from records, these shall be prepared by the Engineer. The Contractor shall, as and when requested, attend to examine and agree the records with the Engineer, and shall sign the same when agreed. If the Contractor does not attend, the records shall be accepted as accurate.

If the Contractor examines and disagrees the records, and/or does not sign them as agreed, then the Contractor shall give notice to the Engineer of the respects in which the records are asserted to be inaccurate. After receiving this notice, the Engineer shall review the records and either confirm or vary them. If the Contractor does not so give notice to the Engineer within 14 days after being requested to examine the records, they shall be accepted as accurate.

The procedures for measurement of the Works are given at Sub-Clause 12. 1 as follows.

(1) The Engineer decides that he requires a part of the Works to be measured and notifies the Contractor.

(2) The Contractor attends and assists the Engineer in making the measurement.

(3) Alternatively, the Contractor fails to attend and the Engineer's measurements are accepted as accurate.

If a part of the Works is to be measured from records of its construction then the details should be specified in the Tender documents. A similar procedure applies in that the Engineer prepares the records and the Contractor examines and agrees or disagrees with the records.

If the Engineer requires the Contractor to carry out the work for either measurement or the preparation of records then this should be stated in the Specification. In practice the Contractor often does play a greater part in this work than is required by the Contract. The Contractor is more likely to have the staff and equipment available and some Contractors prefer to make the measurements themselves, rather than assist the Engineer. The Engineer will then check and confirm the Contractor's measurement.

The Contract does not stipulate any fixed periods or timing for the measurement and this is a matter for the Engineer. The timing of measurement notifications will depend on the progress of the Works and the completion of convenient parts or items in the Bill of Quantities, although any work which is to be buried or covered up must be measured before it is buried or covered. The Contractor will have notified the Engineer under Sub-Clause 7. 3 before the Work is buried or covered up.

The measurement must be completed in time for the Contractor to prepare and submit his Statement at Completion, as Sub-Clause 14. 10, but does not have to be related to interim payments. The provision for interim payments, at Sub-Clause 14. 3, is based on "the estimated value of the Works executed" and not on a final valuation. The estimated value may be based on an interim or approximate measurement and will be adjusted when the final measurement figures have been agreed.

12. 3　Method of Measurement

Except as otherwise stated in the Contract and notwithstanding local practice:

(1) measurement shall be made of the net actual quantity of each item of the Permanent Works; and

(2) the method of measurement shall be in accordance with the Bill of Quantities or other applicable Schedules.

The procedure for the actual measurement of the different work items can be standardized for different projects and for consistency within a project by the use of a published standard method of measurement. The FIDIC Conditions of Contract do not require the use of a standard method of measurement but Sub-Clause 12.2 states that the method of measurement will be in accordance with the Bill of Quantities or other applicable Schedules. If a standard method of measurement, such as the Civil Engineering Standard Method of Measurement published by The Institution of Civil Engineers, is to be used then this requirement should be stated in the Particular Conditions.

Alternatively, the Bill of Quantities should include a detailed explanation of the method of measurement which will be used. For example, the phrase net actual quantity needs to be explained. It will not mean the actual quantity which has been executed by the Contractor. Particularly for work below ground level, the Contractor may have provided method of working. Net actual quantity would then mean the minimum quantities that would be required in order to provide the Permanent Works.

12.4 Evaluation

Except as otherwise stated in the Contract, the Engineer shall proceed in accordance with Sub-Clause 3.5 [Determinations] to agree or determine the Contract Price by evaluating each item of work, applying the measurement agreed or determined in accordance with the Sub-Clauses 12.1 and 12.2 and the appropriate rate or price for the item.

For each item of work, the appropriate rate or price for the item shall be the rate or price specified for such item in the Contractor, if there is no such item, specified for similar work. However, a new rate or price shall be appropriate for an item of work if:

(1) (a) the measured quantity of the item is changed by more than 10% from the quantity of this item in the Bill of Quantities or other Schedule,

(b) this change in quantity multiplied by such specified rate for this item exceeds 0.01 % of the Accepted Contract Amount,

(c) this change in quantity directly changes the Cost per unit quantity of this item by more than 1%, and this item is not specified in the Contract as a 'fixed rate item'; or

(2) (a) the work is instructed under Clause 13 [Variations and Adjustments],

(b) no rate or price is specified in the Contract for this item, and

(c) no specified rate or price is appropriate because the item of work is not of similar character, or is not executed under similar conditions, as any item in the Contract.

Each new rate or price shall be derived from any relevant rates or prices in the Contract, with reasonable adjustments to take account of the matters described in sub-paragraph (a) and/or (b), as applicable. If no rates or prices are relevant for the derivation of a new rate or price, it shall be derived from the reasonable Cost of executing the work, together with reasonable profit, taking account of any other relevant matters.

Until such time as an appropriate rate or price is agreed or determined, the Engineer shall determine a provisional rate or price for the purposes of interim Payment Certificates. Sub-Clause 12. 3 requires the Engineer to agree or determine the Contract Price by applying the measurement and the appropriate rate or price for each item. The appropriate rate or price is stated to be the Contract rate or price for the item, or for similar work, unless:

(1) the measured quantity has changed by more than the amounts stated at Sub-Clause 12. 3 (a) and the item is not specified as a'fixed rate item', or

(2) the work is a Variation under Clause 13 and there is no appropriate rate or price in the Contract.

The percentage figures given at sub-paragraphs (a)(i) and (ii) are probably too low and will result in a requirement to discuss an excessive number of new rates, which may be virtually unchanged from the original rates. The MDB Edition of FIDIC, has used 25% and 0. 25%. Item (a) (iii) refers to changes of Cost, which is defined as expenditure reasonably incurred by the Contractor for the particular item. Only the Contractor knows this figure and he will probably be unwilling, or even unable, to provide an accurate figure.

Any evaluation or new rate or price will be determined by the Engineer in accordance with the procedures in Sub-Clause 3. 5. That is, the Engineer will consult with both Parties and try to reach agreement. Failing agreement the Engineer will make a fair determination. Either Party has the right to invoke the Clause 20 dispute procedures if it is not satisfied with the Engineer's determination.

12. 5   Omissions

Whenever the omission of any work forms part (or all) of a Variation, the value of which has not been agreed, if:

(1) the Contractor will incur (or has incurred) cost which, if the work had not been omitted, would have been deemed to be covered by a sum forming part of the Accepted Contract Amount;

(2) the omission of the work will result (or has resulted) in this sum not forming part of the Contract Price, and

(3) this cost is not deemed to be included in the evaluation of any substituted work;

then the Contractor shall give notice to the Engineer accordingly, with supporting particulars. Upon receiving this notice, the Engineer shall proceed in accordance with Sub-Clause 3. 5 [Determinations] to agree or determine this cost, which shall be included in the Contract Price.

When any work is omitted it is likely that the Contractor will already have incurred some expenditure in the preparation, provision of Goods and ordering Materials, if not in the actual execution of work on the Site. This Sub-Clause requires the Engineer to make a fair assessment of any such Cost.

☞ **疑难词汇** ☜

1. quantities of work 工作量
2. bill of quantities 工程量清单
3. omissions 省略

☞ **疑难语句** ☜

1. If the Contractor fails to attend or send a representative, the measurement made by (or on behalf of) the Engineer shall be accepted as accurate.

如果承包商未能参加或派出一名代表，则由工程师（或工程师授权的他人）进行的测量应被视为准确的，并被接受。

2. Although any work which is to be buried or covered up must be measured before it is buried or covered.

虽然任何可能掩盖或隐蔽的工作应该在掩盖或隐蔽之前完成测量工作。

3. Each new rate or price shall be derived from any relevant rates or prices in the Contract, with reasonable adjustments to take account of the matters described in sub-paragraph (a) and/or (b), as applicable. If no rates or prices are relevant for the derivation of a new rate or price, it shall be derived from the reasonable Cost of executing the work, together with reasonable profit, taking account of any other relevant matters.

每种新的费率或价格是对合同中相关费率或价格在考虑到上述（a）、（b）段所描述的适用的事件以后作出的合理调整。如果没有相关的费率或价格，则新的费率或价格应是在考虑任何相关事件以后，从实施工作的合理费用加上合理利润中得到。

4. The omission of the work will result (or has resulted) in this sum not forming part of the Contract Price.

该工作的省略将导致（或已经导致）这笔金额不构成部分合同价格。

☞ **中文综述** ☜

一、概述

在 FIDIC 合同条款中，测量和估价是比较复杂的。实际中，如果缺乏 FIDIC 经验，从招标到结算的完整过程，承包商很难准确理解 FIDIC 合同的价款和估价原则。例如按 FIDIC 单价合同原则，每一期的付款过程都应该是在凭证齐全准确的前提下精细估价。

二、需测量的工程

"新红皮书"第 12.1 款规定"为了付款，应按照本条规定对工程进行测量和估价"。这句话的直接释义是：付款时，工程师就应该对工程进行测量和估价。对于测量工作，承包商应派出专人协助工程师测量工程的任何部分，凡需根据记录进行测量的任何永久工程，此类记录应由工程师准备。这与国内工程习惯以"竣工图纸为结算依据"是不同的。

按 FIDIC 的推荐，FIDIC "新红皮书"适用于由雇主提供设计的工程。雇主提供设计，意味着雇主设计是合同的一个部分，承包商作为合同当事人，无权单方面修改合同组件的图纸。任何不合"规范"合理要求偏差的工程施工，都会被直接定性为"不符合合同要求"的工程缺陷。所以在施工过程中，承包商应及时就图纸和规范可能出现的问题与工程师沟通，避免返工的发生。

在 FIDIC 条件下，"测量和估价"可以理解为：

1. 完全标准的 FIDIC 施工合同条件过程

即承包商完全按照雇主提供的图纸施工，没有提出任何修改意见，也没有发生变更情况。合同顺利履行完毕，没有任何签证类、索赔类的费用发生。这时应严格按图纸的状况，以及投标工程量计算规则，重新开列与计算清单量。如果与投标时完全相同，就按投标清单执行；如果有偏差，就仅仅是清单问题。这种情况下的工程测量就是指测量图纸。

2. 相对完整的 FIDIC 施工合同过程

即比较正常的工程过程。在工程操作过程中，发生了图纸变更以及其他各种签证。图纸变更归于图纸，核算办法同第 12.1 款（a）项一样是测量图纸，不过此时的图纸是指竣工图纸。签证的部分，就涉及现场尺量工程的过程。任何签证，都不可能反映在图纸上，只能根据现场实际的情况给予确认。常用的方法就是工程中"图纸结算加签证"确定工程造价的方法。

3. 以扩大初步设计图招标投标

确定的承包商进场时，施工图未必出全，工程就开始实施。中期付款时，就需以新的施工图来重新测量工程，以使每一次的工程付款都代表工程实际实施的状况。这个时候的测量，实际也不是指测量工程，仍是指测量图纸，即测量新的施工图。但相对于中标的扩大初步设计图，此时的测量就更表现出实测工程的特性。施工图往往会产生一些扩大初步设计图投标清单中没有的项目，工程量就可能发生变化了，这样也完全地体现出 FIDIC 关于"为了付款，应按照本条规定对工程进行测量和估价"的规定。

三、测量方法

"新红皮书"第 12.2 款是关于工程测量方法的定义，这个定义就是工程量计算规则。一般来说，这个规则都是由专业协会推荐的标准版本，但允许测量师自行为了方便而进行相应的调整。此条款同时规定了工程师对工程合同中的计算规则有最终解释权。

"新红皮书"第 12.2（a）款规定，测量应该是测量每部分永久工程的实际净值，这一条关于"净数量"的概念，在实践中比较容易引起争议。按"新红皮书""以测量工程估价并形成工程价格"的定义，似乎应该是以实物量为基准来形成"净数量"。例如，混凝土灌注桩工程按操作规程是必须要超灌的，否则桩头混凝土质量就无法保证。这种工程惯例及国家规范要求的超灌，就不是合同要求的净数量，而是承包商的措施要求，计量时都不予考虑，费用由承包商投标时在综合单价内综合考虑。

四、估价

按"新红皮书"第 12.1 款测量的基准数据，以及第 12.2 款计算的清单工程量后，就应该按清单计价程序进行组价了。第 12.3 款内容如下：对每一项工作，该项合适的费率或价格应该是合同中对此项工作规定的费率或价格，或者如果没有该项，则为其类似工作的费率或价格。

五、省略

本款是专为省略工程内容扣减承包商相应的工程费用而确定的一个界线。一般来说，分项工程综合单价包括了完成本分项工程所需要的一切工程相关费用，这也同时保证分项工程综合单价不包括其他工程的相关费用。单价合同在综合单价这个特性上是强制性的，也是合同义务与费用一一对应关系在清单中的体现。

这个限定，使分项工程数量的增减对应于工程价格的增减，不会产生分项工程内的费用超扣或分割不清的问题。而与分项工程相关的措施费一般会要求总价包干，不因任何工程变更而变更。所以本条款能够适用的范围，是非常有限的。

"新红皮书"第12.4款规定：当对任何工作的省略构成部分（或全部）变更且对其价值未达成一致时，如果：

（1）承包商将招致（或已经招致）一笔费用，这笔费用应被视为是如果工作未被省略时，在构成部分接受的合同款额的一笔金额中所包含的；

（2）该工作的省略将导致（或已经导致）这笔金额不构成部分合同价格；

（3）这笔费用并不被认为包含在任何替代工作的估价之中。

承包商应随即向工程师发出通知，并附具体的证明资料。在接到通知后，工程师应依据第3.5款【决定】，对此费用作出商定或决定，并将之加入合同价格。

Questions

1. What are the procedures for measurement of the Works under at Sub-Clause 12.1?
2. What is the method of measurement under the New Red Book?

Chapter 13   Variations and Adjustments

13. 1   Introduction

In any construction project there will be a need to change the initial requirements as the construction proceeds on the Site. This may be a matter of the Employer changing his mind about some requirement, or the Engineer may need to issue further information which involves changes to the initial requirements, or it may be necessary to correct a mistake in the information issued to the Contractor. An instruction can be given to change an item of the Works which has been completed and the Cost of making the change will be included in the valuation of the Variation. However, instructions for changes cannot be given after the issue of the Taking-Over Certificate for the Works.

The FIDIC Conditions allow the Engineer, but not the Employer, to issue an instruction to change the Works. The Contractor is not permitted to change the Permanent Works unless the Engineer has instructed or approved the Variation. If the Employer wants to make any changes he must request that the Engineer issues an instruction. If the Employer gives an instruction direct to the Contractor then the Contractor must obtain the Engineer's confirmation and instruction before he executes the change. Strict adherence to these requirements is essential for the Engineer to maintain technical and financial control over the project.

Sub-Clause 3. 3 gives the Engineer the power to issue instructions which may, or may not, constitute a Variation under Clause 13. 1f the Contractor considers that an instruction constitutes a Variation then he should confirm the instruction as a Variation, by acknowledging receipt and stating that it is as required by Sub-Clause 13. 3. 1f the Engineer disagrees then the Contractor must still comply with the instruction but can follow the appropriate claim procedures under Sub-Clause 20. 1.

13. 2   Right to Vary

In the New Red Book, Variations may be initiated by the Engineer at any time prior to issuing the Taking-Over Certificate for the Works, either by an instruction or by a request for the Contractor to submit o proposal.

The Contractor shall execute and be bound by each Variation, unless the Contractor promptly gives notice to the Engineer stating (with supporting particulars) that the Contractor cannot readily obtain the Goods required for the Variation. Upon receiving this notice, the Engineer shall cancel, confirm or vary the instruction.

Each Variation may include:

(a) changes to the quantities of any item of work included in the Contract (however, such changes do not necessarily constitute a Variation);

(b) changes to the quality and other characteristics of any item of work;

(c) changes to the levels, positions and/or dimensions of only pot of the Works;

(d) omission of any work unless it is to be carried out by others;

(e) any additional work, Plant, Materials or services necessary for the Permanent Works, including any associated Tests on Completion, boreholes and other testing and exploratory work; or

(f) changes to the sequence or timing of the execution of the Works.

The Contractor shall not make any alteration and/or modification of the Permanent Works, unless and until the Engineer instructs or approves a Variation.

In Yellow Book, Variations may be initiated by the Engineer at any time prior to issuing the Taking-Over Certificate for the Works, either by an instruction or by a request for the Contractor to submit a proposal. A Variation shall not comprise the omission of any work which is to be carried out by others.

The Contractor shall execute and be bound by each Variation, unless the Contractor promptly gives notice to the Engineer stating (with supporting particulars) that (i) the Contractor cannot readily obtain the Goods required for the Variation, (ii) it will reduce the safety or suitability of the Works, or (iii) it will have an adverse impact on the achievement of the Schedule of Guarantees. Upon receiving this notice, the Engineer shall cancel, confirm or vary the instruction.

Under the New Red Book, the Engineer can issue instructions to change a wide range of matters concerning the Works, as listed at Sub-Clause 13. 1 (a) to (f). However, these are all matters that concern the Permanent Works, which have been defined in the Contract, and do not result in a change to the scope or size of the Works. The Engineer cannot issue instructions under this Clause for additional work unless it is necessary for the Permanent Works, as Sub-Clause 13. 1 (e). If the Employer wants the Contractor to carry out work which changes the scope of the Works then he must negotiate a change to the Contract.

The Contractor can object that he cannot readily obtain the Goods, that is Equipment, Plant, Materials or Temporary Works, and the Engineer can either cancel, confirm or vary the instruction. However, the Contractor cannot object to the instruction because of difficulties in obtaining management staff or labour.

A significant change to previous FIDIC Conditions of Contracts is that the Engineer can initiate the Variation either by issuing an instruction or by a request for the Contractor to submit a proposal. A request for a proposal is not just a matter of submitting a price for a proposed Variation. The Engineer may ask for a detailed technical proposal, together with details of the impact on the programme and on other aspects of the Works.

Where, the Contractor is responsible for a significant part of the design, consideration should be given to restricting the Engineer's power to vary that part of the Works, as stipulated in the Yellow Book. Because the Contractor under the Yellow Book has additional responsibilities, there are additional reasons by which the Contractor can object to the Variation. If the Engineer confirms an instruction following objections by the Contractor then the Employer is taking responsibility for the potential problems which have been notified by the Contractor. If the Variation has design or safety implications then it could also bring additional responsibilities to both the Employer and the Engineer under the applicable law.

13.3   Value Engineering

In the New Red Book, the Contractor may, at any time, submit to the Engineer a written proposal which (in the Contractor's opinion) will, if adopted, (i) accelerate completion, (ii) reduce the cost to the Employer of executing, maintaining or operating the Works, (iii) improve the efficiency or value to the Employer of the completed Works, or (iv) otherwise be of benefit to the Employer.

The proposal shall be prepared at the cost of the Contractor and shall include the items listed in Sub-Clause 13.3 [Variation Procedure]. If a proposal, which is approved by the Engineer, includes a change in the design of part of the Permanent Works, then unless otherwise agreed by both Parties:

(a) the Contractor shall design this part;

(b) subparagraphs (a) to (d) of Sub-Clause 4.1 [Contractor's General Obligations] shall apply; and

(c) if this change results in a reduction in the contract value of this part, the Engineer shall proceed in accordance with Sub-Clause 3.5 [Determinations] to agree or determine a fee, which shall be included in the Contract Price.

Under the New Red Book, the third paragraph of Sub-Clause 13.2 draws a distinction between proposals that include a change in the design of part of the Permanent Works and those that do not include a design change. If the proposal includes a design change then, unless the Parties agree otherwise, the Contractor shall design the changed part of the Works and receive a fee, provided that the reduction in Contract value is greater than any reduction in the value of the Works to the Employer. The fee is calculated by the Engineer, following the Sub-Clause 3.5 procedure. If the proposal does not include a design change then the Contractor will have to rely on any benefit from savings in his own Costs.

In the Yellow Book, The Contractor may, at any time, submit to the Engineer a written proposal which (in the Contractor's opinion) will, if adopted, (i) accelerate completion, (ii) reduce the cost to the Employer of executing, maintaining or operating the Works, (iii) improve the efficiency or value to the Employer of the completed Works, or (iv) otherwise be of benefit to the Employer.

The proposal shall be prepared at the cost of the Contractor and shall include the items listed in Sub-Clause 13. 3 [Variation Procedure] . If the Contractor wishes to submit a proposal that will benefit the Employer in any of the ways listed in the first paragraph of Sub-Clause 13. 2 then he must prepare, at his own Cost, a proposal which includes the information which is required for a Variation proposal under Sub- Clause 13. 3.

The preparation of a value engineering proposal could involve the Contractor in substantial costs which may, or may not, be recovered. Any proposal should be discussed and agreed in principle before the Contractor incurs costs that may not be recoverable. Under the Yellow Book, any value engineering proposal becomes a Variation and is valued as such by the Engineer.

13. 4 Variation Procedure

If the Engineer requests a proposal, prior to instructing a Variation, the Contractor shall respond in writing as soon as practicable, either by giving reasons why he cannot comply (if this is the case) or by submitting:

(a) a description of the proposed work to be performed and a programme for its execution;

(b) the Contractor's proposal for any necessary modifications to the programme according to Sub-Clause 8. 3 [Programme] and to the Time for Completion; and

(c) the Contractor's proposal for evaluation of the Variation.

The Engineer shall, as soon as practicable after receiving such proposal (under Sub-Clause 13. 2 [Value Engineering] or otherwise), respond with approval, disapproval or comments. The Contractor shall not delay any work whilst awaiting a response.

Each instruction to execute a Variation, with any requirements for the recording of Costs, shall be issued by the Engineer to the Contractor, who shall acknowledge receipt. Each Variation shall be evaluated in accordance with Clause 12 [Measurement and Evaluation], unless the Engineer instructs or approves otherwise in accordance with this Clause.

13. 5 Provisional Sums

Each Provisional Sum shall only be used, in whole or in part, in accordance with the Engineer's instructions, and the Contract Price shall be adjusted accordingly. The total sum paid to the Contractor shall include only such amounts, for the work, supplies or services to which the Provisional Sum relates, as the Engineer shall have instructed. For each Provisional Sum, the Engineer may instruct:

(a) work to be executed (including Plant, Materials or services to be supplied) by the Contractor and valued under Sub-Clause 13. 3 [Variation Procedure]; and/or

(b) Plant, Materials or Services to be purchased by the Contractor, from a nominated Subcontractor (as defined in Clause 5 [Nominated Subcontractors]) or otherwise; and for which there shall be included in the Contract Price:

(i) the actual amounts paid (or due to be paid) by the Contractor, and

(ii) a sum for overhead charges and profit, calculated as a percentage of these actual amounts by applying the relevant percentage rate (if any) stated in the appropriate Schedule. If there is no such rate, the percentage rate stated in the Appendix to Tender shall be applied.

A Provisional Sum is defined as a sum of money, which is included in the Contract Price, but has been allocated for a particular part of the Works, or the supply of Plant, Materials or Services, as specified in the Contract. The money can only be used when instructed by the Engineer. The instruction may take the form of a Variation for additional work, which is then valued in accordance with Sub-Clause 13. 3. Alternatively it may be an instruction for the purchase of Plant, Materials or Services. This would be valued as the actual amount paid, based on invoices, plus a percentage for overheads and profit. The percentage must be stated in the Appendix to Tender. Under the Red Book, the Engineer has the option of stating the source to be used, which becomes a nominated Subcontractor; however, under the Yellow Book, this would not be appropriate. The Provisional Sum can only be used for the specified purpose. Any money surplus to these requirements cannot be used for other work and will result in a reduction in the Contract Price. If a sum of money which is included as a Provisional Sum is actually intended to be a contingency sum then this must be clearly defined in the Particular Conditions.

13. 6 Daywork

For work of a minor or incidental nature, the Engineer may instruct that a Variation shall be executed on a daywork basis. The work shall then be valued in accordance with the Daywork Schedule included in the Contract, and the following procedure shall apply. If a Daywork Schedule is not included in the Contract, this Sub-Clause shall not apply.

Before ordering Goods for the work, the Contractor shall submit quotations to the Engineer. When applying for payment, the Contractor shall submit invoices, vouchers and accounts or receipts for any Goods.

Except for any items for which the Daywork Schedule specifies that payment is not due, the Contractor shall deliver each day to the Engineer accurate statements in duplicate which shall include the following details of the resources used in executing the previous day's work:

(a) the names, occupations and time of Contractor's Personnel;

(b) the identification, type and time of Contractor's Equipment and Temporary Works; and

(c) the quantities and types of Plant and Materials used.

One copy of each statement will, if correct, or when agreed, be signed by the Engineer and returned to the Contractor. The Contractor shall then submit priced statements of these resources to the Engineer, prior to their inclusion in the next Statement under Sub-Clause 14. 3 [Application for Interim Payment Certificates].

Payment on a daywork basis means that the Contractor submits daily records of the resources used in the execution of the previous day's work, including the information which is listed at Sub-Clause 13. 6, and is paid at the rates stated in the Daywork Schedule. If there is no Daywork Schedule in the Contract, then payment cannot be made on a daywork basis.

It is therefore important that a Daywork Schedule is included in the Tender documents, completed by the Contractor and included with the Letter of Tender and Letter of Acceptance so as to form part of the Contract. For a Daywork Schedule to be agreed later would require the Employer's agreement, as an addition to the Contract.

Sub-Clause 13. 6 restricts the use of Daywork to work of a minor or incidental nature. Minor or incidental work generally creates more disruption than is normal for the total Cost of the work, so daywork rates are usually high. If the Engineer wants to negotiate a rate on a cost-plus basis he will expect the rates to show a reduction on the daywork rates.

☞ 疑难词汇 ☜

1. variations and adjustments 变更与调整

2. strict adherence to 严格遵守

3. initiated 发起，启动

4. changes to the sequence or timing of the execution of the Works 更改工作顺序或时间

5. omit 省略，遗漏

6. written proposal 书面建议，建议书

7. adverse impact 负面影响

8. value engineering 价值工程

9. anticipated life 预期寿命

10. operational efficiencies 经营效率，运营效率

11. Provisional Sum 暂定金额

12. overhead charges and profits 经常性开支（一般性开支）和利润

13. Contingency sum 意外开支准备金，额外预算费

14. draws a distinction between 在…之间加以区别

15. submit quotation 提出合约

16. benefit from 得益于，从……收益

17. vouchers 付款凭证

18. money surplus 资金结余

19. minor or incidental work 次要或偶然的工作

☞ 疑难语句 ☜

1. If the Employer gives an instruction direct to the Contractor then the Contractor must obtain the Engineer's confirmation and instruction before he executes the change. Strict adherence to these requirements is essential for the Engineer to maintain technical and financial control over the project.

如果雇主直接指示承包商更改工程，在这种情况下，承包商必须在实施更改之前获得工程师认可。严格遵守这些规则对于工程师控制项目的技术和资金是很重要的。

2. The Contractor cannot object to the instruction because of difficulties in obtaining management staff or labour.

承包商不能因管理或用工方面原因拒绝工程师的指示。

3. The Engineer can then either cancel, confirm or vary the instruction. If the Engineer confirms an instruction following objections by the Contractor then the Employer is taking responsibility for the potential problems which have been notified by the Contractor. If the Variation has design or safety implications then it could also bring additional responsibilities to both the Employer and the Engineer under the applicable law.

工程师即可以撤销、批准，也可以更改指示。如果工程师下发了他的指示，但承包商持反对意见，那么雇主将对承包商告知的潜在问题负责。如果更改有设计和安全方面影响，那么，根据现行法律这种更改可能会给雇主和工程师带来额外的责任。

4. Under the New Red Book, the third paragraph of Sub-Clause 13.2 draws a distinction between proposals that include a change in the design of part of the Permanent Works and those that do not include a design change. If the proposal includes a design change then, unless the Parties agree otherwise, the Contractor shall design the changed part of the Works and receive a fee, provided that the reduction in Contract value is greater than any reduction in the value of the Works to the Employer. The fee is calculated by the Engineer, following the Sub-Clause 3.5 procedure. If the proposal does not include a design change then the Contractor will have to rely on any benefit from savings in his own Costs.

根据"新红皮书"，13.2 款第三项对永久性工程的部分设计的改变和不改变的建议进行了区分。如果这个建议包含了设计上的改变，那么，除非合同双方同意，承包商将设计该变化部分并收取费用，如果这项改变设计对雇主来说，在合同价值方面的减少高于工程价值的减少，费用由工程师根据 13.5 款规定的程序计算，如果这项建议不包含设计的改变，那么承包商将从费用节省方面获得收益。

☞ **中文综述** ☜

一、概述

在国际工程施工合同的执行过程中，工程变更不仅具有一定的普遍性，往往也是不可避免的，合同双方及工程师应充分地认识这一点。引起工程变更的因素较多，例如自然条件（主要指水文、地质等因素）的变化、招标文件提供的资料不够齐全、设计（包括设计图纸）的改变等，都可能成为导致工程变更的因素。如果在工程实施阶段因上述因素出现了工程变更，首先应结合工程的实际情况，按照合同规定的条款和条件，对之进行妥善处理，尽可能避免合同双方的争议。对工程变更进行及时、公正和合理的处理，有利于工程建设按合同规定的目标顺利开展，也有利于控制工程建设成本。

工程变更可以视为对原有合同的延续，或对原合同内容的补充。判定一项工作是否构成变更，主要依据是雇主和承包商之间签订的合同文件，以及合同双方在施工阶段达成的谅解或协议。大多数国际工程施工项目都选用某种标准的合同文本，FIDIC 合同条件是目前在国际工程施工领域使用较多的标准合同文本。

二、变更的含义

"新红皮书"第 13 条对变更、变更条件、变更费用以及与变更相关的索赔和价值工程等进行了较为全面具体的界定。第 13.1 款规定：在颁发工程接收证书前的任何时间之内，工程师可通过发布指示或要求承包商递交建议书的方式，提出变更。据此，在工程实施过程中，出现下列一种或若干种情况时，将构成工程变更：

（1）工程师指示（Instruct）增加或减少合同中所包括的任何工作的工程量；

（2）工程师指示删除（Omit）工程中所包括的任何工作（但被删除的工作不能由雇主或其他承包商继续施工）；

（3）工程师指示改变（Change）工程中任何工作的性质、质量或类型；

（4）工程师指示改变工程任何部位的标高、基线、位置和尺寸；

（5）工程师认为完建工程（the Works）所必需的任何附加工作；

（6）工程师指示或因非承包商原因改变工程任何部位的规定顺序或时间安排。

对于以下非承包商的原因导致的额外费用（Additional Cost），在 FIDIC 合同条款使用中，工程师也应按"变更"来处理：

（1）由于工程师提供不正确的数据，使承包商的放线与设计偏离而导致的返工；

（2）进行工程量表中没有规定的勘探和试验作业；

（3）发生应由雇主承担的风险（Employer's Risk），在中止合同前或事件过后继续履行合同时，根据工程师指令进行的任何清理和修补工作；

（4）根据工程师的指示为其他承包商提供的任何服务；

（5）在缺陷责任期内（Defects Liability Period），工程师指示承包商所进行的任何非属于承包商应负责任的修补工作；

（6）特殊风险（Special Risks）对工程造成的损坏；

（7）暂定金额的使用（Use of Provisional Sums）。

三、变更的内容

每项变更可包括：

（1）对合同中任何工作的工程量的改变（此类改变并不一定必然构成变更）；

（2）任何工作质量或其他特性上的变更；

（3）工程任何部分标高、位置和（或）尺寸上的改变；

（4）省略任何工作，除非它已被他人完成；

（5）永久工程所必需的任何附加工作、永久设备、材料或服务，包括任何联合竣工检验、钻孔和其他检验以及勘察工作；

（6）工程的实施顺序或时间安排的改变。

承包商不应对永久工程作任何更改或修改，除非且直到工程师发出指示或同意变更。

四、工程变更程序

1. 变更评估

工程师应在发出变更指示前，对将要变更的工作作出评估，尤其是对承包商建议的工程变更。工程师可以根据承包商提出的初步方案和掌握的资料对变更工作的工程量、变更可能对工程进度的影响、变更的适用价格作出初步分析和评估，为确定变更条件做好基础准备工作。"新红皮书"第13.3款规定："每一项变更应依据第12条［测量与估价］进行估价，除非工程师依据本款另外作出指示或批准"。

2. 发出变更指示

在对将要变更的工作作出评估后，如果认为由承包商实施比较合适，在征得雇主的同意后（如果雇主未将变更的权力授予工程师），工程师可以向承包商发出变更指示；如果雇主已授予变更的权力，则工程师可在授权范围内直接向承包商发出变更指示，也可以间接地通过修改、调整招标图纸及技术规范向承包商发出变更指示。"新红皮书"第13.3款规定："工程师应向承包商发出每一项实施变更的指示，并要求其记录费用，承包商应确认收到该指示。"

3. 确定变更工作的价格

确定变更工作的价格是在承包商提供的变更估价的建议书基础上进行的，工程师应尽快给予确认或提出修改建议。

4. 颁发变更令

变更令记载的主要内容：变更工作的内容说明、性质、工程量、价格、对合同价的增减、适用范围，以及实施变更工作的合同条件和有关技术规范。颁发变更令的目的主要有：一是管理上的需要，即用变更令的方式书面确认工程师与合同双方协商的成果；二是成本控制上的需要。

5. 变更工作的实施

在变更工程的价格确定后，承包商将根据变更指示修改原施工方案或提出新方案并组织变更工作的施工，变更工作随之纳入正常的合同管理和进度控制范围内。没有工程师的书面指示，承包商不能自主地进行任何变更工作。

6. 以适用的货币支付

如果合同规定合同价格以一种以上的货币支付，则在按上述规定已商定、批准或决定调整的同时，应规定以每种适用的货币支付的金额。在规定每种货币的金额时，应参照变更工作费用的实际或预期的货币比例以及为支付合同价格所规定的各种货币比例。

五、价值工程

价值工程（Value Engineering）是"新红皮书"、"新黄皮书"和"新银皮书"中引人的一个全新的概念。"新红皮书"第 13.2 款规定：承包商可随时向工程师递交书面建议，提出（他认为）采用后能够：①加快竣工；②降低雇主的工程施工、维护或运行的费用；③改善雇主的竣工工程的效率或价值；④给雇主带来其他利益。

1. 价值工程的要求

价值工程的建议一般应由承包商自费编制，并应包括第 13.3 款［变更程序］所列内容。如经工程师批准的建议书中包括部分永久工程设计的改变，除非经双方同意：承包商应设计这一部分；并应根据第 4.1 款［承包商的一般义务］中的（a）至（d）项规定办理。如果此决定导致该部分合同价值减少，工程师应根据第 3.5 款［决定］的规定，同意或决定应包括在合同价格内的费用。此项费用应为以下两项金额之差的一半（50%）。

由此项改变引起的合同价值的减少，不包括：

① 按照第 13.7 款［因法律改变的调整］和第 13.8 款［因成本改变的调整］的规定作出的调整；

② 改变后的工程因任何质量、预期寿命或运行效率的降低，对雇主的价值的减少（如有）。

但是，如（1）中金额小于（2）中金额，则不应有此项费用。

2. 价值工程的评判标准

价值工程的评判标准主要集中在该工程能否为雇主创造价值，主要包括以下几个方面：一是，价值工程能够加快竣工；二是降低雇主的工程施工、维护和运行的费用；三是改善雇主的竣工工程的效率或价值；四是给雇主带来其他利益。

承包商可以随时向工程师递交建议。根据第 13.2 款的规定，承包商的价值工程是否被工程师所采纳，应取决于工程师，也就是说，承包商只有建议权，而决定是否采纳是工程师的权力。

六、暂定金额

1. 暂定金额的基本含义

"新红皮书"第 1.1.4.10 款规定，暂定金额是指：合同中指明为暂定金额的一笔金额（如有时），用于按照第 13.5 款［暂定金额］实施工程的任何部分或提供永久设备、材料和服务的一笔金额（如有时）。

从以上定义可以看出，暂定金额的含义主要包括：

（1）在具体项目里，暂定金额可能有，也可能没有。

（2）暂定金额可用于工程建设的各个方面，比如某一部分的施工、某一部分设备、某一部分材料、某些服务等，也可作为不可预见费存在。

（3）哪些项目作为暂定金额，已在招标人的工程量清单中标明，这些金额也包含在合同总价里。

（4）何时动用暂定金额，由工程师决定。当然，动用的前提必须是工程量清单中列明的暂定金额对应项有所实施。动用暂定金额，工程师要明确告知雇主。

暂定金额与国际工程实施的严谨性有关。某项工程到底需要多少资金投入是要严格估算的，这样雇主才能去准确地筹集资金并列出精确的资金计划。如果资金筹集得多了，会增加融资成本，造成资金的闲置，这样无疑会造成较大的浪费；如果估算的资金不够，就会影响工程的进度，而工程进度又会直接影响项目投产的时间，进而产生额外的支出和利润损失。

2. 暂定金额的使用

暂定金额的使用一般可以概括为以下几个方面：

（1）计日工通常被认为是一笔暂定金额。计日工所涉及的人工、材料、设备和工程量相对较小且不容易准确估算。例如：施工中遇有文物、化石需要挖掘；发现难以预见的地下障碍、地下管道需要处理；临时修复被意外事件（如暴雨）破坏的路面等。

（2）由于对工程的某个部分未作出足够详细的规定，从而不能使投标者确定该部分的单价或价格时，可先估计一个暂定金额。为了使报价尽量符合实际，该部分工程可能就以暂定金额的名义由招标人先确定价格，待图纸细化后再根据定价原则由工程师主持商定该合同价格。

（3）招标时不能确定某一具体工作是否包含在合同中，可先估计一个暂定金额。如进场道路，一般情况下雇主负责现场的三通一平（或七通一平），如果在招标时进场道路还不完善，雇主暂时还不能确定是否让承包商承担该工作，这时便可给出道路的图纸或技术要求，让投标人作为暂定金额项目报价，如果中标人的报价合适，则可直接发包给中标人；如果中标人的报价过高，则可另找当地小型承包商负责进场道路的施工。

（4）不可预见费如设计变更、政策变化、物价、汇率浮动、交通管制、环境保护新规定等造成的额外费用，一般雇主会针对不可预见因素给出一个固定金额或百分比，列入暂定金额。

Questions

1. Please discuss the engineer's role in variation under the New Red Book. What is included in each variation?

2. What is Value Engineering? Are there any basic requirements for Value Engineering?

Chapter 14　Contract Price and Payment

14. 1　Introduction

In the Naw Red Book the Contract Price is defined at Sub-Clause 1. 1. 4. 2 as "the price defined in Sub-Clause 14. 1", which includes any adjustments which are provided for in the Contract. The Contract Price must be distinguished from the Accepted Contract Amount, which is defined at Sub-Clause 1. 1. 4. 1 as "the amount accepted in the Letter of Acceptance". The Accepted Contract Amount is fixed, but the Contract Price can change and will probably increase, due to the measurement of actual quantities, Variations and other adjustments. The Contract Agreement states that the Employer will pay the Contractor the Contract Price at the times and in the manner prescribed by the Contract.

The FIDIC Guidance for the Preparation of Particular Conditions includes the statement: "When writing the Particular Conditions, consideration should be given to the amount and timing of payment (s) to the Contractor. A positive cash flow is clearly of benefit to the Contractor, and tenderers will take account of the interim payment procedures when preparing their tenders."

14. 2　The Contract Price

In the New Red Book, the Contract price is defined as:

Unless otherwise stated in the Particular Conditions: (a) the Contract Price shall be agreed or determined under Sub-Clause 12. 3 [Evaluation] and be subject to adjustments in accordance with the Contract; (b) the Contractor shall pay all taxes, duties and fees required to be paid by him under the Contract, and the Contract Price shall not be adjusted for any of these costs except as stated in Sub-Clause 13. 7 [Adjustments for Changes in legislation]; (c) any quantities which may be set out in the Bill of Quantities or other Schedule are estimated quantities and are not to be taken as the actual and correct quantities: (i) of the Works which the Contractor is required to execute, or (ii) for the purposes of Clause 12 [Measurement and Evaluation]; and (d) the Contractor shall submit to the Engineer, within 28 days after the Commencement Date, a proposed breakdown of each lump sum price in the Schedules. The Engineer may take account of the breakdown when preparing Payment Certificates, but shall not be bound by it.

Sub-Clause 14. 1 gives the following four general requirements, which relate to other

Sub-Clauses.

(1) The Contract Price, which is stated in the Contract Agreement to be the amount which the Employer will pay to the Contractor, is agreed or determined by the Engineer. The Engineer will determine the Contract Price in accordance with Sub-Clause 12. 3, as the sum of the valuations of each item of work, including any Variations, together with other adjustments.

(2) Sub-Clause 14. 1 (b) requires the Contractor to pay all taxes, duties and fees. The Employer only reimburses any of these which are the result of changes in legislation as Sub-Clause 13. 7. If the Employer intends to reimburse any other charges they must be defined in the Particular Conditions. The Guidance for the Preparation of Particular Conditions includes suggested Sub-Clauses if Sub-Clause 14. 1 (b) is not to apply.

(3) Sub-Clause 14. 1 (c) must be revised if the quantities in the Bill of Quantities or other Schedules are to be taken as the actual and correct quantities.

(4) Sub-Clause 14. 1 (d) imposes another requirement on the Contractor. Within 28 days from the Commencement Date the Contractor must provide a proposed breakdown of every lump sum price in the Schedules. These breakdowns are only proposals, for the information of the Engineer, but should be consistent with other financial submissions.

14. 3   Advance Payment

The Employer shall make an advance payment when the Contractor submits a guarantee in accordance with this Sub-Clause 14. 2. The total advance payment, the number and timing of installments (if more than one), and the applicable currencies and proportions, shall be as stated in the Appendix to Tender. Unless and until the Employer receives this guarantee, or if the total advance payment is not stated in the Appendix to Tender, this Sub-Clause shall not apply.

The Engineer shall issue an Interim Payment Certificate for the first installment after receiving a Statement (under Sub-Clause 14. 3 [Application for Interim Payment Certificates]) and after the Employer receives (i) the Performance Security in accordance with Sub-Clause 4. 2 [Performance Security], and (ii) a guarantee in amounts and currencies equal to the advance payment. This guarantee shall be issued by an entity and from within a country (or other jurisdiction) approved by the Employer, and shall be in the form annexed to the Particular Conditions or in another form approved by the Employer.

The Contractor shall ensure that the guarantee is valid and enforceable until the advance payment has been repaid, but its amount may be progressively reduced by the amount repaid by the Contractor as indicated in the Payment Certificates. If the terms of the guarantee specify its expiry date, and the advance payment has not been repaid by the date 28 days prior to the expiry date, the Contractor shall extend the validity of the guarantee until the advance payment has been repaid.

The advance payment shall be repaid through percentage deductions in Payment Certificates. Unless other percentages are stated in the Appendix to Tender: (a) deductions shall commence in the Payment Certificate in which the total of all certified interim payments (excluding the advance payment and deductions and repayments of retention) exceeds ten percent (10%) of the Accepted Contract Amount less Provisional Sums; and (b) deductions shall be made at the amortization rate of one quarter (25%) of the amount of each Payment Certificate (excluding the advance payment and deductions and repayments of retention) in the currencies and proportions of the advance payment, until such time as the advance payment has been repaid.

If the advance payment has not been repaid prior to the issue of the Taking-Over Certificate for the Works or prior to termination under Clause 15 [Termination by Employer], Clause 16 [Suspension and Termination by Contractor] or Clause 19 [Force Majeure] (as the case may be), the whole of the balance then outstanding shall immediately become due and payable by the Contractor to the Employer.

If the Employer intends to make an advance payment then the relevant information must be provided in the Appendix to Tender. The figure for the advance payment is given as a percentage of the Accepted Contract Amount and the currency in which it is to be paid must be stated. If the advance payment is to be paid in installments then the number and timing of installments must be stated.

In accordance with Sub-Clause 14. 7 (a), the first installment of the advance payment must be paid with in 42 days from issuing the Letter of Acceptance, or 21 days from receiving the Performance Security under Sub-Clause 4. 2 and the Advance Payment Guarantee and other documents under Sub-Clause 14. 2.

14. 4　Application for Interim Payment Certificates

The Contractor shall submit a Statement in six copies to the Engineer after the end of each month, in a form approved by the Engineer, showing in detail the amounts to which the Contractor considers himself to be entitled, together with supporting documents which shall include the report on the progress during this month in accordance with Sub-Clause 4. 21 [Progress Reports] .

The Statement shall include the following items, as applicable, which shall be expressed in the various currencies in which the Contract Price is payable, in the sequence listed:

(a) the estimated contract value of the Works executed and the Contractor's Documents produced up to the end of the month (including Variations but excluding items described in sub-paragraphs (b) to (g) below);

(b) any amounts to be added and deducted for changes in legislation and changes in cost, in accordance with Sub-Clause 13. 7 [Adjustments for Changes in Legislation] and

Sub-Clause 13. 8 [Adjustrnents for Changes in Cost];

(c) any amount to be deducted for retention, calculated by applying the percentage of retention stated in the Appendix to Tender to the total of the above amounts, until the a-mount so retained by the Employer reaches the limit of Retention Money (if any) stated in the Appendix to Tender;

(d) any amounts to be added and deducted for the advance payment and repayments in accordance with Sub-Clause 14. 2 [Advance Payment];

(e) any amounts to be added and deducted for Plant and Materials in accordance with Sub-Clause 14. 5 [Plant and Materials intended for the Works];

(f) any other additions or deductions which may have become due under the Contract or otherwise, including those under Clause 20 [Claims, Disputes and Arbitration]; and

(g) the deduction of amounts certified in all previous Payment Certificates.

Under the Yellow Book interim payments are made as required by the Schedules, which may not be monthly. Hence, Sub-Clause 14. 3 allows for the periods for payment to be stated in the Contract.

The procedure for the Contractor to receive payments from the Employer starts with the Contractor's application for payment. The Contractor submits a Statement to the Engineer each month giving the amounts that he is claiming, together with supporting documents. The Statement is submitted after the end of each month and the sooner the Contractor collects the necessary information and submits the Statement, the sooner he will be paid. The Statement must be in a form approved by the Engineer and include the items listed as (a) to (g), in the order in which they are listed. Agreement on the form and layout of the Statement is important and if the Engineer has any particular requirements they should be stated in the Particular Conditions.

When submitting the first Statement the Contractor should demonstrate that he has received, or state when he expects to receive, the Employer's approval to the Performance Security. Under Sub-Clause 14. 6 the Engineer will not certify any payment until the Performance Security has been approved by the Employer. Under Sub-Clause 1. 3, the approval must not be unreasonably withheld or delayed. If the Contract includes provision for an advance payment then the Performance Security will already have been approved before payment of the advance payment.

14. 5　Schedule of Payments

If the Contract includes a schedule of payments specifying the installments in which the Contract Price will be paid, then unless otherwise stated in this schedule:

(a) the installments quoted in this schedule of payments shall be the estimated contract values for the purposes of sub-paragraph (a) of Sub-Clause 14. 3 [Application for Interim Payment Certificates];

(b) Sub-Clause 14. 5 [Plant and Materials intended for the Works] shall not apply; and

(c) if these installments are not defined by reference to the actual progress achieved in executing the Works, and if actual progress is found to be less than that on which this schedule of payments was based, then the Engineer may proceed in accordance with Sub-Clause 3. 5 [Determinations] to agree or determine revised installments, which shall take account of the extent to which progress is less than that on which the installments were previously based.

If the Contract does not include a schedule of payments, the Contractor shall submit non-binding estimates of the payments which he expects to become due during each quarterly period. The first estimate shall be submitted within 42 days after the Commencement Date. Revised estimates shall be submitted at quarterly until the Taking-Over Certificate has been issued for the Works.

If the Contract Price is to be paid in installments then the Contract must include a Schedule of Payments, giving the timing and details of the installments, subject to the provisions of Sub-Clause 14. 4. The schedule must be clear and unambiguous and relate to the Contractor's programme and the actual progress which has been recorded on the Site. Subparagraph (c) allows the Engineer to reduce the payment if actual progress is less than had been assumed. Logically the Engineer should also increase the payment if actual progress is greater than had been assumed.

14. 6　Payment

The Employer shall pay to the Contractor:

(a) the first installment of the advance payment within 42 days after issuing the Letter of Acceptance or within 21 days after receiving the documents in accordance with Sub-Clause 4. 2 [Performance Security] and Sub-Clause 14. 2 [Advance Payment], whichever is later;

(b) the amount certified in each Interim Payment Certificate within 56 days after the Engineer receives the Statement and supporting documents; and

(c) the amount certified in the Final Payment Certificate within 56 days after the Employer receives this Payment Certificate.

Payment of the amount due in each currency shall be made into the bank account, nominated by the Contractor, in the payment country (for this currency) specified in the Contract. Interim payments must be made within 56 days after the Engineer receives the Contractor's Statement and supporting documents. For the Final Payment the 56 day period for payment starts when the Employer receives the Payment Certificate. The Employer has the benefit of the cash flow estimates provided under Sub-Clause 14. 4, together with advice from the Engineer, so it should be possible for these periods to be reduced in the

Particular Conditions. Anything which can be done to improve the Contractor's cash flow should result in lower tenders and savings in the overall project cost.

The Employer's obligation is to pay the sum which is certified by the Engineer, without any deductions. If the Employer is entitled to any deduction or payment from the Contractor then the amount will have been claimed under Sub-Clause 2.5, subject to the exceptions listed. The total of any deductions will then be listed in the Engineer's Certificate and should have been included in the Contractor's Statement under Sub-Clause 14.3 (f). If the Employer has a query concerning the Engineer's Interim Payment Certificate then the payment must still be made and any correction included in the next month's certificate.

If the Employer fails to comply with these requirements then the Contractor may give 21 days' notice and then suspend or reduce the rate of work under Sub-Clause 16.1. The Contractor may terminate the Contract if payment is not received within 42 days of the due date under Sub-Clause 16.2 (c).

14.7　Delayed Payment

If the Contractor does not receive payment in accordance with Sub-Clause 14.7 [Payment], the Contractor shall be entitled to receive financing charges compounded monthly on the amount unpaid during the period of delay. This period shall be deemed to commence on the date for payment specified in Sub-Clause 14.7 [Payment], irrespective (in the case of its sub-paragraph (b)) of the date on which any Interim Payment Certificate is issued.

Unless otherwise stated in the particular conditions, these financing charges shall be calculated at the annual rate of three percentage points above the discount rate of the central bank in the country of the currency of payment, and shall be paid in such currency.

The Contractor shall be entitled to this payment without formal notice or certification, and without prejudice to any other right or remedy. Sub-Clause 14.8 gives the procedures for calculating the financing charges which are due to the Contractor if a payment is not made by the due date.

14.8　Statement at Completion

Within 84 days after receiving the Taking-Over Certificate for the Works, the Contractor shall submit to the Engineer six copies of a Statement at completion with supporting documents, in accordance with Sub-Clause 14.3 [Application for Interim Payment Certificates], showing:

(a) the value of all work done in accordance with the Contract up to the date stated in the Taking-Over Certificate for the Works;

(b) any further sums which the Contractor considers to be due; and

(c) an estimate of any other amounts which the Contractor considers will become due to him under the Contract. Estimated amounts shall be shown separately in this Statement at completion.

The Engineer shall then certify in accordance with Sub-Clause 14. 6 [issue of Interim Payment Certificates].

The Statement at completion can only be issued following the issue of the Taking-Over Certificate for all of the Works. Before the issue of this certificate, the Contractor has been able to submit Statements for Interim Payment Certificates. It is in the Contractor's interest to prepare the Statement in advance for issue well within the 84 day period.

14. 9　Final Payment Certificate

14. 9. 1　Application for Final Payment Certificate

Within 56 days after receiving the Performance Certificate, the Contractor shall submit, to the Engineer, six copies of a draft final statement with supporting documents showing in detail in a form approved by the Engineer:

(a) the value of all work done in accordance with the Contract; and

(b) any further sums which the Contractor considers to be due to him under the Contract or otherwise.

If the Engineer disagrees with or cannot verify any part of the draft final statement, the Contractor shall submit such further information as the Engineer may reasonably require and shall make such changes in the draft as may be agreed between them. The Contractor shall then prepare and submit to the Engineer the final statement as agreed. This agreed statement is referred to in these Conditions as the Final Statement.

However if, following discussions between the Engineer and the Contractor and any changes to the draft final statement which are agreed, it becomes evident that a dispute exists, the Engineer shall deliver to the Employer (with a copy to the Contractor) an Interim Payment Certificate for the agreed parts of the draft final statement. Thereafter, if the dispute is finally resolved under Sub-Clause 20. 4 [Obtaining Dispute Adjudication Board's Decision] or Sub-Clause 20. 5 [Amicable Settlement], the Contractor shall then prepare and submit to the Employer (with a copy to the Engineer) a Final Statement.

Sub-Clauses 14. 10 and 14. 11 give the procedures for the Contractor to submit Statements and the Engineer to certify interim payments, following the issue of the Taking-Over Certificate and the Performance Certificate. The Employer must make the interim payments within 56 days from the Contractor's Statement in accordance with Sub-Clause 14. 7 (b).

The Final Statement, following the Performance Certificate, is first submitted as a draft, which is discussed between the Contractor and the Engineer. If the draft statement is agreed then the Contractor submits a Final Statement. However, if there are matters which cannot be agreed they are considered under the Clause 20 disputes procedures. Any sums which have been agreed must be paid on an Interim Payment Certificate and the draft Final Statement remains open until the disputes are eventually resolved. By the time the a-greed matters have been finalized it may be too late for the Employer to pay within 56 days from when the Engineer received the draft Final Statement. The Sub-Clause does not re-quire the Contractor to submit a further interim Statement before the Engineer prepares this Interim Payment Certificate so the Contractor could be entitled to financing charges under Sub-Clause 14. 8.

14. 9. 2   Issue of Final Payment Certificate

Within 28 days after receiving the Final Statement in accordance with Sub-Clause 14. 11 [Application for Final Payment Certificate] and Sub-Clause 14. 12 [Discharge], The Engineer shall issue, to the Employer, the Final Payment Certificate which shall state:

(a) the amount which is finally due; and

(b) after giving credit to the Employer for all amounts previously paid by the Em-ployer and for all sums to which the Employer is entitled, the balance (if any) due from the Employer to the Contractor or from the Contractor to the Employer, as the case may be.

If the Contractor has not applied for a Final Payment Certificate in accordance with Sub-Clause 14. 11 [Application for Final Payment Certificate] and Sub-Clause 14. 12 [Discharge], the Engineer shall request the Contractor to do so. If the Contractor fails to submit an application within a period of 28 days, the Engineer shall issue the Final Pay-ment Certificate for such amount as he fairly determines to be due.

When the Final Statement has eventually been agreed between the Contractor and the Engineer, it is submitted to the Engineer together with the Sub-Clause 14. 12 discharge.

Sub-Clause 14. 13 gives the procedures for the Engineer to issue the Final Payment Certificate. If the Contractor does not make the proper application for the Final Payment Certificate then the Engineer issues a Certificate for the amount he fairly determines to be due. Under this procedure the Contractor has not submitted a written discharge and the Engineer should demonstrate that all claims which have been received have been considered and dealt with in accordance with the Contract. The Employer must pay the amount in the Final Payment Certificate within 56 days from receipt, in accordance with Sub-Clause 14. 7

☞ 疑难词汇 ☜

1. positive cash flow（会计）正现金流量

2. negative cash flow（会计）负现金流量

3. adjustments for changes in legislation 因法律变更的调整数

4. bill of quantities 工程量清单

5. lump sum 总价款

6. measurement of work 工作测量

7. advance payment 预付款

8. interim payment certificate 临时付款证书

9. a proposed breakdown of each lump sum price in the Schedules 资料表中每一项总价款项的价格分解建议表

10. performance security 履约担保

11. provisional sums 暂定金额

12. concurrent 一致的，同时发生的

13. consecutive 连续的，连贯的

14. amortization rate 分期偿还率

15. annexed to 从属于，以……为依据

16. coincides with 与……相一致

17. interest-free loan for mobilization 为了项目启动的无息贷款

18. up to the end of the month 到本月底

19. retention 保留金

20. unambiguous 不含糊的，清楚的

21. correction 修正，补正

22. suspend 延缓，推迟，暂停

23. financing charges 财务费用

24. discount rate of the central bank 中央银行的贴现率

25. without prejudice to 在不损害…的情况下

26. carried forward 结转，结后

27. written discharge 书面结算证明

☞ 疑难语句 ☜

1. Any quantities which may be set out in the Bill of Quantities or other Schedule are estimated quantities and are not to be taken as the actual and correct quantities.

工程量清单或其他报表中可能列出的任何工程量仅为估算的工程量，不得将其视为实际发生的或正确的。

2. The Contractor shall submit to the Engineer，within 28 days after the Commencement Date，a proposed breakdown of each lump sum price in the Schedules. The Engineer may toke account of the breakdown when preparing Payment Certificates，but shall not be bound by it.

在开工日期开始后 28 天之内，承包商应该向工程师提交对资料表中每一项总价款项的价格分解建议表。在编写支付证书时，工程师可以将该价格分解因素考虑在内，但不应受其制约。

3. Deductions shall commence in the Payment Certificate in which the total of all certified interim payments (excluding the advance payment and deductions and repayments of retention) exceeds ten percent (10%) of the Accepted Contract Amount less Provisional Sums.

此种扣减应开始于支付证书中所有被证明了的期中付款的总额（不包括预付款及保留金的扣减与偿还）超过接受的合同款额（减去暂定金额）的 10% 时。

4. Deductions shall be made at the amortization rate of one quarter (25%) of the amount of each Payment Certificate (excluding the advance payment and deductions and repayments of retention) in the currencies and proportions of the advance payment, until such time as the advance payment has been repaid.

按照预付款的货币的种类及比例，分期从每份支付证书中的数额（不包括预付款及保留金的扣减与偿还）中扣除 25%，直至还清全部预付款。

5. Any amount to be deducted for retention, calculated by applying the percentage of retention stated in the Appendix to Tender to the total of the above amounts, until the amount so retained by the Employer reaches the limit of Retention Money (if any) stated in the Appendix to Tender.

作为保留金扣减的任何款额，保留金按投标函附录中标明的保留金百分率乘以上述款项的总额计算得出，扣减直至雇主保留的款额达到投标函附录中规定的保留金限额（如有时）为止。

6. If these installments are not defined by reference to the actual progress achieved in executing the Works, and if actual progress is found to be less than that on which this schedule of payments was based, then the Engineer may proceed in accordance with Sub-Clause 3.5 [Determinations] to agree or determine revised installments, which shall take account of the extent to which progress is less than that on which the installments were previously based.

如果分期支付额不是参照工程实施所达到的实际进度制定的，且如果实际进度落后于支付表中分期支付所依据的进度状况，则工程师可通过考虑所达到的实际进度落后于分期支付所依据的进度的情况，根据第 3.5 款【决定】来商定或决定修正分期支付额。

☞ 中文综述 ☜

一、合同价格的含义

合同价格（The Contract Price）就是承包商完成实际工作，经过工程师测量和估价之后签发付款证书，承包商从雇主所获得的合同金额。"新红皮书"第 14 条对"合同价格和支付"作了规定。根据第 1.1.4.2 款的规定，合同价格被定义为包括对合同进行调整在内的第 14.1 款定义的价格。实践中，需要将合同价格和中标合同金额相区分，中标合同金额在第 1.1.4.1 款中被定义为"中标通知书中认可的价格"。中标合同金额是固定的，但合同价格是可以变更的，并可能由于实际数量的计量、变更和其他调整而有所增减。合同协议书规定雇主向承包商"按合同规定的时间和方式支付合同价格。"

"新红皮书"第14.1款规定：除非专用条件中另有规定，否则合同价格应根据第12.3款［估价］来商定或决定，并应根据本合同对其进行调整；承包商应支付根据合同应支付的所有税费、关税和费用，而合同价格不应因此类费用进行调整（但是第13.7款规定的"法规变化引起的调整"除外）；工程量清单或其他报表中可能列出的任何工程量仅为估算的工程量，不得将其视为：

(1) 要求承包商实施的工程或正确的工程量，或者；

(2) 用于第12条［测量和估价］的实际或正确的工程量。

在开工日期开始后28天之内，承包商应该向工程师提交对资料表中每一项总价款项的价格分解建议表。在编写支付证书时，工程师可以将该价格分解表考虑在内，但不应受其制约。

二、合同价格的种类

1. 中标合同金额

国内工程施工中所说的"合同价"在FIDIC合同条款中被称作"中标合同金额"，它是指雇主在中标函中接受的为承包商承建工程而支付给承包商的价格，即在中标函中所认可的工程施工、竣工和修补任何缺陷所需要的费用。该金额由两部分组成：一是承包商根据招标文件提供的"工程量表"中的估计工程量向雇主签署的工程报价（就是投标书中的总报价），另一部分是暂定金额。

2. 暂定金额

暂定金额是雇主的一笔备用资金，一般包含在承包商的投标报价中，成为其整个报价的一部分。暂定金额的使用由工程师来控制。承包商能得到暂定金额的开支应满足两个条件：一是工程师下达指令，要求承包商实施该工作，二是实施的工作属于暂定金额的工作。同时工程师有权要求承包商提交有关的报价单、凭证、账目、收据等来证明承包商完成该项工作的实际费用。由此可见，暂定金额虽然包含在报价中，但承包商不一定能得到。"新红皮书"第13.5款规定了"暂定金额"。每一笔暂定金额仅按照工程师的指示全部或部分地使用，并相应地调整合同价格。支付给承包商的此类总金额仅应包括工程师指示的且与暂定金额有关的工作、供货或服务的款项。

3. 计日工费

"新红皮书"第13.6款规定了"计日工"。该条规定，对于一些小的或附带性的工作，工程师可指示按计日工作实施变更。这时，工作应按照包括在合同中的计日工作计划表进行估价，并应按下述程序进行。如果合同中未包括计日工作计划表，则本款不适用。在为工程订购货物前，承包商应向工程师提交报价单。当申请支付时，承包商应提交各种货物的发票、凭证，以及账单或收据。

4. 价值工程

"新红皮书"第13.2款规定了"价值工程"。价值工程的规定是为了鼓励承包商在加速施工、节约成本、提高质量等方面提出合理化建议。承包商可以随时向工程师提交一份书面建议，如果该建议被采用，它（在承包商看来）将加速完工，降低雇主实施、维护或运行工程的费用，对雇主而言能提高竣工工程的效率或价值，或为雇主带来其他利益。

"新红皮书"第13.2款（Value Engineering）规定：承包商可以随时向工程师提交一份书面建议，如果该建议被采用，它（在承包商看来）将①加速完工；②降低雇主实施、维护或运行工程的费用；③对雇主而言能提高竣工工程的效率或价值；或④为雇主带来其他利益。

三、支付的种类

1. 开工预付款

开工预付款是指工程承包合同签订后，承包商向雇主呈交了已获得认可的履约保证书及保函（一般保函的金额由雇主在招标时指定，如小浪底工程履约保证金为合同总价的10%）后，工程师开具支付证明，由雇主向承包单位支付的工程预付款，支付的比例可由承包商与雇主在签订合同时商定，预付款的比例一般不高于合同总价的12%。在国际工程承包中，一般在项目的启动阶段，承包商需要投入大笔的资金，为了帮助解决承包商启动资金的困难，"新红皮书"规定，雇主应向承包商支付一定数额的预付款。工程师收到了支付申请后的一段时间内，可以签收预付款凭证，雇主支付预付款。

2. 材料预付款

"新红皮书"第14.5款规定了"用于永久工程的永久设备和材料"。在"新红皮书"中，为了帮助承包商解决订购大量材料和设备占用资金周转的困难，规定雇主在一定条件下应向承包商支付材料、设备预付款。通用条件规定一般材料设备预支额度为其费用的80%，承包商可得到这笔预付款的条件如下：首先，此类材料、设备属于投标附录中所列的支付预付款的材料设备；其次，材料、设备运抵现场并经验收合格；再次，材料、设备的质量和储存条件符合技术条款的要求；最后，承包商按要求提交了订货单及收据价格证明文件。满足以上条件后，承包商申请工程师签发付款文件并与进度款同期支付。

3. 中间支付

中间支付一般包含BOQ支付、到场材料预付款支付、价格调整、变更及索赔支付。

(1) BOQ支付

BOQ是Bill of Quantity的缩写，即工程量清单，是指工程按项目可以量化地支付，一般工程在施工过程中的常规支付都采取这种方式，如开挖量、混凝土量、灌浆等项目。

(2) 价格调整

大型土木工程的施工工期长，劳务和材料市场价格变化较大，对工程的造价有着直接的影响。为使有投标资格的承包商在投标报价时有一个统一的基数，对工程造价有直接影响的材料，一般由雇主指定供应，并指定材料的价格，同时也要确定所使用的劳务价格，以衡量各投标单位报价的水平。在合同实施过程中，由于劳务价格和指定材料价格的变化风险由雇主承担，这些费用的上涨或减少，应在整个合同价中增加或减少，即对合同价格进行调整。

(3) 变更

FIDIC合同中的变更从广义上讲，是指合同文件的任何一部分的实际情况与原招标和签订合同时假定的条件基础相比发生了变化。主要包括以下几方面：

1) 设计图纸的变更。在施工前或施工过程中，对招标图纸任何部分的变更如标高、基线、位置和尺寸的变化等。

2) 施工次序或时间安排的变更。施工次序变更包括工程师批准的施工目标进度中的次序和合同文件中规定的施工次序以及施工工艺的变更。而时间安排的变更是指工程中某一部分或单元的开工或完工时间与原确定的时间相比发生变化。

3）工程数量的减少或增加。对工程量清单中的数量的变动，如果工程师认为有必要，则也要通过变更的形式发出指示。

4）附加或省略作业项目。附加工程量清单中没有的项目或省略工程量清单中已有的项目。

5）工作性质、类型或质量要求变化引起的变更。如工程师认为技术规范有严重的缺陷或在现场不可操作，需要进行必要的修改，或者工程某部分的质量技术要求产生变化均属于变更的范畴。

（4）索赔

索赔（Claim）一般包含工期索赔和费用索赔。工期索赔是指由于非合同当事人原因引起施工进度拖延，要求对进度进行调整的索赔。如由于非承包商原因而导致施工进度拖延，承包商要求顺延合同工期。费用索赔是对非自己原因造成的损失，要求对方给予经济或费用赔偿，以挽回不应由自己承担的经济损失。

4. 保留金

保留金是按合同约定从承包商应得的工程进度款中相应扣减的一笔金额，它保留在雇主手中，作为约束承包商严格履行合同义务的措施之一。当承包商有一般违约行为使雇主受到损失时，可从该项金额内直接扣除损害索赔费。例如，承包商未能在工程师规定的时间内修复缺陷工程部位，雇主雇用其他人完成后，这笔费用可从保留金内扣除。

根据"新红皮书"第 14.9 款的规定，当工程师已经颁发了整个工程的接收证书时，工程师应开具证书将保留金的前一半支付给承包商。如果颁发的接收证书只是限于一个区段或工程的一部分，则应就相应百分比的保留金开具证书并给予支付。这个百分数应该是将估算的区段或部分的合同价值除以最终合同价格的估算值计算得出的比例的 40%。

在缺陷通知期期满时，工程师应立即开具证书将尚未支付的部分保留金支付给承包商。如果颁发的接收证书只限于一个区段，则在这个区段的缺陷通知期期满后，应立即就保留金的后一半的相应百分比开具证书并给予支付。这个百分数应该是将估算的区段或部分的合同价值除以最终合同价格的估算值计算得出的比例的 40%。

5. 延误的支付

如果承包商没有收到根据第 14.7 款［支付］应获得的任何款额，承包商应有权就未付款额按月所计复利收取延误期的融资费。延误期应认为是从第 14.7 款［支付］规定的支付日期开始计算的，而不考虑其中支付证书颁发的日期。除非在专用条件中另有规定，此融资费应以年利率为支付货币所在国中央银行的贴现率加上 3 个百分点进行计算，并用这种货币进行支付。承包商有权得到此类付款而无须正式通知或证明，并且不损害他的任何其他权利或补偿。

6. 竣工结算

"新红皮书"给了承包商收到工程接收证书后 84 天时间，也就是 3 个月，来申报竣工报表。报表内容包括以下几项：

（1）到工程接收证书中指明的竣工日止，根据合同完成全部工作的最终价值。

（2）承包商认为应该支付给他的其他款项，如要求的索赔款、应退还的部分保留金等。

（3）承包商认为根据合同应支付给他的估算总额。所谓"估算总额"是指这笔金额还未经过工程师审核同意。估算总额应在竣工结算报表中单独列出，以便工程师签发支付证书。

工程师接到竣工报表后，应对照竣工图进行工程量的详细核算，对其他支付要求进行审查，然后再依据检查结果签署竣工结算的支付证书。此项签证工作，工程师也应在收到竣工报表后 28 天内完成。雇主根据工程师的签证予以支付。

7. 最终结算

最终结算是指颁发履约证书后，对承包商完成全部工作价值的详细结算以及根据合同对应付给承包商的其他费用进行核实，确定合同的最终价格。颁发履约证书后的 56 天内，承包商应向工程师提交最终报表草案以及工程师要求提交的有关资料。最终报表草案要详细说明根据合同完成的全部工程价值和承包商依据合同认为还应支付给他的任何进一步款项，如剩余的保留金及缺陷通知期内发生的索赔费用等。工程师审核后与承包商协商，对最终报表草案进行适当的补充或修改后形成最终报表。承包商将最终报表送交工程师的同时，还需向雇主提交一份"结清单"，进一步证实最终报表中的支付总额，作为同意与雇主终止合同关系的书面文件。工程师在接到最终报表和结清单附件后的 28 天内签发最终支付证书，雇主应在收到证书后的 56 天内支付。

Questions

1. What is the procedure for payment?

2. What steps are required for contractor applying for payment?

3. How many kinds of payment are defined in the New Red Book?

Chapter 15　Termination

15.1　Introduction

Termination is a serious step and is never one to be taken lightly. It is important that determination provisions are followed precisely. If a dispute arises, those procedures will usually be carefully considered and strictly applied. These issues recently came before the TCC in London, in the case of *Obrascon Huarte Lain SA v Her Majesty's Attorney General for Gibraltar*❶ where Mr Justice Akenhead had to consider whether or not the employer, in a tunnel project at Gibraltar airport, was entitled to terminate the contract. The contract was the FIDIC Conditions of Contract for Plant and Design-Build for Electrical and Mechanical Plant, and for Building and Engineering Works, Designed by the Contractor, 1st edition, 1999 (better known as the "Yellow Book").

Sub-Clause 15. 1 of Yellow Book states that: "If the Contractor fails to carry out any obligation under the Contract, the Engineer may by notice require the Contractor to make good the failure and to remedy it within a specified reasonable time."

Sub-Clause 15. 2 lists the circumstances in which an Employer may terminate upon the giving of 14 days' notice, including if the Contractor:

(a) fails to comply…with a notice under Sub-Clause 15. 1……

(b) …plainly demonstrates the intention not to continue performance of his obligations under the Contract;

(c) without reasonable excuse fails;

(d) to proceed with the Works in accordance with Clause 8.

The FIDIC contract has a warning mechanism whereby termination could be avoided by the Contractor's compliance with the Sub-Clause 15. 1 notice: "Commercial parties would sensibly understand that this contractual chance is a warning as well to the Contractor and the remedy is in its hands in that sense."

Further, termination could not legally occur if the Contractor has been prevented or hindered from remedying the failure within the specified reasonable time. Under English law, there is an implied term that the Employer shall not prevent or hinder the Contractor from performing its contractual obligations and usually an implied term of mutual cooperation. If after a notice has been served, the Employer hindered or prevented the Contractor

---

❶　[2014] EWHC 1028 (TCC) TCC means Technology Consultancy Centre (技术咨询中心).

from remedying the breach, the Employer could not rely on the Contractor's failure in order to terminate the Contract.

15.2　Termination by Employer

Clause 15 describes the circumstances in which the Employer is entitled to terminate the Contract, the procedures that must be followed and the financial arrangements that will apply.

Termination is an extremely serious step, which inevitably causes hardship to both Parties and should not be invoked without considerable discussion and attempts to overcome any problems and rectify the situation. If the Contractor objects to the termination and a DAB or Arbitrator later decides that the Employer was not entitled to terminate then the financial consequences to the Employer would be substantial.

If the Employer does decide to terminate the Contract it is essential that he follows the correct procedures. The governing law may also have requirements in addition to, or which supersede, the Contract procedures.

15.2.1　Notice to Correct

If the Contractor fails to carry out any obligation under the Contract, the Engineer may by notice require the Contractor to make good the failure and to remedy it within a specified reasonable time. When the Engineer writes a letter to the Contractor requiring him to make good a failure to carry out some obligation, it may refer to a relatively minor matter or it may be an obligation which is crucial to the success of the project. However, it could be the first step towards termination of the Contract.

A Notice to Correct under Sub-Clause 15.1 is the starting point of one of the routes towards termination of the Contract by the Employer. To avoid possible disputes as to whether the termination procedure was followed correctly, any Notice to Correct should refer specifically to Sub-Clause 15.1. The issue of such a notice may be a sensible additional step in some of the alternative routes to termination, in order to emphasise the seriousness of the situation as perceived by the Engineer and to give the Contractor a final warning as to the consequences of failure to comply with the particular obligation.

15.2.2　Termination by Employer

The Employer shall be entitled to terminate the Contract if the Contractor:

(a) fails to comply with Sub-Clause 4.2 [Performance Security] or with a notice under Sub-Clause 15.1 [Notice lo Correct];

(b) abandons the Works or otherwise plainly demonstrates the intention not to continue performance of his obligations under the Contract;

(c) without reasonable excuse fails:

[i] to proceed with the Works in accordance with Clause 8 [Commencement, Delays and Suspension], or

[ii] to comply with a notice issued under Sub-Clause 7.5 [Rejection] or Sub-Clause 7.6 [Remedial Work], within 28 days after receiving it;

(d) subcontracts the whole of the Works or assigns the Contract without the required agreement;

(e) becomes bankrupt or insolvent, goes into liquidation, has a receiving or administration order made against him, compounds with his creditors, or carries on business under a receiver, trustee or manager for the benefit of his creditors, or if any act is done or event occurs which (under applicable Laws) has a similar effect to any of these acts or events; or

(f) gives or offers to give (directly or indirectly) to any person any bribe, gift, gratuity, commission or other thing of value, as an inducement or reward:

(i) for doing or forbearing to do any action in relation to the Contract, or

(ii) for showing or forbearing to show favour or disfavour to any person in relation to the Contract;

or if any of the Contractor's Personnel, agents or Subcontractors gives or offers (directly or indirectly) to any person any such inducement or reward as is described in this sub-paragraph (f), However, lawful inducements and rewards to Contractor's Personnel shall not entitle termination.

In any of these events or circumstances, the Employer may, upon giving 14 days' notice to the Contractor, terminate the Contract and expel the Contractor from the Site. However, in the case of sub-paragraph (e) or (f), the Employer may by notice terminate the Contract immediately. The Employer's election to terminate the Contract shall not prejudice any other rights of the Employer, under the Contract or otherwise.

The Contractor shall then leave the Site and deliver any required Goods, all Contractor's Documents, and other design documents made by or for him, to the Engineer. However, the Contractor shall use his best efforts to comply immediately with any reasonable instructions included in the notice (i) for the assignment of any subcontract, and (ii) for the protection of life or property or for the safety of the Works.

After termination, the Employer may complete the Works and/or arrange for any other entities to do so. The Employer and these entities may then use any Goods, Contractor's documents and other design documents made by or on behalf of the Contractor.

15. 2. 3   Valuation at Date of Termination

As soon as practicable after a notice of termination under Sub-Clause 15.2 [Termination by employer] has taken effect, the engineer shall proceed in accordance with Sub-Clause 3.5 [Determinations] to agree or determine the value of the Works, Goods and Contractor's Documents, and any other sums due to the Contractor for work executed in accordance with the Contract.

The Engineer will agree or determine the sums due to the Contractor as soon as practicable after the notice of termination. Whilst the agreement of the value of some items may require lengthy negotiations, any measurement of work executed or agreement of Materials on Site must be carried out immediately, preferably during the period between the notice and the Contractor's departure from the Site.

15.2.4 Payment after Termination

After a notice of termination under Sub-Clause 15.2 (Termination by Employer) has taken effect, the Employer may:

(a) proceed in accordance with Sub-Clause 2.5 [Employer's Claims];

(b) withhold further payments to the Contractor until the costs of execution, completion and remedying of any defects, damages for delay in completion (if any), and all other costs incurred by the Employer, have been established; and/or

(c) recover from the Contractor any losses and damages incurred by the Employer and any extra costs of completing the Works, after allowing for any sum due to the Contractor under Sub-Clause 15.3 [Valuation at Date of Termination]. After recovering any such losses, damages and extra costs, the Employer shall pay any balance to the Contractor.

Subparagraphs (a) to (c) refer to three procedures whereby the Employer may recover money from the Contractor. However, the word "may" in the opening sentence of this Sub-Clause could lead to confusion. The choice of (a), (b) and/or (c) will depend on the circumstances and the Employer must follow the Contract procedures.

Subparagraphs (a) and (b) refer to procedures for the correction of problems caused by the Contractor whose Contract has been terminated. Subparagraph (a) requires that claims which would be covered by Sub-Clause 2.5 are to follow the procedure of Sub-Clause 2.5. Similarly claims under (b) arose from actions by this Contractor and should, as far as is practical, follow the same procedure.

The procedure for subparagraph (c) is more difficult. If the termination occurs early in the project, or here is a delay before a new Contractor can start on Site, the extra Costs incurred by the Employer could be substantial and may be disputed by the Contractor. Any such claim by the Employer would also seem to be covered by Sub-Clause 2.5. The Employer must ensure that all the necessary records are kept to substantiate any such claim.

15.3 Suspension and Termination by Contractor

Payment by the Employer to the Contractor, in accordance with the provisions of the Contract, is an essential requirement of any construction contract. This obligation on the Employer is clearly stated in the FIDIC Contract Agreement and the procedures for payment are given at Clause 14. When a Contractor prepares his Tender he will base his calculations on the assumption that the money he pays out, for labour and Materials, will be reimbursed in accordance with the provisions of the Contract. If this does not happen then the Contractor may have no alternative but to stop work. Clause 16 enables the Contractor to reduce the rate of work, suspend all work or terminate the Contract if the Employer fails to comply with his obligations for payment or to provide the information concerning his financial arrangements as required by Sub-Clause 2. 4.

15. 3. 1　Contractor's Entitlement to Suspend Work

If the Engineer fails to certify in accordance with Sub-Clause 14. 6 [Issue of Interim Payment Certificates] or the Employer fails to comply with Sub-Clause 2. 4 [Employer's Financial Arrangements] or Sub-Clause14. 7 [Payment], the Contractor may, after giving not less than 21 days' notice to the Employer, suspend work (or reduce the rate of work) unless and until the Contractor has received the Payment Certificate, reasonable evidence or payment, as the case may be and as described in the notice.

If the Contractor subsequently receives such Payment Certificate, evidence or payment (as described in the relevant Sub-Clause and in the above notice) before giving a notice of termination, the Contractor shall resume normal working as soon as is reasonably practicable.

If the Contractor suffers delay and/or incurs cost as a result of suspending work (or reducing the rate of work) in accordance with this Sub-Clause, the Contractor shall give notice to the Engineer and shall be entitled subject to Sub-Clause 20. 1 [Contractor's Claims] to:

(a) an extension of time for any such delay, if completion is or will be delayed, under Sub-Clause 8. 4 [Extension of Time for Completion]; and

(b) payment of any such Cost plus reasonable profit, which shall be included in the Contract Price.

After receiving this notice, the engineer shall proceed in accordance with Sub-Clause 3. 5 [Determinations] to agree or determine these matters.

The Contractor is entitled to reduce the rate of work or suspend work if:

(a) the Employer fails to provide information concerning his Financial arrangements as Sub-Clause 2. 4, or

(b) the Engineer fails to issue an Interim Payment Certificate as Sub-Clause 14. 6, or

(c) the Employer fails to pay the Contractor the sum due as Sub-Clause 14. 7.

If the Contractor wishes to invoke the provisions of this Sub-Clause he must give at least 21 days' notice and describe the information, Certificate or payment which he has not received. If the information, Certificate or payment is not received during the notice period then the Contractor can reduce or suspend work, but must resume normal working as soon as is reasonably practicable if the information, Certificate or payment is received before he gives a notice of termination under Sub-Clause 16. 2.

When the Contractor takes action to reduce or suspend work he will inevitably incur additional Costs and delay, which may delay completion. The Contractor should then give notice under Sub-Clause 16. 1 and follow the procedures of Sub-Clauses 8. 4 and 20. 1. The Engineer will endeavour to reach agreement or make a determination in accordance with

Sub-Clause 3. 5. The Contractor's Costs would include the Cost of resuming work and he is also entitled to profit an those Costs.

15. 3. 2   Termination by Contractor

The Contractor shall be entitled to terminate the Contract if:

(a) the Contractor does not receive the reasonable evidence within 42 days after giving notice under Sub-Clause 16. 1 [Contractor's Entitlement to Suspend Work] in respect of a failure to comply with Sub-Clause 2. 4 [Employer's financial Arrangements];

(b) the Engineer fails, within 56 days after receiving a Statement and supporting documents, to issue the relevant Payment Certificate;

(c) the Contractor does not receive the amount due under an Interim payment Certificate within 42 days after the expiry of the time stated in Sub-Clause 14. 7 [Payment] within which payment is to be made (except for deductions in accordance with Sub-Clause 2. 5 [Employer's Claims]);

(d) the Employer substantially fails to perform his obligations under the Contract;

(e) the Employer fails to comply with Sub-Clause 1. 6 [Contract Agreement] or Sub-Clause 1. 7 [Assignment];

(f) a prolonged suspension affects the whole of the Works as described in Sub-Clause 8. 11 [Prolonged Suspension]; or

(g) the Employer becomes bankrupt or insolvent, goes into liquidation, has a receiving or administration order made against him, compounds with his creditors, or carries on business under a receiver, trustee or manager for the benefit of his creditors, or if any act is done or event occurs which (under applicable laws) has a similar effect to any of these acts or events.

In any of these events or circumstances, the Contractor may, upon giving 14 days' notice to the Employer, terminate the Contract. However, in the case of sub-paragraph (f) or (g), the Contractor may by notice terminate the Contract immediately.

Before taking action the Contractor must ensure that he has legally acceptable proof that the Employer has failed to meet the relevant obligation. In the examples such as failure to make payment, this should be easy to establish. However, for a provision such as (d) "the Employer substantially fails to perform his obligations under the Contract" it will be more difficult to establish proof that would satisfy the Dispute Adjudication Board or Arbitration Tribunal if the Employer should dispute the termination. Any significant failure on the part of the Employer would presumably have been the subject of correspondence and probably have already resulted in claims under other Clauses of the Contract.

15. 3. 3   Cessation of Work and Removal of Contractor's Equipment

After a notice of termination under Sub-Clause 15. 5 [Employer's Entitlement to Termination], Sub-Clause 16. 2 [Termination by Contractor] or Sub-Clause 19. 6 [Optional termination, Payment and Release] has taken effect, the Contractor shall promptly:

(a) cease all further work, except for such work as may have been instructed by the

Engineer for the protection of life or property or for the safety of the Works;

(b) hand over Contractor's Documents, Plant, Materials and other work, for which the Contractor has received payment; and

(c) remove all other Goods from the Site, except as necessary for safety, and leave the Site.

This Sub-Clause gives the requirements for the Contractor to leave the Site and applies to Sub-Clauses 15. 5 and 19. 6 as well as to Sub-Clause 16. 2.

15.3.4　Payment on Termination

After a notice of termination under Sub-Clause 16. 2 [Termination by Contractor] has taken effect, the Employer shall promptly:

(a) return the Performance Security to the Contractor;

(b) pay the Contractor in accordance with Sub-Clause 19. 6 [Optional termination, Payment and Release]; and

(c) pay to the Contractor the amount of any loss of profit, other loss or damage sustained by the Contractor as a result of this termination.

Under Sub-Clause 16. 2 the termination is caused by failure by the Employer, so the Contractor is entitled to receive back his Performance Security and receive loss of profit and other losses or damage in addition to payment as Sub-Clause 19. 6.

☞ 疑难词汇 ☜

1. Gibraltar airport 直布罗陀机场

2. to put right/to make good 改正，恢复正常

3. supersede 取代，代替

4. reasonable excuse 合理解释

5. gratuity 酬金，小费

6. inducement 诱因，诱惑

7. reward 奖励，报酬

8. expel 驱逐

9. minor obligation 次要责任

10. allow for 考虑到，虑及

11. substantiate 证实，证明

12. ad hoc 临时的，特别的

13. resume 重新开始，继续

14. goes into liquidation 破产清算

15. cessation 停止，中止

☞ 疑难语句 ☜

1. Termination is an extremely serious step, which inevitably causes hardship to both Parties and should not be invoked without considerable discussion and attempts to over-

come any problems and rectify the situation.

终止协议是很严肃的问题，会不可避免地伤害合同双方，在没有充分讨论和试图克服问题或改正现状的情况下不能加以使用。

2. If the Contractor fails to carry out any obligation under the Contract, the Engineer may by notice require the Contractor to make good the failure and to remedy it within a specified reasonable time.

如果承包商不能根据合同规定履行义务，工程师可以以通知的形式要求承包商充分认识到失败，并在规定的合理时间内进行补救。

3. The issue of such a notice may be a sensible additional step in some of the alternative routes to termination, in order to emphasise the seriousness of the situation as perceived by the Engineer and to give the Contractor a final warning as to the consequences of failure to comply with the particular obligation.

发出通知是在可选择终止合同方法中的明智的附加步骤，也是为了从工程师角度强调这种状况的严肃性，并且给承包商的不能遵守特定义务结果的最后通牒。

4. Becomes bankrupt or insolvent, goes into liquidation, has a receiving or administration order made against him, compounds with his creditors, or carries on business under a receiver, trustee or manager for the benefit of his creditors, or if any act is done or event occurs which (under applicable Laws) has a similar effect to any of these acts or events.

破产或无力偿还债务，或停业清理，或已由法院委派其破产案财产管理人或遗产管理人，或为其债权人的利益与债权人达成有关协议，或在财产管理人、财产委托人或财务管理人的监督下营业，或承包商所采取的任何行动或发生的任何事件（根据有关适用的法律）具有与前述行动或事件相似的效果。

☞ **中文综述** ☜

一、概述

合同的权利义务终止，又称合同的终止或合同的消灭，是指依法生效的合同，因具备法定的或者当事人约定的情形，造成合同权利义务的消灭。合同终止后，债权人不再享有合同权利，债务人也不必再履行合同义务。

根据我国《合同法》第九十一条的规定，如出现合同中债务已经依约履行，合同解除，债务相互抵消，债务人依法将标的物提存，债权人免除债务，或者债权债务同归于一人中的任一情形的，合同即告终止，此为法定的合同终止。另外，当事人之间也可以通过约定的方式终止合同。合同的终止并不是合同责任的终止。如果一方当事人严重违约而引起另一方当事人行使解除权，此时因解除而终止合同的并不能免除违约方的违约责任，也不应影响权利人行使请求损害赔偿的权利。

《最高人民法院关于审理建设工程施工合同纠纷案件适用法律问题的解释》分别对发包人和承包人的合同解除权作出了相应规定。在我国，建设工程施工合同的解除条件是结合建设工程施工合同的特点对《合同法》法定解除条件的适用。同时，规定了在承包人有过错的情况下，发包人请求解除建设工程施工合同的情形。例如，承包人在合同约定的期限内没有完工，且在发包人催告的合理期限内仍未完工的；承包人已经完成的工程质量不合格，且拒绝修复的；或者在工程施工承包过程中擅自将己方承包的建设工程非法转包或违法分包的等，进一步明确了建设工程合同适用合同法分则承揽合同关于定作人的法定解除权的规定。

另外，该《解释》规定了发包人有违约行为或违法行为时承包人的法定解除权，即发包人如未按约定支付工程价款的，或者提供的主要建筑材料、建筑构配件和设备不符合强制性标准，或者不履行合同约定的协助义务的，致使承包人无法施工，且在催告的合理期限内仍未履行相应义务，承包人即有权向法院或者仲裁机构请求解除建设工程施工合同。

二、雇主终止合同

合同终止是"新红皮书"的一项重要内容。在合同一方当事人未能履行其义务、未能完成其义务或妨碍另一方履行义务等事项发生时，当事人的行为即构成合同项下的违约。

根据"新红皮书"第15.2款的规定，在下述情形下，雇主有权终止合同：

（1）承包商未能遵守第4.2款［履约担保］的规定，或根据第15.1款［通知改正］的规定发出通知的要求；

（2）放弃工程，或明确表现出不愿意继续按照合同履行其义务的意向；

（3）无合理解释，未能按照第8条［开工、延误和暂停］的规定进行工程；或没能在收到按照第7.5款［拒收］或第7.6款［修补工作］的规定发出通知后28天内，遵守通知要求；

（4）未经必要的许可，将整个工程分包出去，或将合同转让给他人；

（5）破产或无力偿债，停业清理，已有对其财产的接管令或管理令，与债权人达成和解，或为其债权人的利益在财产接管人、受托人或管理人的监督下营业，或采取了任何行动或发生任何事件（根据有关适用法律）具有与前述行动或事件相似的效果；

（6）（直接或间接）向任何人付给或企图付给任何贿赂、礼品、赏金、回扣或其他贵重物品，以引诱或报偿他人：（i）采取或不采取有关合同的任何行动；或（ii）对与合同有关的任何人做出或不做有利或不利的表示；或任何承包商人员、代理人或分包商（直接或间接）向任何人付给或企图付给本款（6）项所述的任何此类引诱物或报偿。但对给予承包商人员的合法奖励和奖赏无权终止。

雇主有权因上述列明的承包商违约或第15.5款规定的雇主认为方便的时候终止合同。第19.6款也规定，如果不可抗力事件持续84天并对全部工程的进度造成实际影响，任何一方均可终止合同。

三、承包商终止合同

"新红皮书"、"新黄皮书"都规定了承包商终止合同的事项。按照"新红皮书"第16.2款的规定，如出现下列情况，承包商有权终止合同：

（1）承包商在根据第16.1款［承包商暂停工作的权利］的规定，就雇主未能遵循第2.4款［雇主的资金安排］规定的事项发出通知后42天内，承包商仍未收到合理的解释；

（2）工程师未能在收到报表和证明文件后56天内发出有关的付款证书；

（3）在第14.7款规定的付款时间到期后42天内，承包商仍未收到根据期中付款证书的应付款额（按照第2.5款［雇主的索赔］规定的扣减部分除外）；

（4）雇主实质上未能根据合同规定履行其义务；

（5）雇主未遵守第1.6款［合同协议书］或第1.7款［权益转让］的规定；

（6）第 8.11 款［拖长的暂停］所述的拖长的停工影响了整个工程；

（7）雇主破产或无力偿债，停业清理，已有对其财产的接管令或管理令，与债权人达成和解，或为其债权人的利益在财产接管人、受托人或管理人的监督下营业，或采取了任何行动或发生任何事件（根据有关适用法律）具有与前述行动或事件相似的效果。

在上述任何时间或情况下，承包商可通知雇主 14 天后终止合同。但在（6）或（7）项情况下，承包商可发出通知立即终止合同。承包商做出终止合同的选择，不应影响其根据合同或其他规定所享有的其他任何权利。

四、合同终止时的通知程序

由于终止合同是一项重大的合同行为，因此，各版 FIDIC 合同均要求雇主或承包商履行一定的程序。按照 FIDIC "新红皮书" 第 15 条的规定，在雇主终止合同时，终止合同的程序如下：如果承包商未能根据合同履行任何义务，工程师可通知承包商，要求其在规定的合理时间内，纠正并补救上述未履约。在分包合同终止时，不同的分包合同规定了不同的终止分包合同的通知程序。

根据 1994 年 FIDIC 分包合同第 18.1 款的规定，如果发生了分包商的违约，则 "承包商可根据分包合同的规定，在通知分包商后，立即终止对分包商的雇用"。如果分包合同规定了合同终止时的通知程序，承包商或分包商应遵守通知程序的要求，任何一方都应十分关注通知的程序。

五、雇主方便时的终止

与 1987 年第四版 "红皮书" 不同，"新红皮书" 第 15.5 款规定，雇主可以在他认为方便的时候终止合同，这项规定是：雇主应有权在他方便的任何时候，向承包商发出终止通知，终止合同。此项终止应在承包商收到该项通知或雇主退回履约担保两者中较晚的日期后第 28 天生效。雇主不应为了自己实施或安排另外的承包商实施工程，而依据本款终止合同。在终止后，承包商应根据第 16.3 款［停止工作和承包商设备的撤离］的规定办理，并应根据第 19.6 款［自主选择终止、付款和解除］的规定得到付款。

根据第 15.5 款的规定，"新红皮书" 赋予了雇主可以任意终止合同的权利，而无论承包商是否存在违约行为，无论是轻微的还是重大的、实质性的违约。在雇主任意终止合同时，根据本款的规定：

（1）雇主可以在任何时间内终止合同，无论承包商是否违约，但雇主应提前 28 天通知承包商；

（2）如果雇主根据该款的规定终止合同，则不能由他人继续完成工程；

（3）承包商有权获得第 16.3 款和第 19.6 款规定的付款。

雇主可以随意终止合同，这是雇主的权利，但这可能与雇主的利益相违背，但如果雇主确实遇到了资金问题，无法继续支持工程项目的建设，雇主可以根据本款的规定终止合同，但这是雇主的违约行为，雇主需要为此承担违约的后果，赔偿承包商的损失。

Questions

1. In what situations does the Employer terminate the contract?

2. In what situations does the Contractor terminate the contract?

3. Discuss the payment after termination.

Chapter 16　Risk and Responsibility

16. 1　Introduction

16. 1. 1　What is risk?

The word "risk" is used with many different meanings. The European Commission suggests that a risk is any factor, event or influence that threatens the successful completion of a project in terms of time, cost or quality. However, there are many other definitions, such as:

(a) A situation where there exists no knowledge of its outcome.

(b) The variation in possible outcomes that exist in nature in a given situation.

(c) A high probability of failure.

(d) Lack of predictability about structure, outcome, or consequences in decision or planning situations.

(e) The chance of something happening that will have an impact on objectives.

Although the risk concept has been defined in many ways, it is characterized by two main factors:

(a) The likelihood of a particular hazard actually taking place.

(b) The impact or consequences of that.

Actually, many risk standards suggest it is important to understand these two component elements to fully define a risk. While some definitions of risk focus only on the probability of occurrence of an event that may possibly affect the achievement of a given process, more comprehensive definitions consider both the probability of the occurrence and its consequences.

16. 1. 2　Types of risk in construction projects

The first category of risk is often referred to as "pure and particular risk" . It includes damage to persons and property (such as fire, storm, water, collapse, vibration, etc.). Contract conditions often make it a contractual obligation to take out insurance cover against these risks.

The second category is "fundamental risk" . This includes external factors such as: damage due to war, nuclear pollution and supersonic bangs; government policy on taxes, labour, safety or other laws; malicious damage; and industrial disputes. Such incidents are all the subject of statutory liability and no insurance cover is normally available or needed.

The third category, often referred to as "speculative risk", is something which can be apportioned in advance as decided by the parties to the contract. This may include losses in time and money, which result from unexpected ground conditions, exceptionally adverse weather, unforeseeable shortages of labour or materials, and other similar matters beyond the control of the Contractor.

There are also risks of losses of time and money due to: delays and disputes (possession of site, late supply of information, inefficient execution of work, etc.); poor direction, supervision or communication; delays in payment; and delays in resolving disputes.

16.1.3   Risk and Responsibility in FIDIC

The FIDIC New Red Book states clearly that the Contractor is responsible for the execution and completion of the Works and will remedy any defects in the Works. In return, the Employer will pay the Contract Price to the Contractor. Clause 17 refers to risks and responsibilities for which one Party indemnifies the other Party against losses and some additional risks for which the Employer accepts responsibility for the Cost of repairing any damage to the Works. These are not all-inclusive lists and must be considered in conjunction with the risks and responsibilities stated or implied in other clauses of the Contract.

Clause 17 also contains an important Sub-Clause which limits the liability of the Parties for consequential loss and also limits the total liability of the Contractor.

The legal meaning of the phrase "indemnify and hold harmless" should be checked under the governing law.

16.2   Indemnities

The Contractor shall indemnify and hold harmless the Employer, the Employer's Personnel, and their respective agents, against and from all claims, damages, losses and expenses (including legal fees and expenses) in respect of:

(a) bodily injury, sickness, disease or death, of any person whatsoever arising out of or in the course of or by reason of the Contractor's design [if any], the execution and completion of the Works and the remedying of any defects, unless attributable to any negligence, willful act or breach of the Contract by the Employer, the Employer's Personnel, or any of their respective agents; and

(b) damage to or loss of any property, real or personal (other than the Works), to the extent that such damage or loss:

(i) arises out of or in the course of or by reason of the Contractor's design (if any), the execution and completion of the Works and the remedying of any defects, and

(ii) is attributable to any negligence, willful act or breach of the Contract by the Contractor, the Contractor's Personnel, their respective agents, or anyone directly or indirectly employed by any of them.

The Employer shall indemnify and hold harmless the Contractor, the Contractor's Personnel, and their respective agents, against and from all claims, damages, losses and expenses (including legal fees and expenses) in respect of (a) bodily injury, sickness, disease or death, which is attributable to any negligence, willful act or breach of the Contract by the Employer, the Employer's Personnel, or any of their respective agents, and (b) the matters for which liability may be excluded from insurance cover, as described in sub-paragraphs (d) (i), (ii) and (iii) of Sub-Clause 18. 3 [Insurance Against Injury to Persons and Damage to Property].

Sub-Clause 17. 1 includes separate indemnities from the Contractor and the Employer. The indemnities cover similar losses, which are different due to the different roles of the Parties. Both indemnities cover the other Party's personnel as well as that Party itself. The extension of the normal contractual obligations to the Contract. Employer's Personnel includes anyone who has been notified to the Contractor. It is important that any specialist advisers or other visitors to Site are notified to the Contractor so as to be covered by the indemnity. Contractor's Personnel includes employees of Subcontractors and any other personnel assisting the Contractor in the execution of the Works, but the names of the individuals do not have to be notified to the Engineer.

These indemnities must be considered in conjunction with the insurance provisions at Clause 18 and cover losses that may be excluded from the insurance cover. The indemnities must also be considered together with the indemnities at other Sub-Clauses, such as: Sub-Clause 1. 13 failure to give notices required by Law and comply with regulations; Sub-Clause 4. 2 claims under Performance Security; Sub-Clause 4. 14 interference with the convenience of the public; Sub-Clause 4. 16 claims from transport of Goods; Sub-Clause 5. 2 objection to nominated Subcontractor; Sub-Clause17. 5 intellectual and industrial property rights.

16. 3   Contractor's Care of the Works

The Contractor shall take full responsibility for the care of the Works and Goods from the Commencement Date until the Taking-Over Certificate is issued (or is deemed to be issued under Sub-Clause 10. 1 [Taking Over of the Works and Sections]) for the Works, when responsibility for the care of the Works shall pass to the Employer If a Taking-Over Certificate is issued (or is so deemed to be issued) for any Section or part of the Works, responsibility for the care of the Section or part shall then pass to the Employer.

After responsibility has accordingly passed to the Employer, the Contractor shall take responsibility for the care of any work which is outstanding on the date stated in a Taking-Over Certificate, until this outstanding work has been completed.

If any loss or damage happens to the Works, Goods or Contractor's Documents during the period when the Contractor is responsible for their care, from any cause not listed in Sub-Clause 17. 3 [Employer's Risks], the Contractor shall rectify the loss or damage at the Contractor's risk and cost, so that the Works, Goods and Contractor's Documents

Chapter 16　Risk and Responsibility

conform with the Contract.

The Contractor shall be liable for any loss or damage caused by any actions performed by the Contractor after a Taking-Over Certificate has been issued. The Contractor shall also be liable for any loss or damage, which occurs after a Taking-Over Certificate has been issued and which arose from a previous event for which the Contractor was liable.

16. 4　Employer's Risks

The risks referred to in Sub-Clause 17. 4 below are:

(a) war, hostilities, invasion, act of foreign enemies;

(b) rebellion, terrorism, revolution, insurrection, military or usurped power, or civil war, within the Country;

(c) riot, commotion or disorder within the Country by persons other than the Contractor's Personnel and other employees of the Contractor and Subcontractors;

(d) munitions of war, explosive nation by radio-activity, with table to the Contractor's use materials, ionising radiation except as may be attributable to the Contractor's use of such munitions, explosives, radiation or radio-activity;

(e) Pressure waves caused by aircraft or other aerial devices travelling at sonic or supersonic speeds;

(f) Use or occupation by the Employer of any part of the permanent works , except as may be specified in the Contract;

(g) design of any part of the Works by the Employer's Personnel or by others for whom the Employer is responsible; and

(h) any operation of the forces of nature which is Unforeseeable or against which an experienced Contractor could not reasonably have been expected to have taken adequate preventative precautions.

16. 5　Consequences of Employer's Risks

If and to the extent that any of the risks listed in Sub-Clause 17. 3 above results in loss or damage to the Works, Goods or Contractor's Documents, the Contractor shall promptly give notice to the Engineer and shall rectify this loss or damage to the extent required by the Engineer.

If the Contractor suffers delay and/or incurs Cost from rectifying this loss or damage, the Contractor shall give a further notice to the Engineer and shall be entitled subject to Sub-Clause 20. 1 [Contractor's Claims] to:

(a) an extension of time for such delay, if completion is or will be delayed, under Sub-Clause 8. 4 [Extension of Time for Completion]; and

(b) payment of any such Cost, which shall be included in the Contract Price. In the

160

case of sub-paragraphs (f) and (g) of Sub-Clause 17. 3 [Employer's Risks], reasonable profit on the Cost shall also be included.

After receiving this further notice, the Engineer shall proceed in accordance with Sub-Clause 3. 5 [Determinations] to agree or determine these matters.

Some of the items listed at Sub-Clause 17. 3 are similar to events which are noted elsewhere in the Contract as giving justification for a claim by the Contractor. Any claims should always be considered together with the provisions for Force Majeure at Clause 19. The distinction is that the Employer's risk is only for rectifying the loss or damage which has occurred to the Works, Goods or Contractor's Documents. It does not cover other Costs that may have been incurred by the Contractor. When damage occurs the Contractor must give the usual notices to the Engineer but is only required to rectify the loss or damage to the extent which is required by the Engineer.

16. 6   Intellectual and Industrial Property Rights

In this Sub-Clause, "infringement" means an infringement (or alleged infringement) of any patent, registered design, copyright, trade mark, trade name, trade secret or other intellectual or industrial property right relating to the works; and "claim" means a claim (or proceedings pursuing a claim) alleging an infringement.

Whenever a Party does not give notice to the other Party of any claim within 28 days of receiving the claim, the first Party shall be deemed to have waived any right to indemnity under this Sub-Clause.

The Employer shall indemnify and hold the Contractor harmless against and from any claim alleging an infringement which is or was:

(a) an unavoidable result of the Contractor's compliance with the Contract; or

(b) result of any Works being used by the Employer:

The Contractor shall indemnify and hold the Employer harmless against and from any other claim which arises out of or in relation to (i) the manufacture, use, sale or import of any Goods, or (ii) any design for which the Contractor is responsible.

If a Party is entitled to be indemnified under this Sub-Clause, the indemnifying Party may (at its cost) conduct negotiations for the settlement of the claim, and any litigation or arbitration which may arise from it. The other Party shall, at the request and cost of the indemnifying Party, assist in contesting the claim. This other Party (and its Personnel) shall not make any admission which might be prejudicial to the indemnifying Party, unless the indemnifying Party failed to take over the conduct of any negotiations, litigation or arbitration upon being requested to do so by such other Party.

16.7   Limitation of Liability

Neither Party shall be liable to the other Party for loss of use of any Works, loss of profit, loss of any contract or for any indirect or consequential loss or damage which may be suffered by the other Party in connection with the Contract, other than under Sub-Clause16.4 [Payment on Termination] and Sub-Clause 17.1 [Indemnities].

The total liability of the Contractor to the Employer, under or in connection with the Contract other than under Sub-Clause 4.19 [Electricity, Water and Gas], Sub-Clause 4.20 [Employer's Equipment and Free-Issue Material], Sub-Clause 17.1 [Indemnities] and Sub-Clause 17.5 [Intellectual and Industrial Property Rights], shall not exceed the sum stated in the Particular Conditions or (if a sum is not so stated) the Accepted Contract Amount.

This Sub-Clause shall not limit liability in any case of fraud, deliberate default or reckless misconduct by the defaulting Party.

The Contractor's total liability to the Employer is restricted to the Accepted Contract Amount or the sum stated in the Particular Conditions, except under the Sub-Clauses listed. There is no similar limitation on the Employer's liability.

Both Parties' liability for fraud and certain other causes remains in accordance with the applicable law and is not limited by this Sub-Clause. The meaning and enforcement of this Sub-Clause could be controversial and will depend on any relevant provisions in the applicable law.

☞ 疑难词汇 ☜

1. indemnities 保护，保障
2. consequential loss 间接损失
3. negligence 粗心大意
4. willful 故意的
5. hostilities 战争
6. invasion 入侵
7. rebellion 叛乱
8. force majeure 不可抗力
9. terrorism 恐怖主义
10. insurrection 暴动
11. usurped power 篡权
12. commotion 骚动，暴乱
13. ionising radiation 电离辐射
14. strikes or lockouts 罢工或停工
15. infringement 侵犯，违反（知识产权）

16. admission 承认，坦白，录用

17. inferred from 从……推断出

18. deliberate default 故意违约

19. reckless misconduct 轻率的不当行为

20. defaulting Party 违约方

☞ 疑难语句 ☜

1. Giving justification for a claim by the Contractor 给承包商一个索赔的理由

2. The Contractor shall be liable for any loss or damage caused by any actions performed by the Contractor after a Taking-Over Certificate has been issued. The Contractor shall also be liable for any loss or damage, which occurs after a Taking-Over Certificate has been issued and which arose from a previous event for which the Contractor was liable.

承包商在（工程）接收证书发放后，应对由其自身原因产生的任何损失和损害承担责任。同时，对于接收证书颁发后出现，并且是由于在此之前承包商的责任而导致的任何损失或损害，承包商也应负有责任。

3. For a purpose other than that indicated by, or reasonably to be inferred from.

不是为合同中指明或可合理推论出来的目的。

4. In conjunction with anything not supplied by the Contractor, unless such use was disclosed to the Contractor prior to the Base date or is stated in the Contract.

与非承包商提供的任何事物联合使用，除非此类使用在基准日期之前已向承包商公开说明或在合同中指出。

☞ 中文综述 ☜

一、概述

为了有效地分担和规避风险，"新红皮书"对雇主和承包商风险和风险规避作了规定。一般而言，在雇主和承包商之间划分风险责任时，主要基于三个基本原则：

（1）承包商在投标阶段是否可以合理预见，以基准日（投标截止日期前第 28 天）作为划分合同风险责任的时间点。

（2）所发生的事件属于有经验的承包商不能合理预见，而非承包商的投标失误或管理责任。

（3）通过保险也不能合理或全部转移的风险应由雇主承担。

因此，在基准日后发生的作为一个有经验承包商在投标阶段不可能合理预见的风险事件，按承包商受到的实际影响给予补偿；若雇主获得好处，也应取得相应的利益。对于某一不利于承包商的风险损害是否应给予补偿，工程师不是简单地根据承包商的报价内是否已包括此事件的费用，而是以有经验的承包商在投标阶段能否合理预见作为判定准则。

二、保障

"新红皮书"的保障条款是针对合同双方设定的，即最大限度地保障合同双方当事人的利益，同时对于各方因各自的责任造成损失的补救作了较为完整的规定。"新红皮书"第 17.1 款规定：承包商应保障和保护雇主、雇主的人员，以及他们各自的代理人免遭与

下述有关的一切索赔、损害、损失和开支（包括法律费用和开支）：

（1）由于承包商的设计（如有时），施工、竣工以及任何缺陷的修补导致的任何人员的身体伤害、生病、病疫或死亡，由于雇主、雇主的人员或他们各自的代理人的任何渎职、恶意行为或违反合同而造成的除外，以及；

（2）物资财产，即不动产或私人财产（工程除外）的损伤或毁坏，当此类损伤或毁坏是：

1）由于承包商的设计（如有时），施工、竣工以及任何缺陷的修补导致的，以及；

2）由于承包商、承包商的人员，他们各自的代理人，或由他们直接或间接雇用的任何人的任何渎职、恶意行为或违反合同而造成的。

根据保障条款的规定，承包商不仅对"免责"事项引发的后果负责，还要对"免除"合同另一方在此类事件中可能承受的"任何伤害"负责。FIDIC的这个"免责"责任，非常有利于被保护方的利益。

三、承包商对工程的照管

从工程开工日期起直到颁发（或认为根据第10.1款【对工程和区段的接收】已颁发）接收证书的日期为止，承包商应对工程的照管负全部责任。此后，照管工程的责任移交给雇主。如果就工程的某区段或部分颁发了接收证书（或认为已颁发），则该区段或部分工程的照管责任即移交给雇主。

在责任相应地移交给雇主后，承包商仍有责任照管任何在接收证书上注明的日期内应完成而尚未完成的工作，直至此类扫尾工作已经完成。在承包商负责照管期间，如果工程、货物或承包商的文件发生的任何损失或损害不是由于第17.3款【雇主的风险】所列的雇主的风险所致，则承包商应自担风险和费用弥补此类损失或修补损害，以使工程、货物或承包商的文件符合合同的要求。承包商还应为在接收证书颁发后由于他的任何行为导致的任何损失或损害负责。

四、雇主的风险与后果

FIDIC关于雇主风险的规定主要体现在17.4款之中，根据17.4款规定，雇主风险主要表现为：

（1）战争、敌对行动（不论宣战与否）、入侵、外敌行动；

（2）工程所在国内的叛乱、恐怖活动、革命、暴动、军事政变或篡夺政权，或内战；

（3）暴乱、骚乱或混乱，完全局限于承包商的人员以及承包商和分包商的其他雇用人员中间的事件除外；

（4）工程所在国的军火、爆炸性物质、离子辐射或放射性污染，由于承包商使用此类军火、爆炸性物质、辐射或放射性活动的情况除外；

（5）以音速或超音速飞行的飞机或其他飞行装置产生的压力波；

（6）雇主使用或占用永久工程的任何部分，合同中另有规定的除外；

（7）因工程任何部分设计不当而造成的，而此类设计是由雇主的人员提供的，或由雇主所负责的其他人员提供的；

（8）一个有经验的承包商不可预见且无法合理防范的自然力的作用。

如果上述第17.3款所列的雇主的风险导致了工程、货物或承包商的文件的损失或损害，则承包商应尽快通知工程师，并且应按工程师的要求弥补此类损失或修复此类损害。

如果为了弥补此类损失或修复此类损害使承包商延误工期和（或）增加了费用，则承包商应进一步通知工程师，并且根据第 20.1 款【承包商的索赔】要求工期延长或要求雇主获得任何此类发生的费用，并将之加在合同价格中或者加上合理的利润。

"新红皮书"中关于雇主风险及处理原则的规定，与第 19 章不可抗力的规定及处理原则很相近，包括条款规定和处理方式。唯一不同的是雇主风险导致的索赔，承包商可以索赔利润；而不可抗力导致的索赔，承包商不能索赔利润。

五、知识产权

知识产权是人们对其智力成果所享有的民事权利。概括起来，在建筑工程施工领域，知识产权有以下几个特征：其一，知识产权是无形财产权，包括各种施工技术，施工组织活动等；其二，知识产权具有双重性，既有某种人身权（如签名权）的性质，又包含财产权的内容，但商标权是一个例外，它只保护财产权，不保护人身；其三，知识产权具有专有性，知识产权为权利主体所专有，权利人以外的任何人，未经权利人的同意或者法律的特别规定，都不能享有或者使用这种权利；其四是地域性，某一国法律所确认和保护的知识产权，只在该国领域内发生法律效力。FIDIC 合同条件中的知识产权是指与工程有关的专利权、已登记的设计、版权、商标、商品名称、商业机密或其他知识产权或工业产权。

"新红皮书"第 17.5 款"侵权"的含义是指对与工程有关的任何专利权，已注册的设计、版权、商标、商品名称、商业秘密或其他知识产权的侵权（或声称的侵权）；"索赔"是指声称侵权的索赔（或为索赔进行的诉讼活动）。如果一方在收到此类索赔后 28 天内未向任何索赔事件的另一方发出通知，则认为前者已经放弃了根据本款得到保障的一切权利。

雇主应保障和保护承包商免遭侵害，主要基于以下两种情况：

（1）由于承包商遵循合同而必然引起的结果；

（2）由于雇主使用任何工程引起的结果。

如果一方有权根据本款得到保障，则保障方可以（自费）为解决该索赔进行谈判和进行由此索赔而引起的任何诉讼或仲裁。应保障方的要求并在由其负担费用的情况下，被保障方应协助对此类索赔进行争辩。该被保障方（包括其人员）不应承认任何有损于保障方的谈判、诉讼或仲裁，除非保障方未能按照被保障方的要求进行谈判、诉讼或仲裁。

Questions

1. How to define the risks?

2. How many types of niks are defined in construction projects?

3. How to understand indemnities under the FIDIC New Red Book?

Chapter 17   Insurance

17. 1   Construction Risks

By nature, construction work is hazardous, and accidents are frequent and often severe. The annual toll of deaths, bodily injuries, and property damage in the construction industry is extremely high. The potential severity of accidents and the frequency with which they occur require that the contractor protect itself with a variety of complex and expensive insurance coverages. Without adequate insurance protection, the contractor would be constantly faced with the possibility of serious or even ruinous financial loss.

As discussed previously in this book, construction projects usually have in force several simultaneous contractual arrangements: those between the Employer and the engineer, between the Employer and the general contractor, and between the general contractor and its several subcontractors. Contracts that provide for design-construct and construction management services. Construed as a whole, these contracts establish a complicated structure of responsibilities for damages arising out of construction operations. Liability for accidents can devolve to the Employer or architect/engineer, as well as to the prime contractor and subcontractors whose equipment and employees perform the actual work. Construction contracts typically require the contractor to assume the Employer's and engineer's legal liability for construction accidents or to provide insurance for the Employer's direct protection. Consequently, a contractor's insurance program normally includes coverages to protect parties other than itself and to protect itself from liabilities not legally its own.

17. 2   The Insurance Policy

An insurance policy is a contract under which the insurer promises, for a consideration, to assume financial responsibility for a specified loss or liability. Under the insurance contract the insurer has a duty to defend the contractor in an action brought against it if the complaint alleges facts that are potentially within the coverage of the policy, and to indemnify the contractor from loss covered by the policy. The policy contains many provisions pertaining to the loss against which it affords protection. Because of its intimate association with the public welfare, the insurance field is controlled and regulated by state statutes. Each country has an insurance regulatory agency that administers that country's insurance code, a set of statutory provisions that imposes regulations on insurance companies concerning investments, reserves, annual financial statements, and periodic examinations. The organizational structure, financial affairs, and business methods of insurance companies are controlled.

A loss suffered by a contracting firm as a result of its own deliberate action cannot be recovered under an insurance policy. However, negligence or oversight on the part of the contractor will not generally invalidate the insurance contract. The contractor must pay a premium as the consideration for the insurance company's promise of protection against a designated loss. Most types of insurance require that the premium be paid before the policy becomes effective. In the event of a loss covered by an insurance policy, the contractor cannot recover more than the loss; that is, a profit cannot be made at the expense of the insurance company.

17. 3   Insurance Clauses under FIDIC

Clause 18 covers the requirements for construction insurances for the Works and Contractor's Equipment, injury to persons, damage to property and for the Contractor's Personnel.

The arrangement of Sub-Clauses under the New Red Book has changed completely from the previous FIDIC Contracts. Whilst the basic requirements are similar, many of the details have changed and policies which met the requirement of the previous Conditions will need to be checked and modified to meet the new requirements.

The FIDIC Contracts Guide acknowledges that all the insurance cover described in this Clause may not be available. The available cover will depend on the type of Works and the Country in which the cover is being sought. It is therefore essential that the Employer checks on the available cover when preparing the Particular Conditions. Specialist advice from an insurance expert will be necessary.

When all or part of the design is being carried out by the Contractor then Professional Indemnity Insurance to cover the design liability may also be required. This may cause a problem because of the fitness for purpose requirement at Sub-Clause 4. 1 (RB) and Clause 5 (YB).

17. 4   General Requirements for Insurances

17. 4. 1   Conclusion of Insurance Contract

In Clause 18. 1, insuring Party means, for each type of insurance, the Party responsible for effecting and maintaining the insurance specified in the relevant Sub-Clause.

Wherever the Contractor is the insuring Party, each insurance shall be effected with insurers and in terms approved by the Employer. These terms shall be consistent with any terms agreed by both Parties before the date of the Letter of Acceptance. This agreement of terms shall take precedence over the provisions of this Clause.

Wherever the Employer is the insuring Party, each insurance shall be effected with insurers and in terms consistent with the details annexed to the Particular Conditions.

17. 4. 2　Joint Insured

If a policy is required to indemnify joint insured, the cover shall apply separately to each insured as though a separate policy had been issued for each of the joint insured. If a policy indemnifies additional joint insured, namely in addition to the insured specified in this Clause, (i) the Contractor shall act under the policy on behalf of these additional joint insured except that the Employer shall act for Employer's Personnel, (ii) additional joint insured shall not be entitled to receive payments directly from the insurer or to have any other direct dealings with the insurer, and (iii) the insuring Party shall require all additional joint insured to comply with the conditions stipulated in the policy.

17. 4. 3　Responsibilities of the Insuring Party

(1) Each policy insuring against loss or damage shall provide for payments to be made in the currencies required to rectify the loss or damage. Payments received from insurers shall be used for the rectification of the loss or damage.

(2) The relevant insuring Party shall, within the respective periods stated in the Appendix to Tender (calculated from the Commencement Date), submit to the other Party:

(a) evidence that the insurances described in this Clause have been effected; and

(b) copies of the policies for the insurances described in Sub-Clause 18. 2 [insurance for Works and Contractor's Equipment] and Sub-Clause 18. 3 [insurance against Injury to Persons and Damage to Property].

(3) When each premium is paid, the insuring Party shall submit evidence of payment to the other Party. Whenever evidence or policies are submitted the insuring Party shall also give notice to the Engineer.

(4) Each Party shall comply with the conditions stipulated in insurance policies. The insuring Party shall keep the insurers any relevant changes to the execution of the Works and each of the informed of ensure that insurance is maintained in accordance with this Clause.

(5) Neither Party shall make any material alteration to the terms of any insurance without the prior approval of the other Party. If an insurer makes (or attempts to make) any alteration, the Party first notified by the insurer shall promptly give notice to the other Party.

(6) If the insuring Party fails to effect and keep in force any of the insurances it is required to effect and maintain under the Contract, or fails to provide satisfactory evidence and copies of policies in accordance with this Sub-Clause, the other Party may (at its option and without prejudice to any other right or remedy) effect insurance for the relevant coverage and pay the premiums due. The insuring Party shall pay the amount of these pre-

miums to the other Party, and the Contract Price shall be adjusted accordingly.

(7) Nothing in this Clause limits the obligations, liabilities or responsibilities of the Contractor or the Employer, under the other terms of the Contractor otherwise. Any amounts not insured or not recovered from the insurers shall be borne by the Contractor and/or the Employer in accordance with these obligations, liabilities or responsibilities.

17. 5　Insurance for Works and Contractor's Equipment

The Insuring Party shall insure the Works, Plant, Materials and Contractor's Documents for not less than the full reinstatement cost including the costs of demolition, removal of debris and professional fees and profit. This insurance shall be effective from the date by which the evidence is to be submitted under sub-paragraph [a] of Sub-Clause 18. 1 [General Requirements For Insurances], until the date of issue of the Taking-Over Certificate for the Works.

The Insuring Party shall maintain this insurance to provide cover until the date of issue of the Performance Certificate, for loss or damage for which the Contractor is liable arising from a cause occurring prior to the issue of the Taking-Over Certificate, and for loss or damage caused by the Contractor in the course of any other operations (including those under Clause 11 [Defects Liability]).

The Insuring Party shall insure the Contractor's Equipment for not less than the full replacement value, including delivery to Site. For each item of Contractor's Equipment, the insurance shall be effective while it is being transported to the Site and until it is no longer required as Contractor's Equipment.

17. 6　Insurance against Injury to Persons and Damage to Property

The Insuring Party shall insure against each Party's liability for any loss damage, death or bodily injury which may occur to any physical property (except things insured under Sub-Clause 18. 2 [insurance for Works and Contractor's Equipment]) or to any person (except persons insured under Sub-Clause 18. 4 [insurance for Contractor's Personnel], which may arise out of the Contractor's performance of the Contract and occurring before the issue of the Performance Certificate.

This insurance shall be for a limit per occurrence of not less than the amount stated in the Appendix to Tender, with no limit on the number of occurrences. If an amount is not stated in the Appendix to Tender, with no limit on the number Sub-Clause shall not apply.

Unless otherwise stated in the Particular Conditions, the insurances specified in this Sub-Clause:

(a) shall be effected and maintained by the Contractor as insuring Party;

(b) shall be in the joint names of the Parties；

(c) shall he extended to cover liability for all loss and damage to the Employer's property (except things insured under Sub-Clause 18. 2) arising out of the Contractor's performance of the Contract；and

(d) may however exclude liability to the extent that it arises from：

(i) the Employer's right to have the Permanent works executed on, over, under, in or through any land, and to occupy this land for the Permanent works (ii) damage which is an unavailable result of the Contractor's obligations to execute the Works and remedy any defects, and (iii) a cause listed in Sub-Clause 17. 3 [Employer's risks], except to the extent that cover is available at commercially reasonable terms.

The minimum amount of third party insurance required by this Sub-Clause must be stated in the Appendix to Tender. If no amount is stated then the Sub-Clause will not apply. The Contractor will then need to ensure that he has adequate insurance to cover his liabilities to third parties.

No date is given for the cover to commence but the insurance covers events arising out of the Contractor's performance of the Contract and so must commence before the Contractor takes any action in connection with the Contract. The insurance must cover any such event up to the issue of the Performance Certificate

17. 7　Insurance for Contractor's Personnel

The Contractor shall effect and maintain insurance against liability for claims, damages, losses and expenses (including legal fees and expenses) arising from injury, sickness, disease or death of any person employed by the Contractor or any other of the Contractor's Personnel.

The Insurance shall be maintained in full force and effect during the whole time that these personnel are arising in the execution of the Works. For a Subcontractor's employees, the insurance may be effected by the Subcontractor, but the Contractor shall be responsible for compliance with this Clause. The insurance to cover liabilities for claims concerning Contractor's Personnel must be maintained for the whole time that such persons are assisting with the execution of the Works.

Sub-Clauses 18. 2 and 18. 3 refer to "the insuring Party", which is stated to be the Contractor but could be the Employer if this is required by the Particular Conditions. However, Sub-Clause 18. 4 does not refer to the insuring Party but states that the insurance shall be effected by the Contractor.

☞ 疑难词汇 ☜

1. insurance cover 保险，保险范围

2. checks on 检查，核实

3. take precedence over 优于

4. indemnity insurance 损失补偿保险

5. fitness for purpose 适用性，适合用途

6. Insuring Party 投保方

7. insurer 保险公司，承保人

8. annexed to 所附于

9. joint insured 联合被保险人

10. act for 代理

11. premium 保险费

12. full reinstatement cost 全部复原成本

13. demolition 拆除，拆迁

14. debris full reinstatement cost 碎片，残骸

15. Base Date 基准日期

16. deductibles 免赔额

17. dispense with 无需，免除

18. queried 质疑，对……表示疑问

☞ **疑难语句** ☜

1. Liability for accidents can devolve to the Employer or architect/engineer.

事故责任可能转移给雇主或工程师。

2. The available cover will depend on the type of Works and the Country in which the cover is being sought.

可行的保险范围取决于工程的种类以及所在国保险险种覆盖范围。

3. Wherever the Contractor is the insuring Party, each insurance shall be effected with insurers and in terms approved by the Employer. These terms shall be consistent with any terms agreed by both Parties before the date of the Letter of Acceptance. This agreement of terms shall take precedence over the provisions of this Clause.

当承包商作为投保方时，承包商应按照雇主批准的承保人及条件办理保险。这些条件应与中标函颁发日期前达成的条件保持一致，且此达成一致的条件优先于本条的各项规定。

4. Each Party shall comply with the conditions stipulated in insurance policies. The insuring Party shall keep the insurers any relevant changes to the execution of the Works and each of the informed of ensure that insurance is maintained in accordance with this Clause.

每一方当事人应按照保险合同规定执行。投保方应确保保险人知道工程执行过程中的改变，并确保保险条件与本条的规定一致。

5. If the insuring Party fails to effect and keep in force any of the insurances it is required to effect and maintain under the Contract，or fails to provide satisfactory evidence and copies of policies in accordance with this Sub-Clause, the other Party may（at its op-

tion and without prejudice to any other right or remedy) effect insurance for the relevant coverage and pay the premiums due. The insuring Party shall pay the amount of these premiums to the other Party, and the Contract Price shall be adjusted accordingly.

如果（投）保险方未能按合同要求办理保险并使之保持有效，或未能按本款要求提供另一方满意的证明和保险单的副本，则另一方可以（按他自己的决定且不影响任何其他权利或补救的情况下）为此类违约相关的险别办理保险并支付应交的保险费。保险方应向另一方支付此类保险费的款额，同时合同价格应作相应的调整。（在这段翻译中，如果保险方是承包商，另一方则是雇主。反之亦然。）

6. The Insuring Party shall insure the Works, Plant, Materials and Contractor's documents for not less than the full reinstatement cost including the costs of demolition, removal of debris and professional fees and profit. This insurance shall be effective from the date by which the evidence is to be submitted under sub-paragraph (a) of Sub-Clause 18.1 [General Requirements for Insurances], until the date of issue of the Taking-Over Certificate for the Works.

保险方应为工程、永久设备、材料以及承包商的文件投保，该保险的最低限额应不少于全部复原成本，包括补偿拆除和移走废弃物以及专业服务费和利润。此类保险应自根据第18.1款【有关保险的总体要求】提交证明之日起，至颁发工程的接收证书之日止保持有效。

7. This insurance shall be for a limit per occurrence of not less than the amount stated in the Appendix to Tender, with no limit on the number of occurrences. If an amount is not stated in the Appendix to Tender, with no limit on the number Sub-Clause shall not apply.

该保险每一次事故的最低限额应不少于投标函附录中规定的数额，对于事故的数目并无限制。如果在投标函附录中没有注明此类金额，则本款将不再适用。

❧ 中文综述 ❧

一、概述

国际工程项目的特殊性和复杂性，决定了施工承包企业在承包工程过程中需要承担过多的风险，如气候变化、不可预见的地质变化、安全事故等。国际工程项目承包因涉及国际政治、经济、进出口贸易、国际关系、风俗习惯不同等一系列不确定因素，风险则更大。所以国际工程项目的风险管理尤为重要。风险防范的方法有很多，其中工程保险是一种十分有效的转移风险的手段。

建筑工程保险对各种建筑工程项目提供全面保障。既对在施工期间工程本身、施工机具或工地设备所遭受的损失予以赔偿，也对因施工而给第三方造成的物质损失或人员伤亡承担赔偿责任。

建筑工程保险责任通常有以下几个方面：

(1) 自然灾害（包括洪水、水灾、冰灾、海啸、风暴、雪暴、雪崩、地崩、山崩、冻灾、地震、雷击等）；

(2) 意外事故，如火灾和飞行物体坠落或飞机坠毁；

（3）盗窃；

（4）职工缺乏经验、疏忽、过失或其他恶意行为；

（5）原材料和工艺缺陷引起的事故；

（6）爆炸及其他不可预料的突然事故等。

根据"新红皮书"第18条的规定，投保方可以是雇主，也可以是承包商。投保方根据需要和约定以单方或以双方的名义对工程进行保险，而且保险对于被保险的任何一方都单独适用。在没有通知另一方并得到另一方批准的情况下，任何一方无权对保险单的一般条件进行更改。如果一方未能维持保险单有效，而按照合同条款的规定该保险单是应该保持有效的，那么另一方可以办理相关保险范围的保险并支付相应的保险费。

在18条中，"保险方"的含义是指根据相关条款的规定投保各种类型的保险并保持其有效的一方。当雇主作为投保方时，他应按照专用条件后所附详细说明的承保人及条件办理保险。如果某一保险单被要求对联合被投保人进行保障，则该保险应适用于每一单独的被投保人，其效力应和向每一联合被投保人颁发了一张保险单的效力一致。如果某一保险单保障了另外的联合被投保人，即本条款规定的被投保人以外的被投保人，则：①承包商应代表此类另外的联合被投保人根据保险单行动（雇主代表雇主的人员行动的情况除外）；②另外的联合被保险人应无权直接从承保人处获得支付，或者直接与承保人办理任何业务；③保险方应要求所有另外的联合被保险人遵循保险单规定的条件。

为防范损失或损害，对于所办理的每份保险单应规定按照修复损失或损害所需的货币种类进行补偿。从承保人处得到的赔偿金应用于修复和弥补上述损失或损害。

保险方在支付每一笔保险费后，应将支付证明提交给另一方。在提交此类证明或投保单的同时，保险方还应将此类提交事宜通知工程师。每一方都应遵守每份保险单规定的条件。保险方应将工程实施过程中发生的任何有关的变动通知给承保人，并确保保险条件与本条的规定一致。没有另一方的事先批准，任一方都不得对保险条款作出实质性的变动。如果承保人作出（或欲作出）任何实质性的变动，承保人先行通知的一方应立即通知另一方。

如果保险方未能按合同要求办理保险并使之保持有效，或未能按本款要求提供令另一方满意的证明和保险单的副本，则另一方可以（按他自己的决定且不影响任何其他权利或补救的情况下）为此类违约相关的险别办理保险并支付应交的保险费。保险方应向另一方支付此类保险费的款额，同时合同价格应作相应的调整。

二、工程和承包商设备的保险

保险方应为工程、永久设备、材料以及承包商的文件投保，该保险的最低限额应不少于全部复原成本，包括补偿拆除和移走废弃物以及专业服务费和利润。对于每项承包商的设备，该保险应保证其运往现场的过程中以及设备停留在现场或附近期间，均处于被保险之中，直至不再将其作为承包商的设备使用为止。除非专用条件中另有规定，否则本款规定的保险：

（1）应由承包商作为投保方办理并使之保持有效；

（2）应以合同双方联合的名义投保，联合的合同双方均有权从承保人处得到支付，仅为修复损失或损害的目的，该支付的款额由合同双方共同占有或在各方间进行分配；

（3）此保险应补偿除第17.3款［雇主的风险］所列雇主的风险之外的任何原因导致

的所有损失和损害；

(4) 补偿由于雇主使用或占用工程的另一部分而对工程的某一部分造成的损失或损害，以及雇主的风险所导致的损失或损害。

三、人员伤亡和财产损害的保险

保险方应为履行合同引起的，并在履约证书颁发之前发生的任何物资财产的损失或损害，或任何人员的伤亡引起的任一方的责任办理保险。该保险每一次事故的最低限额应不少于投标函附录中规定的数额，对于事故的数目并无限制。除非专用条件中另有规定，"新红皮书"第 18.2 款中规定的保险：

(1) 应由承包商作为保险方办理并使之保持有效；

(2) 应以合同双方联合的名义投保；

(3) 应保证弥补由于承包商履行合同而导致的雇主的财产的一切损失和损害（根据第 18.2 款的规定被投保的物品除外）；

(4) 不承保下述情况引起的责任：

1) 雇主有权在任何土地上，越过该土地，在该土地之下、之内或穿过其间实施永久工程，并为永久工程占有该土地；

2) 承包商履行实施工程并修补缺陷而导致的无法避免的损害；

3) 第 17.3 款【雇主的风险】所列雇主的风险所导致的情况，根据商业合理条件可以投保的除外。

四、承包商的人员的保险

承包商应为由于承包商或任何其他承包商的人员雇用的任何人员的伤害、疾病、病疫或死亡所导致的一切索赔、损害、损失和开支（包括法律费用和开支）的责任投保，并使之保持有效。雇主和工程师也应能够依此保险单得到保障，但此类保险不承保由雇主或雇主的人员的任何行为或疏忽造成的损失和索赔。该保险应在此类人员协助实施工程的整个期间保持完全有效。对于分包商的雇员，此类保险可由分包商来办理，但承包商应负责使分包商遵循本条的要求。

Questions

1. What is the insurance policy? What is the joint insured? What are the responsibilities of the Insuring Party?

2. What is subrogation and how does it affect builder's risk coverage?

3. Why it is necessary for a contractor to have completed operations insurance?

Chapter 18　Force Majeure

18. 1　Introduction

The term "force majeure" comes from French law, where it translates as "superior force" (as opposed to "vis majeure" or "vis major" which refers to an act of God). Whilst in France, the term has a defined legal meaning, in English law it is dealt with in different ways by different forms of contract.

Very broadly, it relates to exceptional, unforeseen events or circumstances that are beyond the reasonable control of a party to a contract and which prevent or impede performance of their obligations under the contract. Generally it cannot be an event that the party could reasonably have avoided or overcome, or an event attributable to the other party.

Clauses referring to force majeure attempt to set out the circumstances to which the term applies to and prescribe how such situations should be treated. Depending on the provisions of the contract, the following may be considered to constitute force majeure:

(a) Unforeseen changes to legislation.

(b) Wars and other hostilities (such as terrorism).

(c) Fires.

(d) Exceptionally adverse weather.

(e) Civil unrest, such as riots or revolution.

(f) Strikes (other than by the contractor or subcontractors).

(g) Natural catastrophes such as earthquakes, floods and volcanoes.

(h) Epidemics or pandemics.

In some contracts, force majeure is considered a "relevant event", that may allow the contractor to claim an extension of time if they have been prevented or impeded from performing their obligations under the contract. Although, if the contractor has continued to perform their duties, despite the occurrence, they may not be able to make a claim.

As these conditions tend not to be defined, it can be difficult to determine whether they have arisen or not. For example, when does a virulent virus constitute an epidemic? This has become particularly significant in recent years due to the increasing number of exceptionally adverse weather events (in particular flooding), as well events such as foot and mouth, swine flu and restrictions on air travel due to volcanic ash clouds.

Whilst clients will generally accept the contractor cannot perform their duties under the contract where there is genuine force majeure, problems arise when the client believes the contractor is unnecessarily claiming force majeure for commercial gain and that the situation could have been foreseen, avoided or mitigated. Disputed claims are particularly common in relation to exceptionally adverse weather as the term is not always defined.

Force Majeure clauses need to be flexible enough to cover events which are by their very definition are unforeseeable, but specific enough to prevent disputes arising. Some forms of construction no longer use the phrase force majeure, but instead include clauses to deal with the specific circumstances that might arise.

In situations where a contractual obligation becomes incapable of being performed, the occurrence might be considered to be a "frustration event" resulting in termination of the contract. Frustration occurs when circumstances that are not the fault of either party mean it is impossible to continue with the contract. The contract will come to an end without any party being considered to be in breach.

In FIDIC, Clause 19 defines Force Majeure and gives the procedures that must be followed and the consequences if a Force Majeure event occurs. Force Majeure is a new concept for FIDIC Contracts, but is covered by the law of many countries. Any provisions of the governing law which cover Force Majeure or refer to situations such as unexpected circumstances must be checked.

Sub-Clause 19.7 refers to events or circumstances outside the control of the Parties and is not limited to the definition of Force Majeure. The procedures for payment on termination under Sub-Clauses 19.6 and 19.7 do not include provision for the resolution of any disputes, but the procedures of Sub-Clause 20.1 would apply.

18.2　Definition of Force Majeure

In this Clause, Force Majeure means an exceptional event or circumstance:

(a) which is beyond a Party's control;

(b) which such Party could not reasonably have provided against before entering into the Contract;

(c) which having arisen, such Party could not reasonably have avoided or overcome; and

(d) which is not substantially attributable to the other Party.

Force Majeure may include, but is not limited to, exceptional events or circumstances of the kind listed below, so long as conditions (a) to (d) above are satisfied:

(i) war, hostilities (whether war be declared or not), invasion, act of foreign enemies;

(ii) rebellion, terrorism, revolution, insurrection, military or usurped power or civil war;

(iii) riot, commotion, disorder, strike or lockout by persons other than the Contractor's Personnel and other employees of the Contractor and Subcontractors;

　(iv) munitions of war, explosive materials, ionizing radiation or contamination by radio-activity, except as may be attributable to the Contractor's use of such munitions, explosives, radiation or radio-activity; and

　(v) natural catastrophes such as earthquake, hurricane, typhoon or volcanic activity.

Sub-Clause 19. 1 gives the four conditions thereof which must all be met for an event or circumstance to qualify as Force Majeure. The event or circumstance does not have to be Unforeseeable, but it must prevent the Party from performing one or more of its obligations.

These conditions are similar to the conditions for unexpected circumstances which are included in the Civil Codes of some countries. A comparison with the conditions and consequences as given in the governing law, as stated in the Appendix to Tender, will be necessary. If the governing law is more advantageous to the Contractor then the claim may be submitted under these provisions, or as otherwise in connection with the Contract under Sub-Clause 20. 1.

A non-exclusive list of five examples is given, all of which are events outside the control of either Party. The list is significant as the Contractor's right to claim for Cost as well as delay depends on the category of the Force Majeure, as provided at Sub-Clause 19. 4. The list includes events which are also listed at Sub-Clause 17. 3 as Employer's risk. The distinction is that the Employer's risk relates to loss or damage to the works, goods or Contractor's Documents together with delay or Cost from rectifying this loss or damage. Force Majeure refers to the situation when either Party is prevented from performing any of its obligations under the Contract.

For Force Majeure, the relevant forces of nature are described in more detail as such as earthquake, hurricane, lightning, typhoon or volcanic activity, although Force Majeure is not limited to these examples.

18. 3　Notice of Force Majeure

If a Party is or will be prevented from performing any of its obligations under the Contract by Force Majeure, then it shall give notice to the other Party of the event or circumstances constituting the Force Majeure and shall specify the obligations, the performance of which is or will be prevented. The notice shall be given within 14 days after the Party became aware (or should have become aware) of the relevant event or circumstance constituting Force Majeure.

The Party shall, having given notice, be excused performance of such obligations for so long as such Force Majeure prevents it from performing them.

Notwithstanding any other provision of this Clause, Force Majeure shall not apply to obligations of either Party to make payments to the other Party under the Contract.

Each Party shall at all times use all reasonable endeavours to minimize any delay in the performance of the Contract as a result of Force Majeure. A Party shall give notice to the other Party when it ceases to be affected by the Force Majeure.

Sub-Clauses 19. 2 and 19. 3 refer to the notices that must be given within 14 days of the Party becoming aware of the relevant event or circumstance, or when the Party should have become aware of it. Another notice must be given when the Party is no longer affected by the Force Majeure. The notice under Sub-Clause 19. 2 may duplicate a notice given under another Sub-Clause. To avoid potential confusion and problems it is important that each notice refers to every Sub-Clause under which it is given and includes exactly the information that is stipulated in each Sub-Clause. If the Force Majeure prevents the performance of obligations by both Parties then they must each give the due notices to the other. For Force Majeure to apply the Party must be prevented from performing an obligation. It is not sufficient that performance may be more difficult or more expensive.

Sub-Clause 19. 2 also includes the effect of the Force Majeure that: the Party shall, having given notice, be excused performance of such obligations for so long as such Force Majeure continues.

For a Party to be excused from performing some obligation, it be prevented from performing that particular obligation by the Force Majeure. All other obligations, which are not prevented by the Force Majeure, must be performed as required by the Contract. In particular, the final paragraph of Sub-Clause 19. 2 states that the obligation to make payments is not affected by the provisions for Force Majeure. If the Force Majeure has serious consequences for the Works as a whole then the Engineer may consider suspension under Sub-Clause 8. 8.

There is apparently no need for the Engineer or other Party to confirm or agree that the event constitutes Force Majeure or the performance of the obligation has been prevented. However, it is clearly advisable for the Contractor to ensure that the Engineer agrees that the event constitutes Force Majeure before he assumes that he can be excused from some obligation and stops work an the relevant item of work. Under Sub-Clause 19. 3 both Parties must use all reasonable endeavours to minimize any delay in the performance of the Contract, which repeats the usual legal obligation to mitigate damage due to an event outside the Party's control. The application of the phrase "all reasonable endeavours" is a subjective interpretation which may be argued and would be determined initially by the Engineer and then, if necessary, by the Dispute Adjudication Board.

18. 4　Consequences of Force Majeure

If the Contractor is prevented from performing any of his obligations under the Contract by Force Majeure of which notice has been given under Sub-Clause 19. 2 [Notice of Force Majeure], and suffers delay and/or incurs Cost by reason of such Force Majeure, the Contractor shall be entitled subject to Sub-Clause 20. 1 [Contractor's Claims] to:

(a) an extension of time for any such delay, if completion is or will be delayed, under Sub-Clause 8. 4 [Extension of Time for Completion]; and

(b) if the event or circumstance is of the kind described in subparagraphs (i) to (iv) of Sub-Clause 19. 1 [Definition of Force Majeure] and, in the case of sub-paragraphs (ii) to (iv), occurs in the Country, payment of any such Cost.

After receiving this notice, the Engineer shall proceed in accordance with Sub-Clause 3. 5 [Determinations] to agree or determine these matters.

If the Contractor suffers delay or additional Cost due to the Force Majeure then the rights to claim depend on which category of the list at Sub-Clause 19. 1 is appropriate. An extension of time can be claimed, as Sub-Clause 8. 4 (b), if completion is, or will be, delayed. However, Cost can only be claimed following the warlike events at subparagraphs (i) to (iv) of Sub-Clause 19. 1 and not as a consequence of natural catastrophes. If the event is a war, hostilities, invasion or act of foreign enemies, as paragraph (i) then fine event may occur anywhere in the world, although it would be necessary to prove the effect on the Contract. Paragraphs (ii) to (iv) refer to more localised situations and only events in the Country are covered.

18. 5　Optional Termination, Payment and release

If the execution of substantially all the Works in progress is prevented for a continuous period of 84 days by reason of Force Majeure of which notice has been given under Sub-Clause 19. 2 [Notice of Force Majeure], or for multiple periods which total more than 140 days due to the same notified Force Majeure, then either Party may give to the other Party a notice of termination of the Contract. In this event, the termination shall take effect 7 days after the notice is given, and the Contractor shall proceed in accordance with Sub-Clause 16. 3 [Cessation of Work and Removal of Contractor's Equipment].

Upon such termination, the Engineer shall determine the value of the work done and issue a Payment Certificate which shall include:

(a) the amounts payable for any work carried out for which a price is stated in the Contract;

(b) the Cost of Plant and Materials ordered for the Works which have been delivered to the Contractor, or of which the Contractor is liable to accept delivery; this Plant and Materials shall become the property of (and be at the risk of) the Employer when paid for by the Employer, and the Contractor shall place the same at the Employer's disposal;

(c) any other Cost or liability which in the circumstances was reasonably incurred by the Contractor in the expectation of completing the Works;

(d) the Cost of removal of Temporary Works and Contractor's Equipment from the Site and the return of these items to the Contractor's works in his country (or to any other destination at no greater cost); and

(e) the Cost of repatriation of the Contractor's staff and labour employed wholly in connection with the Works at the date of termination.

Under Sub-Clause 19.6, either Party may give a notice of termination of the Contract. The procedures are a mixture of the provisions for termination of Clauses 15 and 16, which reflects the fact that Force Majeure is not caused by any default by either Party.

18.6　Release from Performance Under the Law

Notwithstanding any other provision of this Clause, if any event or circumstance outside the control of the Parties (including, but not limited to, Force Majeure) arises which makes it impossible or unlawful for either or both Parties to fulfill its or their contractual obligations or which, under the law governing the Contract, entitles the Parties to be released from further performance of the Contract, then upon notice by either Party to the other Party of such event or circumstance:

(a) the Parties shall be discharged from further performance, without prejudice to the rights of either Party in respect of any previous breach of the Contract; and

(b) the sum payable by the Employer to the Contractor shall be the same as would have been payable under Sub-Clause 19.6 (optional Termination, Payment and Release) if the Contract had been terminated under Sub-Clause 19.6.

Sub-Clause 19.7 is much wider than the Force Majeure provisions of Sub-Clause 19.1 and acknowledges that situations can arise when it is impossible for the Contract to continue. This is a very serious action and should only be taken after legal advice and consideration of the applicable law.

☞ 疑难词汇 ☜

1. superior force 超级力量（"vis majeure" or "vis major" 不可抗力）
2. force majeure 不可抗力
3. unexpected circumstances 意想不到的事件
4. natural catastrophes 自然灾害
5. civil unrest 国内动乱
6. virulent virus 烈性病毒
7. foot and mouth 口足病
8. swine flu 猪流感
9. insurrection 暴动，叛乱
10. strike 罢工
11. hostilities 敌对状态，战争
12. commotion 暴乱，骚动
13. terrorism 恐怖行为

14. ionizing radiation 核电辐射

15. contamination 污染

16. lockout 停工，封锁

17. governing law 准据法

18. hurricane 飓风，暴风

19. volcanic activity 火山活动

20. duplicate 复制，重复

21. mitigate damage 减轻损害

22. be excused from performing obligation 免于履行义务

23. subjective interpretation 主观解释

☞ **疑难语句** ☜

1. The distinction is that the Employer's risk relates to loss or damage to the works, goods or Contractor's Documents together with delay or Cost from rectifying this loss or damage. Force Majeure refers to the situation when either Party is prevented from performing any of its obligations under the Contract.

它们的区别是雇主的风险是与工程，货物和承包商文件相关的损失和损害，以及因修复这些损失和损害的延期和费用有关。不可抗力是指合同任一方受阻而不能履行合同义务。

2. The Party shall, having given notice, be excused performance of such obligations for so long as such Force Majeure prevents it from performing them.

在发出通知后，该方应在此类不可抗力持续期间免除此类义务的履行。

☞ **中文综述** ☜

一、概述

1. 不可抗力的含义

不可抗力是指非由当事人的主观意志决定，也非当事人能力能抗拒的客观情势。我国《民法通则》第一百五十三条规定，不可抗力是指"不能预见、不能避免并不能克服的客观情况"。

（1）不能预见

预见性取决于人的预见能力，人的预见能力的提高，必将影响到预见的范围。某种现象过去不能预见，现在却可以预见；现在不能预见，将来未必不能预见。所以，决定人们对某种现象是否可以预见，应以当时的技术水平为依据。因此，一般认为，应以普通人的预见能力而不是具体当事者的预见能力为标准，来判断对某种现象是否可以预见。

（2）不可避免并不能克服

不可避免和不能克服，表明事件的发生和事件造成的损害具有必然性。所谓"不能避免"是指当事人已经尽了最大的努力，仍然不能避免某种事件的发生。所谓"不能克服"是指当事人在事件发生以后，已尽了最大的努力仍不能克服事件所造成的损害后果。

（3）客观情况

所谓"客观情况"是指实际存在的事实。

此外，不可抗力必须影响到合同的正常履行。如果在合同履行中遇到不能预见、不能避免和不能克服的客观事件，但并没有导致当事人不能按合同履行，此种事件在法律上没有任何意义，不应被视为合同法意义上的不可抗力。

2. 不可抗力的构成条件

根据上述不可抗力的含义，构成不可抗力须具备如下条件：

（1）是在合同成立后发生的；

（2）不是由于任何一方当事人的过失或疏忽而造成的；

（3）意外事故的发生是任何一方当事人不能预见、无法避免、无法预防的。

不可抗力事故包括自然原因引起的，如地震、海啸、水灾、风灾、旱灾、大雪等；另一种是社会原因引起的，如战争、罢工、政府封锁、禁运。

不可抗力事故发生后的法律后果，一般均可以使当事人有解除合同或要求延迟履行合同的权利。具体需视不可抗力的大小和持续时间决定。如不可抗力使合同的履行成为不可能，则可解除合同。如只是暂时阻碍了合同的履行，则只能延迟履行合同。

二、FIDIC 合同条件中对于不可抗力的定义

"新红皮书"第 19 条针对工程项目实施过程中可能遇到的不可抗力事件进行了如下描述。

"不可抗力"的含义是指如下所述的异常事件或情况：

（1）一方无法控制的；

（2）该方在签订合同前，无法进行合理准备的；

（3）情况发生时，该方无法合理回避或克服的；

（4）主要不是由于另一方造成的。

只要满足上述条件，不可抗力可包括（但不限于）下列各种特殊事件或情况：战争、敌对行动（不论宣战与否）、入侵、外敌行动；叛乱、恐怖活动、革命、暴动、军事政变或篡夺政权，或内战；承包商人员和承包商及其分包商的其他雇员以外的人员的骚乱、混乱、罢工或停工；战争军火、爆炸物资、离子辐射或放射性污染，但因承包商使用此类军火、炸药、辐射或放射性的情况除外；自然灾害，如地震、飓风、台风或火山活动。

上述 FIDIC 关于工程项目的不可抗力的定义具有广泛的代表性，但若与某些工程合同适用的法律不一致，则应在具体的合同条款中加以修改。

三、不可抗力范围的确认

"新红皮书"明确指出，一个事件或情况只有在同时满足第 19.1 款中的 4 个条件时，才能称为不可抗力。只要合同双方当事人同意，可以把其他可能发生的情况列入不可抗力的范围之内。在规定不可抗力事件范围时，一定要注意以下问题：

（1）不能把政府政策所不允许的内容列入不可抗力的事件范围。例如，在美国一般就不能将由于"社会力量"引起的意外事故列入不可抗力事件的范围。

（2）在确定不可抗力事件的范围时，应该区别不同项目的具体情况，作出不同的规定。不能脱离项目的实际仅作泛泛的规定，而漏掉可能发生的一些重要的不可抗力事件，致使合同一方，特别是承包商，承担自身难以控制的责任和义务。

（3）对于不可抗力事故范围规定的用词，一定要具体、确切、明了，不能使用一些模棱两可、含糊不清的词语。

四、不可抗力的处理

"新红皮书"规定，不可抗力事件发生后，主要由雇主承担由不可抗力引发的损失，并给予承包商合理的补偿。承包商可以根据不可抗力条款进行索赔。

1. 不可抗力的通知及减少延误的责任

在不可抗力事件发生后，承包商已经或将要无法履行合同义务，那么在承包商注意到此事件后的 14 天内，应通知雇主有关情况，并详细说明他已经或将要无法履行的义务和工作。此后，承包商可在此不可抗力持续期间，免去履行此类义务。当不可抗力的影响终止时，承包商也应通知雇主。

2. 不可抗力的后果有利于承包商

如果由于发生不可抗力，承包商无法履行其合同义务，并且已经按照要求通知了雇主，则承包商有权按照程序索赔自己遭受的工期和费用损失。从"新红皮书"第 19.4 款可以看出，发生不可抗力事件之后，在风险承担上 FIDIC 是有利于承包商的。

3. 合同的终止、付款和解除

"新红皮书"第 19.6 款规定：如果由于不可抗力，导致整个工程已经持续 84 天无法继续施工，或停工时间累计已经超过了 140 天，则任一方可向对方发出终止合同的通知，通知发出 7 天后合同终止即生效。承包商按照合同终止时的规定撤离现场。如果因不可抗力合同已经中止，工程师应估算已完成的工作的价值，并向承包商颁发支付证书。

本款中的责任分担对于承包商是合理的。若一种特殊的不可抗力事件发生后，使得双方不可能再继续履行义务，也没有复工的希望，则不应再按照一般的不可抗力事件来处理。如果再等待很多天才可以终止合同的话，则双方只能招致更大的损失，此时，应依据第 19.7 款解除履约。

Questions

1. How to define the concept of Force Majeure? What is the scope of Force Majeure?
2. What are the Consequences of Force Majeure under FIDIC?

Chapter 19　Claims

19.1　Introduction

The procedures for the resolution of claims are arguably the most important part of any Conditions of Contract. Certainly the claims provisions are the most frequently used Clauses in any Contract. The FIDIC Conditions include provisions for the submission, consideration and resolution of claims and disputes in a number of different Clauses. This chapter gives a general review of the procedures for the submission, response and resolution of claims, draws attention to the need for co-ordination between different Clauses, and lists some of the Clauses which include similar procedures. These procedures may have been modified in the Particular Conditions and the actual Contract should be checked to ascertain the detailed procedures for the particular project.

Unexpected situations are an inevitable feature of every construction project. Delays and additional costs may lead to claims. Claims may arise under any of the Contracts for a particular project, and may be Employer/Contractor, Contractor/Subcontractor or Employer/Consultant.

The 1999 FIDIC Conditions of Contract for Construction include procedures which must be followed for the Employer to claim against the Contractor as well as for the Contractor to claim against the Employer. This is a new procedure for FIDIC, which will help with the efficient administration of the project but will need to be studied carefully by both the Employer, the Engineer and the Contractor.

19.2　Claims and the Conditions of Contract

The Conditions of Contract give the rights and obligations of the Employer and the Contractor to the Contract, other people, such as the Engineer, a Consultant or a Subcontractor may be involved in the preparation, analysis or administration of the claim but cannot be the principal who makes or receives the claim. While it may be legally possible for an outside person to claim that either the Employer or the Contractor has caused them damage by negligence or failing to comply with some legal obligation.

All claims that are made because of problems which arose under or in connection with a particular Contract must follow the procedures laid down in that Contract. The claim may be made:

(1) in accordance with a Clause which states that the Contractor may be entitled to additional time or money in certain circumstances, or the Employer may be entitled to claim money from the Contractor;

(2) because one Party alleges that the other Party has failed to fulfill an obligation which is required by a Clause in the Contract;

(3) because one Party alleges that it is entitled to payment for some other reason, possibly because of some legal entitlement, which applies regardless of whether it is mentioned in the Contract.

19. 3　Contractor's Claims

19. 3. 1　"Contractual" Claims

Since the first edition of the FIDIC Red Book was published in 1957, the FIDIC contracts have contained provisions entitling the Contractor to claim additional money or time (or both) from the Employer when the Contractor encounters specifically defined unforeseeable conditions. The 1999 edition of the Red and Yellow Books each contain about 30 sub-clauses specifying events which, should they occur, will entitle the Contractor to claim from the Employer.

The sub-clauses in the New Red Book which entitle the Contractor to claim additional money or time are listed below :

(1) 1. 9 [Red Book only] Delayed: Drawings or Instructions

Contractor may claim extension of time, Cost and reasonable profit if Engineer fails to issue a notified instruction or drawing within a reasonable time.

(2) 2. 1 Right to Access to the Site

Contractor may claim extension of time, Cost and reasonable profit if Employer fails to give right of access to Site within time stated in the Contract.

(3) 4. 7 Setting Out

Contractor may claim extension of time, Cost and reasonable profit for errors in original setting-out points and levels of reference.

(4) 4. 12 Unforeseeable Physical Conditions

Contractor may claim extension of time and Cost if he encounters physical conditions which are Unforeseeable.

(5) 4. 24 Fossils

Contractor may claim extension of time and Cost attributable to an instruction to Contractor to deal with an encountered archaeological finding.

(6) 7. 4 Testing

Contractor may claim extension of time, Cost and reasonable profit if testing is delayed by (or on behalf of) the Employer.

(7) 8. 4 Extension of Time for Completion

Contractor may claim extension of time if completion (see Sub-Clauses 8. 2 & 10. 1) is or 8. 5 Delays Caused by Authorities, Contractor may claim extension of time if Country's 6 public authority causes Unforeseeable delay.

(8) 8. 9 Consequences of Suspension

Contractor may claim extension of time and Cost if Engineer instructs a suspension of progress.

(9) 10. 2 Taking Over of Parts of the Works

Contractor may claim Cost and reasonable profit attributable to the taking over of a part of the Works.

(10) 10. 3 Interference with Tests on Completion

Contractor may claim extension of time, Cost and reasonable profit if Employer delays a Test on Completion.

(11) 11. 8 Contractor to Search Contractor may claim Cost and reasonable profit if instructed to search for cause of a defect for which he is not responsible.

(12) 12. 3 Evaluation

Contractor's entitlement to new rates or prices for work whose quantity has been changed or which is varied.

(13) 12. 4 Omissions

Contractor may claim a Cost which, although it had been included in a BOQ item, he would not recover because the item was for work which has been omitted by Variation.

(14) 13. 2 Value Engineering

Contractor may claim half of the saving in contract value of his redesigned post-contract alternative proposal, which was approved without prior agreement of such contract value and of how saving would be shared.

(15) 13. 3 Variation Procedure

The Contract Price shall be adjusted as a result of Variations.

(16) 13. 7 Adjustments for Changes in Legislation

Contractor may claim extension of time and Cost attributable to a change in the Laws of the Country.

(17) 14. 4 Schedule of Payments

If interim payment installments were not defined by reference to actual progress, and actual progress is less than that on which the schedule of payments was originally based, these installments may be revised.

(18) 14. 8 Delayed Payment

Contractor may claim financing changes if he does not receive payment in accordance with Sub-Clause 14. 7.

(19) 16. 1 Contractor's Entitlement to Suspend Work

Contractor may claim extension of time, Cost and reasonable profit if Engineer fails to certify or if Employer fails to pay amount certified or fails to evidence his financial arrangements, and Contractor suspends work.

(20) 16. 4 Payment on Termination

Contractor may claim losses and damages after terminating Contract.

(21) 17. 1 Indemnities

Contractor may claim cost attributable to a matter against which he is indemnified by Employer.

(22) 17. 4 Consequences of Employer's Risks

Contractor may claim extension of time, Cost and (in some cases) reasonable profit if Works, Goods or Contractor's Documents are damaged by an Employer's risk as listed in Sub-Clause 17. 3.

(23) 18. 1 General Requirements for Insurances

Contractor may claim cost of premiums if Employer fails to effect insurance for which he is the "Insuring Party".

(24) 19. 4 Consequences of Force Majeure

Contractor may claim extension of time and (in some cases) Cost if Force Majeure prevents him from performing obligations.

(25) 19. 6 Optional Termination, Payment and Release

Contractor's work and other Costs are valued and paid after progress is prevented by a prolonged period of Force Majeure and either Party then gives notice of termination.

(26) 19. 7 Release from Performance

If it becomes impossible or unlawful to perform contractual obligations, Contractor may be released and can claim as in 19. 6.

19. 3. 2　Notice Periods

If the Contractor considers himself to be entitled to any extension of time for the completion of the works or for any additional payments under any clause of the contract he should give notice to the Engineer.

The notice shall describe the event of circumstances giving rise to the claim and shall be given as soon as practicable. In any event is the notice must be given not later than 28 days after the Contractor became aware or should have become aware of the relevant event or circumstance giving rise to the claim. In practice it may be easier to establish whether notice was given within 28 days after the Contractor should have become aware of the relevant event or circumstance giving rise to the claim. Generally there is no need for this notice to indicate how much extension of time or additional payments may be claimed or to state the clause or other contractual basis of the claim.

Notices must comply with Sub-Clause 1. 3. Sub-Clause 4. 21 requires progress reports to list all notices which have been given under Sub-Clause 20. 1.

The notice is to be sent to the Engineer with a copy to the Employer in accordance with Sub-Clause 1. 3. The recipient is not required to respond other than to acknowledge receipt, people should not regard the notice as an aggressive act but merely as an act which enables the Employer to be aware of the possibility that the Contractor has an enhanced entitlement. This first notice is the start of the detail procedure specified in Sub-Clause 20.1. The Contractor must ensure that notices are given in due time in order to protect his rights under the contract. Failure to give notice in accordance with the first paragraph of Sub-Clause 20.1 deprives the Contractor of all his entitlement to any extension of time and/or compensation.

Notices enable the Engineer to make his own observations and make his own records of the events giving rise to the claim. They also enable the Engineer to consider what possible actions he may take to overcome the problem. Notices put the problems on record and enable the Contractor to receive prompt decisions on his entitlement. A further, and possibly more drastic consequence of the notices will enable the Employer to take a decision to determine the contract.

Whether a failure to give a notice or provide information can remove legal entitlement is a matter which may depend on the applicable law. However it is clear that under this contract notice is essential for the Contractor to establish his legal entitlements. Sub-Clause 20.1 imposes procedural obligations on the recipient of the Contractor's claims and submissions. By comparison with the Contractor's procedural failures it will be noted that no consequences are stated in respect of the failures of such recipients.

19.3.3 The Claims Procedure

Sub-Clause 20.1 provides for the following procedure:

(1) If the Contractor considers himself to be entitled to an extension of the Time for Completion and/or additional payment under any clause of the Conditions or otherwise, the Contractor must give notice to the Engineer (or to the Employer, under the Silver Book) as soon as practicable and "not later than 28 days after the Contractor became aware, or should have become aware, of the event or circumstance" giving rise to the claim.

The Contractor has merely to give a bare notice of claim within 28 days. A one- or two-sentence letter will do. The Contractor does not need to state the amount or time claimed nor the contractual basis of the claim nor provide any supporting documents.

If the Contractor fails to give such notice of claim within 28 days: "the Time for Completion shall not be extended, the Contractor shall not be entitled to additional payment, and the Employer shall be discharged from all liability in connection with the claim" (Sub-Clause 20.1).

(2) When the Contractor gives such a notice under the Sub-Clause, he is required, as in the case of the old Red Book and the Orange Book, to "keep such contemporary records as may be necessary to substantiate any claim" and the Engineer (or the Employer, under the Silver Book) is authorized to monitor the Contractor's record-keeping and/or instruct the Contractor to keep additional contemporary records (Sub-Clause 20.1).

(3) Within 42 days after the Contractor became aware, or should have become aware, of the event or circumstance giving rise to the claim, or within such other period as the En-

gineer (or the Employer, under the Silver Book) may approve, the Contractor is required to send to the Engineer (or Employer) "a fully detailed claim" which includes "full supporting particulars of the basis of the claim and of the extension of time and/or additional payment claimed". If the event or circumstance giving rise to the claim has "a continuing effect", further procedures need to be complied with.

(4) Within 42 days after receiving a claim or any further particulars supporting a previous claim, or within such other period as may be proposed by the Engineer (or the Employer, under the Silver Book) and approved by the Contractor, the Engineer (or Employer) must respond "with approval, or with disapproval and detailed comments". He may also request any necessary further particulars "but shall nevertheless give his response on the principles of the claim within such time".

This is the first time a FIDIC contract has required the Engineer or the Employer to respond to the claim of a Contractor within a given time period or in a given manner.

(5) The requirements of Sub-Clause 20.1 are expressly stated to be "in addition to those of any other Sub-Clause which may apply to a claim". Thus, the Contractor must comply with the claims procedure provided for in Sub-Clause 20.1 in addition to the requirements of the clause in the contract which may have given him the substantive right to claim.

(6) Sub-Clause 20.1 further provides in part that: "If the Contractor fails to comply with this or another Sub-Clause in relation to any claim, any extension of time and/or additional payment shall take account of the extent (if any) to which the failure has prevented or prejudiced proper investigation of the claim…"

Thus, the extension of time or additional payment is required to take account of any damage the Employer may have suffered as the result of the Contractor's failure to comply with the claims procedure in the contract.

19.4　Claims by the Employer

19.4.1　Procedure and Notice of the Employer's claim

FIDIC contracts are aimed at the early resolution of any queries at the time when the claim arises, with the likelihood that plant, manpower and witnesses are still on site. The starting moment of the procedure is given by occurrence of an event or circumstance giving rise to a claim as a result of which the Employer considers himself entitled to any payment under or in connection with the Contract and/or (in all the Books apart from the Gold Book) to any extension of the Defects Notification Period. It then involves the following stages:

(1) the Employer or Engineer /Employer's Representative (G) is required to give notice and particulars to the Contractor. The time within which notice must be given;

(2) the contract administrator is then required to proceed in accordance with Sub-

Clause 3. 5 to agree or determine the Employer's claim.

The notice can be given in a short letter, which should set out the event or circumstance giving rise to the claim as a result of which the Employer considers himself entitled to payment and/or an extension of the Defects Notification Period.

Generally, the notice must comply with the requirements of Sub-Clause 1. 3 and must be given in writing. It is not clear if the particulars are to be delivered at the same time with the notice. The clause does not impose this and there is no time limit or frame stated in the clause. So, the contract provides a lot of flexibility when regulates the procedure of the Employer's claims. Once received by the Contractor, it should also be listed in the progress reports in accordance with Sub-Clause 4. 21 (f).

19. 4. 2　The period within the notice must be given

The period within which notice must be given under Red and Yellow Books is "as soon as practicable after the Employer became aware of the event or circumstances giving rise to the claim". This requires the Employer to have actual knowledge of the event or circumstance before he must give notice. Relating to the extension of the defects Notification Period, any notice should be given before the expiry of that period. Also, Sub-Clause 11. 3 restricts the extension to no more than two years.

No sanction is specified if the Employer fails to give notice to the Contractor within the required time. This brings some scholars to the conclusion that Sub-Clause 2. 5 provides a simpler claim mechanism with no time bar.

There is no similar provision to Sub-Clause 20. 1 which says that any claim to time or money will be lost if no notice is given within the specified time limit. As a consequence, it has generally been considered that a failure by the employer to bring a claim "as soon as practicable" would not be treated as a condition precedent. This said that any notice relating to the extension of the Defects Notification Period had of course to be made before the current end of that period.

☞ 疑难词汇 ☜

1. ascertain 查明，确定
2. be discharged from 被允许……免于
3. substantiate 证实，加强
4. contemporary records 同期记录
5. prevented or prejudiced 阻止和损害
6. sanction 制裁，处罚
7. harsh 严厉的，严酷的
8. imaginable 可能的，可想象的
9. on the merits of the claim 依据索赔
10. deduct 扣除，扣掉
11. onerous 繁琐，麻烦

☞ **疑难语句** ☜

1. The 1999 edition of the Red and Yellow Books each contain about 30 sub-clauses specifying events which, should they occur, will entitle the Contractor to claim from the Employer.

FIDIC "新红皮书"和"黄皮书"都包含了大约 30 个条款，这些条款强调，如果这些条款规定的事实发生，承包商将有权向雇主索赔。

2. The Employer shall be discharged from all liability in connection with the claim.

雇主将被免除与索赔有关的所有责任。

3. Without admitting the Employer's liability. 在不必事先承认雇主责任的情况下。

4. In order to avoid losing the right to claim, many Contractors will use a standard form to submit notices for every imaginable event, many of which will not be followed by a detailed claim.

为了避免失去索赔的权利，许多承包商使用标准格式对每一个可能构成索赔的事件通知（工程师），而这些事件很大一部分并不构成索赔的内容。

☞ **中文综述** ☜

一、索赔概述

根据索赔行为及产生的后果，应该认为索赔的本意是主张自身权益，是一种当一方受到损失时向另一方提出补偿的要求。它是一种正当权利的要求，并不意味着对过错方的惩罚，所以其基调是温和的。无论是在一方违约而使另一方蒙受损失情况下的索赔，还是因自然灾害引起的索赔，都是一种正当权利的要求。索赔不是法律上的概念，在 FIDIC 合同条款中，索赔被作为一个独立的章节，可以说明索赔是建筑工程管理的重要手段和必要环节，它可以是承包商向雇主的索赔，也可以是雇主向承包商的索赔。索赔需遵守一定的索赔程序，按照索赔程序提交索赔要求和索赔证据。只有当索赔没有得到被索赔方的认可或接受，索赔方仍然坚持通过索赔来维护自己的权益时，索赔方才可能转向法律途径，通过仲裁或诉讼解决问题。

二、索赔起因

1. 合同文件引起的索赔

（1）合同文件组成引起的索赔

建设工程施工合同是一个由合同协议书、通用条款、专用条款、中标函等多种法律文件组成的综合体，有些合同文件还可能是在投标后修改拟定的。如果投标前后合同条款或图纸发生不一致，或雇主与承包商对合同条款以及合同文件内容等理解不一致，都可能引发索赔。

（2）合同缺陷引起的索赔

合同缺陷是指合同条款规定不严谨甚至前后矛盾，合同中有遗漏或者错误。它不仅包括条款中的缺陷，也包括技术规程和图纸上的缺陷。工程师有权对此作出解释，但如果承包商执行工程师的解释后引起了成本增加或工期延误，则有权提出索赔。

2. 不可抗力和不可预见因素引起的索赔

（1）不可抗力的自然因素引起的索赔

不可抗力的自然因素是指飓风、超标准的洪水等自然灾害。"新红皮书"规定，由这类自然灾害引起的损失应由雇主承担，但是同时也指出，承包商在这种情况下应采取措施，尽力减小损失。对由于承包商未尽力而使承包商损失扩大的部分，雇主不再承担赔偿责任。

(2) 不可抗力的社会因素引起的索赔

不可抗力的社会因素是指发生战争、核装置的污染和冲击波、暴乱、承包商和其分包商以外人员的动乱和骚扰等而使承包商受到的损害。这些风险一般应由雇主承担，承包商不对此造成的工程损失或人身伤亡负责，且应得到损害前已完成的永久工程的付款和合理利润以及一些修复费用和重建费用。这些费用还包括由于特殊风险而引起的费用的增加。

(3) 不可预见的外界条件引起的索赔

不可预见的外界条件是指有经验的承包商在招标阶段根据招标文件中提供的资料和现场勘察结果，都无法合理预见到的外界条件，如地下水、地质断层、溶洞等，但其中不包括气候条件（异常恶劣天气条件除外）。遇到此类条件，承包商受到损失或增加额外支出，经工程师确认，承包商可获得经济补偿和批准工期顺延的天数。如工程师认为承包商在提交投标书前根据介绍的现场情况、地质勘探资料应能预见到此类情况，承包商在投标时理应予以考虑，可不同意索赔。

(4) 施工中遇到地下文物或构筑物引起的索赔

在挖方工程中，如发现图纸中未注明的文物（不管是否有价值）或人工障碍（如公共设施、隧道、旧建筑物等），承包商应立即报告工程师，请其现场检查，共同讨论处理方案。如果新施工方案导致工程费用增加，如原计划的机械开挖方式改为人工开挖方式等，承包商有权提出费用索赔和工期索赔。

3. 雇主方原因引起的索赔

(1) 拖延提供现场及通道引起的索赔

因施工现场的搬迁工作进展不顺利等原因，雇主没能如期向承包商移交合格的、可以直接进行施工的现场，会导致承包商提出误工的费用索赔和工期索赔。

(2) 拖延支付工程款引起的索赔

合同中均有支付工程款的时间限制，如果雇主不能按时支付工程进度款，承包商可按合同规定向雇主索付利息。严重拖欠工程款而使得承包商资金周转困难时，承包商除向雇主提出索赔要求外，还有权放慢施工进度，甚至可以因雇主违约而解除合同。

(3) 指定分包商违约引起的索赔

指定分包商违约常常表现为未能按分包合同规定完成应承担的工作而影响了总承包商的施工，雇主对指定分包商的不当行为也应承担一定的责任。总承包商除根据与指定分包商签订的合同索赔窝工损失外，还有权向雇主提出延长工期的索赔要求。

(4) 雇主提前占用部分永久工程引起的索赔

工程实践中，雇主经常因经济效益等原因使部分单项工程提前投入使用，或提前占用部分工程。如果合同未规定可提前占用部分工程，则提前使用永久工程的单项工程或部分工程所造成的后果，责任由雇主承担；另一方面，提前占用工程若影响承包商的后续工程施工，增加施工困难，则承包商有权提出索赔。

(5) 雇主要求提前完成施工任务引起的索赔

由于雇主改变原合同工期规定，或者改变了部分工程的施工内容而必须延长工期，但是雇主又坚持按原工期完工，迫使承包商赶工，并投入更多的机械、人力来完成工程，从而导致成本增加。承包商可以要求赔偿赶工措施费用，例如加班工资、新增设备租赁费和使用费、增加的管理费用、分包的额外成本等。

4. 工程师方原因引起的索赔

（1）延误提供图纸或拖延审批图纸引起的索赔

如工程师延误向承包商提供施工图纸，或者拖延审批承包商负责设计的施工图纸，因此使施工进度受到影响，承包商可以索赔工期，还可以对延误导致的损失要求经济补偿。

（2）重新检验引起的索赔

工程师为了对工程的施工质量进行严格控制，除了要进行合同中规定的检查试验外，还有权要求重新检验和检查。例如对承包商的材料进行多次抽样检验，或对已施工的工程进行部分拆卸或挖开检查以及要求在现场进行工艺试验等。如果这些检查或检验表明其质量未达到技术规程所要求的标准，则检查或检验费用由承包商承担；如检查或检验证明符合合同要求，则承包商除了可向雇主提出偿付这些检查费用和修复费用外，还可以对由此引起的其他损失，如工期延误、工人窝工等，要求赔偿。

（3）工程质量要求过高引起的索赔

合同中的技术规程对于工程质量，包括材料质量、设备性能和工艺要求等，均作了明确规定。但在施工过程中，工程师有时可能不认可某种材料，而迫使承包商使用比合同文件规定的标准更高的材料，或者提出更高的工艺要求，则承包商可以就此要求对其损失进行补偿或重新核定单价。

（4）对承包商的施工进行不合理干预引起的索赔

合同规定承包商有权采取任何可以满足合同规定的进度和质量要求的施工顺序和方法。如果工程师不是以建议的方式，而是对承包商的施工顺序及施工方法进行不合理地干预，甚至正式下达指令要求承包商执行，则承包商可以就这种干预所引起的费用增加和工期延长提出索赔。

（5）暂停施工引起的索赔

项目实施过程中，工程师有权根据承包商违约或破坏合同的情况，或者因现场气候条件不利于施工以及为了工程的合理进行（如分项工程或工程任何部位的安全）而有必要停工时，下达暂停施工的指令。如果这种暂停施工的命令并非因承包商的责任或原因所引起的，则承包商有权要求工期赔偿，同时可以就其停工损失获得合理的额外费用补偿。

三、承包商的索赔

根据"新红皮书"的规定，承包商对雇主的索赔有很多依据，承包商对雇主的索赔主要包括：

1. 雇主拖延图纸或指示

如果因工程师未能在一合理的且已在（附有详细证据的）通知中说明的时间内颁发承包商在通知中要求的图纸或指示，而导致承包商延误和（/或）招致费用增加时，承包商应向工程师发出进一步的通知，且按照第 20.1 款【承包商的索赔】进行索赔。

2. 承包商进入现场的权利

如果由于雇主一方未能在规定时间内给予承包商进入现场和占用现场的权利，致使承

包商延误了工期和（或）增加了费用，承包商应向工程师发出通知，并依据第 20.1 款
【承包商的索赔】进行索赔。

3. 雇主对承包商放线使用的位置、标高或尺寸或准线基础数据负责

如果由于这些参照项目的差错而不可避免地对实施工程造成了延误和（或）导致了费
用，而且一个有经验的承包商无法合理发现这种差错并避免此类延误和（或）费用，承包
商应向工程师发出通知并有权依据第 20.1 款【承包商的索赔】进行索赔。

4. 不可预见的外界条件

承包商遇到了不可预见的外界条件，发出了通知，且因此遭到了延误和（或）导致了
费用，承包商应有权依据第 20.1 款【承包商的索赔】进行索赔。

5. 化石

承包商一旦发现此类物品，应立即通知工程师，工程师可发出关于处理上述物品的指
示。如果承包商由于遵守该指示而引起延误和（/或）招致了费用，则应进一步通知工程
师并有权依据第 20.1 款【承包商的索赔】进行索赔。

6. 检验

如果由于遵守工程师的指示或因雇主的延误而使承包商遭受了延误和（/或）导致了
费用，则承包商应通知工程师并有权依据第 20.1 款【承包商的索赔】进行索赔。

7. 竣工时间的延长

如果承包商认为他有权获得竣工时间的延长，承包商应按第 20.1 款【承包商的索赔】
的规定，向工程师发出通知。当依据第 20.1 款确定每一延长时间时，工程师应复查以前
的决定并可增加（但不应减少）整个延期时间。

8. 暂停引起的后果

如果承包商在遵守工程师根据第 8.8 款【工程暂停】所发出的指示以及/或在复工时
遭受了延误和/或导致了费用，则承包商应通知工程师并有权依据第 20.1 款【承包商的索
赔】进行索赔。

9. 对部分工程的接收

如果由于雇主接收和（或）使用该部分工程（合同中规定的及承包商同意的使用除
外），而使承包商招致了费用，承包商应通知工程师并有权依据第 20.1 款【承包商的索
赔】获得有关费用以及合理利润的支付，并将之加入合同价格。

10. 对竣工检验的干扰

若延误进行竣工检验致使承包商遭受了延误和（或）导致了费用，则承包商应通知工
程师并有权依据第 20.1 款【承包商的索赔】进行索赔。

11. 承包商的检查

如果工程师要求的话，承包商应在其指导下调查产生任何缺陷的原因。除非此类缺陷
已依据第 11.2 款【修补缺陷的费用】，由承包商支付费用进行了修补，否则调查费用及合
理的利润应由工程师依据第 3.5 款【决定】，作出商定或决定，并加入合同价格。承包商
可以据此向雇主索赔。

12. 估价

每种新的费率或价格是对合同中相关费率或价格在考虑到任何相关事件以后作出的合
理调整。如果没有相关的费率或价格，则新的费率或价格应是在考虑任何相关事件以后，

从实施工作的合理费用加上合理利润中得到。

13. 省略

当对任何工作的省略构成部分（或全部）变更且对其价值未达成一致时，如果：① 承包商将招致（或已经招致）一笔费用，这笔费用应被视为是如果工作未被省略时，在构成部分接受的合同款额的一笔金额中所包含的；② 该工作的省略将导致（或已经导致）这笔金额不构成部分合同价格；并且③ 这笔费用并不被认为包含在任何替代工作的估价之中，承包商应随即向工程师发出通知，并附具体的证明资料。在接到通知后，工程师应依据第3.5款【决定】，对此费用作出商定或决定，并将之加入合同价格。

14. 价值工程

承包商可以随时向工程师提交一份书面建议，如果该建议被采用，它（在承包商看来）将①加速完工，②降低雇主实施、维护或运行工程的费用，③对雇主而言能提高竣工工程的效率或价值，或④为雇主带来其他利益。如果此改变造成该部分工程的合同价值减少，工程师应依据第3.5款【决定】，商定或决定一笔费用，并将之加入合同价格。

15. 变更程序

合同价格将依据变更而调整。

16. 法规变化引起的调整

如果承包商由于此类在基准日期后所作的法律或解释上的变更而遭受了延误（或将遭受延误）和/或承担（或将承担）额外费用，承包商应通知工程师并有权依据第20.1款【承包商的索赔】进行索赔。

17. 支付表

如果分期支付额不是参照工程实施所达到的实际进度制定的，且如果实际进度落后于支付表中分期支付所依据的进度状况，则工程师可通过考虑所达到的实际进度落后于分期支付所依据的进度的情况，根据第3.5款【决定】来商定或决定修正分期支付额。

18. 延误的支付

如果承包商没有收到根据第14.7款【支付】应获得的任何款额，承包商应有权就未付款额按月所计复利收取延误期的融资费。即承包商可以进行索赔。

19. 承包商有权暂停工作

如果工程师未能按照第14.6款【期中支付证书的颁发】开具支付证书，或者雇主未能按照第2.4款【雇主的资金安排】或第14.7款【支付】的规定执行，则承包商可提前21天以上通知雇主，暂停工作（或降低工作速度），除非并且直到承包商收到了支付证书、合理的证明或支付（视情况而定并且遵守通知的指示）。

20. 终止时的支付

在根据第16.2款【承包商提出终止】发出的终止通知生效后，雇主应尽快：①将履约保证退还承包商，② 根据第19.6款【可选择的终止、支付和返回】向承包商进行支付，以及③ 向承包商支付因终止合同承包商遭受的任何利润的损失或其他损失或损害的款额。

21. 保障

雇主应保障和保护承包商、承包商的人员，以及他们各自的代理人免遭与下述有关的一切索赔、损害、损失和开支（包括法律费用和开支）：①由于雇主、雇主的人员或他们各自的代理人的任何渎职、恶意行为或违反合同而造成的身体伤害、生病、病疫或死亡；②没有承保的责任。

22. 雇主的风险造成的后果

如果上述第 17.3 款所列的雇主的风险导致了工程、货物或承包商的文件的损失或损害，则承包商应尽快通知工程师，并且应按工程师的要求弥补此类损失或修复此类损害。

23. 有关保险的总体要求

当雇主作为保险方时，他应按照专用条件后所附详细说明的承保人及条件办理保险。

24. 不可抗力引起的后果

如果由于不可抗力，承包商无法依据合同履行他的任何义务，而且已经根据第 19.2 款【不可抗力的通知】，发出了相应的通知，并且由于承包商无法履行此类义务而使其遭受工期的延误和（或）费用的增加，则可根据第 20.1 款【承包商的索赔】进行索赔。

25. 可选择的终止、支付和返回

如果由于不可抗力，整个工程的施工无法进行已经持续了 84 天，且已根据第 19.2 款【不可抗力的通知】发出了相应的通知，或如果由于同样原因停工时间的总和已经超过了 140 天，则任一方可向另一方发出终止合同的通知。承包商可据此提出相关索赔。

26. 根据法律解除履约

除非本条另有规定，如果合同双方无法控制的任何事件或情况（包括，但不限于不可抗力）的发生使任一方（或合同双方）履行他（或他们）的合同义务已变为不可能或非法，或者根据本合同适用的法律，合同双方均被解除进一步的履约，承包商可以据此索赔。

四、雇主的索赔

在 FIDIC "新红皮书" 的通用合同条款中，雇主的索赔主要包括：

1. 缺陷通知期索赔

根据 "新红皮书" 第 11.3 款规定，如果由于某项缺陷或损害达到使工程、区段或主要永久设备（视情况而定，并且在接收以后）不能按照预定的目的进行使用，则雇主有权依据合同要求延长工程或区段的缺陷通知期。但缺陷通知期的延长不得超过 2 年。第 2.5 款规定，如果雇主认为按照任何合同条款的规定他有权获得支付或缺陷通知期的延长，则雇主或工程师应向承包商发出通知并说明细节。

2. 不合格工程的拒收和再次检验

"新红皮书" 第 7.5 款规定，如果经检查、检验、测量或试验，发现任何永久设备、材料或工艺有缺陷或不符合合同要求，工程师可拒收此永久设备、材料或工艺，并通知承包商，同时说明理由。承包商应立即修复上述缺陷并保证使被拒收的项目符合合同规定。若工程师要求对此永久设备、材料或工艺再次进行检验，则检验应按相同条款和条件重新进行。如果此类拒收和再次检验致使雇主产生了额外费用，则承包商应向雇主支付这笔费用。

3. 雇用他人完成修复工作

"新红皮书" 第 7.6 款规定，不论先前是否进行了任何检验或颁发了证书，工程师仍可以指示承包商：将工程师认为不符合合同规定的永久设备或材料从现场移走并进行替换；把不符合合同规定的任何其他工程移走并重建。如果承包商未能遵守该指示，则雇主有权雇用其他人来实施工作，并予以支付。除承包商有权从该工作所得的付款范围外，他应向雇主支付因其未完成工作而导致的费用。

4. 赶工导致费用增加

"新红皮书"第8.6款规定，除了由于第8.4款［竣工时间的延长］中所列原因导致的迟延，工程师可以指示承包商提交一份修改的进度计划以及证明文件，详细说明承包商为加快施工并在竣工时间内完工拟采取的修正方法。如果这些修正方法导致雇主增加了费用，则除第8.7款中所述的误期损害赔偿费（如有）外，承包商还应向雇主支付该笔附加费用。

5. 误期损害赔偿费

"新红皮书"第8.7款规定，如果承包商未能遵守第8.2款约定的竣工时间，承包商应为此违约向雇主支付误期损害赔偿费。

《标准施工招标文件》第11.5款约定，由于承包人原因造成工期延误，承包人应支付逾期竣工违约金。《建设工程施工合同（示范文本）》第14.2款规定，因承包人原因不能按照协议书约定的竣工日期或工程师同意顺延的工期竣工的，承包人应承担违约责任。

6. 承包商延误检验

"新红皮书"第9.2款规定，如果承包商无故延误竣工检验，工程师可通知承包商要求他在收到该通知后21天内进行此类检验。承包商应在该期限内他可能确定的某日或数日内进行检验，并将此日期通知工程师。若承包商未能在21天的期限内进行竣工检验，雇主的人员可着手进行此类检验，其风险和费用均由承包商承担。

7. 雇主自行清理现场

"新红皮书"第11.11款规定，在收到履约证书时，承包商应从现场运走任何剩余的承包商的设备、剩余材料、残物、垃圾或临时工程。若在雇主颁发履约证书后28天内上述物品还未被运走，则雇主可对此留下的任何物品予以出售或另作处理。雇主应有权获得为此类出售或处理及整理现场所发生的或有关的费用的支付。

8. 履约担保

"新红皮书"第4.2款规定，承包商未履行合同约定的义务，雇主可以依据履约担保的索赔范围，索赔承包商的应付金额。

9. 承包商使用现场水电服务

"新红皮书"第4.19款规定，为工程之目的承包商有权使用现场供应的电、水、气及其他服务，其详细规定和价格见规范。承包商应自担风险和自付费用，提供使用及计量此类服务所需的仪器。此类服务的消耗数量和应支付的款额（按其价格），应由工程师作出同意或决定。承包商应向雇主支付该项款额。

10. 使用雇主设备

"新红皮书"第4.20款规定，工程师应对使用雇主的设备的合适数量及应支付的款额（按指定价格）作出商定或决定。承包商应向雇主支付该项款额。

11. 雇主直接对指定分包商付款

根据"新红皮书"第5.4款的规定，雇主依据合同约定直接向指定分包商付款时，承包商应向雇主偿还这笔由雇主直接支付给指定分包商的款额。

12. 工程未通过竣工验收

　　根据"新红皮书"第9.4款（c）项的规定，当整个工程或某区段未能通过所进行的重复竣工检验时，如果雇主同意颁发接收证书，承包商应根据合同中规定的所有其他义务继续工作，并且合同价格应按照可以适当弥补由于此类失误而给雇主造成的价值损失数额予以扣除。

　　13. 承包商未修复缺陷

　　"新红皮书"第11.4款规定，如果承包商未能在合理时间内修复任何缺陷或损害，雇主（或其代表）可确定一日期并通知承包商，要求在该日或该日之前修复缺陷或损害。如果承包商到该日期尚未修复缺陷或损害，并且依据约定，这些修复工作应由承包商承担费用，雇主可（自行选择）：①以合理的方式由他本人或他人进行此项工作，承包商承担费用，但承包商对此项工作不再承担责任；并且承包商应依据第2.5款的约定，向雇主支付其因修复缺陷或损害发生的合理费用；② 要求工程师依据第3.5款［决定］，同意或决定合同价格的合理减少额；③在缺陷或损害使雇主实质上丧失了工程或工程的任何主要部分的整个利益时，终止整个合同或者不能按预期使用功能使用的该项主要部分。在不影响依据合同或其他规定所享有的任何其他权利的情况下，雇主还应有权收回为整个工程或该部分工程（视情况而定）所支付的全部费用以及融资费用、拆除工程、清理现场和将永久设备和材料退还给承包商所支付的费用。

　　五、索赔的程序

　　根据FIDIC"新红皮书"第20条规定，索赔程序可以分为两个部分：一是常规索赔程序，二是争议索赔程序。

　　（一）常规索赔程序

　　常规索赔程序是指索赔双方就索赔事项友好解决，没有争议存在。常规索赔程序包括：

　　1. 索赔通知

　　"新红皮书"第20.1款规定，如果承包商根据本合同条件的任何条款或参照合同的其他规定，认为他有权获得任何竣工时间的延长和（或）任何附加款项，他应通知工程师，说明引起索赔的事件或情况。该通知应尽快发出，并应不迟于承包商开始注意到，或应该开始注意到，这种事件或情况之后28天。

　　2. 索赔记录

　　"新红皮书"第20.1款规定：承包商应在现场或工程师可接受的另一地点保持用以证明任何索赔可能需要的同期记录。工程师在收到根据本款发出的上述通知后，在不必事先承认雇主责任的情况下，监督此类记录的进行，并（或）可指示承包商保持进一步的同期记录。承包商应允许工程师审查所有此类记录，并应向工程师提供复印件（如果工程师指示的话）。

　　3. 索赔报告

　　"新红皮书"第20.1款规定：在承包商开始注意到，或应该开始注意到，引起索赔的事件或情况之日起42天内，或在承包商可能建议且由工程师批准的此类其他时间内，承包商应向工程师提交一份足够详细的索赔，包括一份完整的证明报告，详细说明索赔的依据以及索赔的工期和（或）索赔的金额。

　　4. 工程师的批复意见

工程师在审议了索赔报告后，需给出意见函，并将该函件抄送雇主。"新红皮书"第20.1款规定：工程师在收到索赔报告或对过去索赔的任何进一步证明资料后 42 天内，或在工程师可能建议并经承包商认可的此类其他期限内，做出回应，表示批准或不批准并附具体意见。他还可以要求任何必要的进一步资料。

5. 雇主的批复意见

雇主在审议完索赔报告和工程师的批复意见后，给予索赔。

（二）争议索赔程序

如果任何一方对 DAB 的裁决结果持否定意见，或者说对索赔裁决结果不予认可，持反对意见的一方应在 28 日内，将不满决定通知另一方，否则任一方无权着手争议的仲裁。28 日内未发出不满通知，该决定则成为最终的对双方均具有拘束力的解决方案。"新红皮书"第 20.5 款规定：如果已按上述第 20.4 款发出了表示不满的通知，双方应在着手仲裁前，努力以友好方式解决争端。但是，除非双方另有协议，仲裁可在表示不满的通知发出后第 56 天或其后着手进行，即使未曾做过友好解决的努力。

Questions

1. In what situations does the New Red and Yellow Books entitle the Contractor to claim additional money or time ?

2. Describe the claim procedure under Sub-Clause 20. 1.

3. In what situations the employer be entitled to claim against the contractor?

4. In what situations the contractor be entitled to claim against the employer?

Chapter 20　The Dispute Adjudication Board

20. 1　Different Methods of Dispute Resolution in Construction Disputes

The construction industry is regarded as one of the most conflict and dispute ridden industries, which has resulted in it being one of the most claim orientated sectors. Over the years, various methods of alternative dispute resolution (ADR)❶ have been introduced into the construction industry as a mean to avoid lengthy and expensive litigation.

The possible ADR processes available to construction disputes are: mediation; adjudication; arbitration; expert determination and court proceedings. Each possible method will be considered in turn. It is common (and advisable) for a construction contract to specify one or more methods of dispute resolution.

20. 1. 1　Adjudication

Adjudication is a process in which a neutral third party will give a decision on a dispute. The Housing Grants, Construction and Regeneration Act 1996 (the Construction Act)❷ states that parties to a construction contract may refer their disputes to an adjudicator. Adjudication has become known as a "pay first, argue later" way for parties to resolve their disputes.

A successful party to adjudication can apply to the Technology and Construction Court to enforce an adjudicator's decision. The decision of the adjudicator will be binding, unless or until it is revised in arbitration or litigation.

(1) Benefits of Adjudication

---

❶　ADR: In the late 1980s and early 1990s, many people became increasingly concerned that the traditional method of resolving legal disputes in the United States, through conventional litigation, had become too expensive, too slow, and too cumbersome for many civil lawsuits (cases between private parties). This concern led to the growing use of ways other than litigation to resolve disputes. These other methods are commonly known collectively as alternative dispute resolution (ADR). Alternative dispute resolution (ADR) is generally classified into at least four types: negotiation, mediation, collaborative law, and arbitration.

❷　The Housing Grants, Construction and Regeneration Act 1996 is an Act of Parliament of the United Kingdom. Its long title shows that it is a piece of omnibus legislation. An Act to make provision for grants and other assistance for housing purposes and about action in relation to unfit housing; to amend the law relating to construction contracts and architects; to provide grants and other assistance for regeneration and development and in connection with clearance areas; to amend the provisions relating to home energy efficiency schemes; to make provision in connection with the dissolution of urban corporations, housing action trusts and the Commission for New Towns; and for connected purposes.

(a) The adjudicator is a neutral person who is not involved in the day to day running of the construction contract.

(b) Adjudication is a quick process, which is designed to ensure that cash flow is maintained during the construction process.

(c) Although it is still possible to go to the Court, in most cases the decision of the adjudicator decides the dispute.

(d) Adjudication is less expensive than court proceedings.

(2) Disadvantages of adjudication

(a) The dispute needs to have been aired between the parties before adjudication can be commenced.

(b) The adjudicator's powers are limited.

(c) Court proceedings are still required to enforce the adjudicator's decision if the "losing" party does not pay.

20. 1. 2   Expert Determination

Expert determination is often used to resolve issues or disputes of a specialist nature, such as construction, and is one of the most informal systems of dispute resolution. Expert determination is often used when there is a valuation dispute. If an expert is to be used to determine the dispute, the parties will agree this by contract and will agree that the expert determination will be binding.

(1) Benefits of Expert Determination

(a) It is an economic way of finally resolving valuation disputes.

(b) It is less expensive and a quicker and a less formal method of dispute resolution.

(2) Disadvantages of Expert Determination

(a) The use of experts is much less tied to legal processes and therefore it is more difficult to challenge the decision of an expert.

(b) An expert's report cannot generally be enforced without further court or arbitration proceedings.

20. 1. 3   Litigation

Whilst there are many methods of ADR, court proceedings are still one of the most common forms of resolving disputes within the construction industry. The Technology and Construction Court (TCC)❶ is a specialist court which deals with technology and construc-

---

❶   The Technology and Construction Court (commonly abbreviated in practice to the TCC) is a sub-division of the Queen's Bench Division, part of the High Court of Justice, which together with the Crown Court and the Court of Appeal, is one of the Senior Courts of England and Wales. The Civil Procedure Rules, which regulate procedure civil procedure in the High Court, allocate non-exhaustive categories of work to the court, principally, as the name suggests, disputes in the areas of construction and technology.

However, since its formation in its current guise in October 1998, the court's jurisdiction has expanded such that many civil claims which are factually or technically complex are now heard in the TCC, beyond its traditional case load. For example, large-scale group personal injury claims are heard by the court, as are disputes arising out of the EU's complicated public procurement regime.

tion disputes and is governed not only by the Civil Procedure Rules but also by the Technology and Construction Court Guide. A specialist TCC judge will deal with cases in the TCC.

(1) Advantages of Litigation

(a) The claim process will be managed by a judge throughout.

(b) Complex issues can be dealt with.

(c) The parties will obtain a binding and enforceable decision.

(2) Disadvantages of Litigation

(a) Only claims which are over the value of £ 250,000 can be dealt with at the TCC. Any claims below this sum will be dealt with at the County Court.

(b) It is often a slow process.

(c) It is likely to be the most expensive way of resolving a dispute.

(d) The proceedings will be in public and are therefore not confidential, except in certain very limited circumstances.

20.1.4　Mediation

Mediation is commonly used within the construction industry to resolve disputes. The Technology and Construction Court Guide provides guidance on the conduct of litigation within the construction industry and states that the court should encourage parties to use alternative dispute resolution (ADR), which in most cases, will be mediation.

(1) Benefits of Mediation

(a) The mediator will be an independent person, who will not make a decision, judge or advise, but will facilitate discussions between the parties, with the aim of resolving the dispute. Mediators are generally highly experienced in the area of the dispute, and may even by TCC judges.

(b) It can help maintain a business relationship.

(c) It is relatively quick, with mediations usually lasting 1~2 days.

(d) It is usually considerably less costly than litigation.

(e) Everything that happens in a mediation is confidential.

(f) A mediator will encourage the parties to find a solution to the dispute which will suit both the parties' needs.

(2) Disadvantages of Mediation

(a) In some cases there may be a concern that, during mediation, parties may disclose an important aspect of their argument or commercial position, which (despite the confidential nature of mediation) could benefit the other party if the matter went to trial.

(b) If the parties do not come to an agreement, the dispute will remain unresolved and the cost of mediation will have been wasted.

20.1.5　Arbitration

Arbitration is another alternative to litigation and is a process in which the parties will agree to refer the dispute to a third party, the arbitrator. Disputes are resolved on the basis of material facts, documents and relevant principles of law. Arbitrations in the UK are governed by the Arbitration Act 1996 which ensures that arbitrations are fair, cost-effective and rapid, as well as ensuring that the law is followed wherever possible and the language used is friendly and accessible. Arbitration is often used in the context of international construction disputes, but can equally be used for pure domestic disputes.

(1) Benefits of Arbitration

(a) Like mediation, arbitration is a confidential process.

(b) Parties can agree on an arbitrator who has relevant experience in the matter.

(c) Compared to court proceedings, it is a relatively quick process.

(d) It is highly flexible compared to court proceedings.

(2) Disadvantages of Arbitration

(a) It is the parties' responsibility to bear the costs of both the arbitrator and the venue where the arbitration is to take place.

(b) There are limited powers of compulsion or sanction available to the arbitrator if one party fails to comply with the directions set by the arbitrator.

(c) There are limited appeal rights available during arbitration.

(d) Costs can be similar to litigation at court.

20. 2   Introduction to DAB

The first recorded use of a dispute board was on Boundary Dam in Washington in the 1960s (known as the "Joint Consulting Board"). It then received a boost due to the publication of a report by the US National Committee on Tunnelling Technology entitled "Better Contracting for Underground Construction" . As a result, a dispute board was established for the Eisenhower Tunnel project in Colorado and its success gradually led to the widespread use of dispute boards throughout the US.

Dispute boards went international with the El Cajon Dam and Hydropower Project in Honduras. This project was part funded by the World Bank who, mindful of the inexperience of the Honduras Electricity Company in managing such a major project with international contractors, pushed for a US-style dispute board. The use of the dispute board was perceived as successful, leading to further use on international projects.

At the same time as this development of dispute boards was taking place, FIDIC was facing criticism over the role of the "Engineer" within its standard form contracts. Although the Engineer was empowered to make determinations under the contracts, contractors were distrustful of the independence of the Engineer given that they were appointed by the employer. These two streams came together in the new FIDIC "rainbow" suite of contracts introduced in 1999. The FIDIC approach to dispute boards was to make the decisions binding (the same approach as the FIDIC contracts had always taken to the decisions of the Engineer) rather than mere recommendations and so the DAB as we know it today was established.

A DAB is a panel of experienced, respected, impartial and independent reviewers. The board is normally organized before construction begins and meets at the job site periodically. The DAB members are provided with the contract documents, plans and specifications and become familiar with the project procedures and the participants and are kept abreast of job progress and developments. The DAB meets with the Employer's and Contractor's representatives during regular site visits and encourages the resolution of disputes at job level. When any dispute flowing from the contract or the work cannot be resolved by the parties it is referred to the DAB for Decision.

The DAB procedure was conceived as a method of primary dispute resolution. Thus the procedures should facilitate prompt reference of disputes to the board as soon as job level negotiations have reached an impasse. If a dispute arises between the Employer and the Contractor then it is referred to the DAB, under Sub-Clause 20.4. The wording of Sub-Clause 20.4 is not restricted to disputes as a result of a claim being rejected, but includes disputes of any kind whatsoever, in connection with or arising out of the Contract or the execution of the Works.

The DAB comprises either one or three people. The one-person Board is chosen by agreement at the start of the project. For the three-person Board each side proposes one person for the other side's agreement and the Chairman is chosen by agreement. Failing agreement, the selection is made by an independent organization, such as FIDIC or the Institution of Civil Engineers, named in the Appendix to Tender.

20.3   Appointment of the Dispute Adjudication Board

Disputes shall be adjudicated by a DAB in accordance with Sub-Clause 20.4. The Parties shall jointly appoint a DAB by the date stated in the Appendix to Tender.

The DAB shall comprise, as stated in the Appendix to Tender, either one or three suitably qualified persons ("the members"). If the number is not so stated and the Parties do not agree otherwise, the DAB shall comprise three persons. If the DAB is to comprise three persons, each Party shall nominate one member for the approval of the other Party. The Parties shall consult both these members and shall agree upon the third member, who shall be appointed to act as chairman. However, if a list of potential members is included in the Contract, the members shall be selected from those on the list, other than anyone who is unable or unwilling to accept appointment to the DAB.

The terms of remuneration of either the sole member or each of the three members, including the remuneration of any expert whom the DAB consults, shall be mutually agreed upon by the Parties when agreeing the terms of appointment. Each Party shall be responsible for paying one-half of this remuneration.

If at any time the Parties so agree, they may jointly refer a matter to the DAB for it to give its opinion. Neither Party shall consult the DAB on any matter without the agreement of the other Party. If at any time the Parties so agree, they may appoint a suitably qualified person or persons to replace (or to be available to replace) any one or more members of the DAB. Unless the Parties agree otherwise, the appointment will come into effect if a member declines to act as a result of death, disability, resignation or termination of appointment. If any of these circumstances occurs and no such replacement is available, a replacement shall be appointed in the same manner as the replaced person was required to have been nominated or agreed upon, as described in this Sub-Clause.

The appointment of any member may be terminated by mutual agreement of both Parties, but not by the Employer or the Contractor acting alone. Unless otherwise agreed by both Parties, the appointment of the DAB (including each member) shall expire when the discharge referred to in Sub-Clause14.12 (discharge) shall have become effective.

It is important that any person appointed to a DAB has appropriate construction experience, including experience of claims and dispute resolution, knowledge of contract interpretation knowledge of the DAB procedures. The DAB acts as a team, not as representatives of the Parties, so ideally there should be a balance of experience and professional expertise within the team. Whilst this may be difficult to achieve for the members nominated by the separate Parties, it should be considered in the choice of the Chairman. It is always useful for the Parties to discuss their prospective nominees before making a final decision.

Training courses for DAB members have already been established and no doubt will develop further as the 1999 FIDIC Contracts are used more extensively. Lists of suitable people have been prepared by several organizations, including FIDIC, The Institution of Civil Engineers (ICE) in London, The International Chamber of Commerce in Paris and other organizations in different countries.

20.4 Obtaining Dispute Adjudication Board's Decision

If a dispute (of any kind whatsoever) arises between the Parties in connection with, or arising out of, the Contract or the execution of the Works, including any dispute as to any certificate, determination, instruction, opinion or valuation of the Engineer, either Party may refer the dispute in writing to the DAB for its decision, with copies to the other Party and the Engineer. Such reference shall state that it is given under this Sub-Clause.

For a DAB of three persons, the DAB shall be deemed to have received such reference on the date when it is received by the chairman of the DAB.

Both Parties shall promptly make available to the DAB all such additional information, further access to the Site, and appropriate facilities, as the DAB may require for the purposes of making a decision on such dispute. The DAB shall be deemed to be not acting as arbitrator(s).

Within 84 days after receiving such reference, or within such other period as may be proposed by the DAB and approved by both Parties, the DAB shall give its decision, which shall be reasoned and shall state that it is given under this Sub-Clause. The decision shall be binding on both Parties, who shall promptly give effect to it unless and until it shall be revised in an amicable settlement or an arbitral award as described below.

If either Party is dissatisfied with the DAB's decision, then either Party may, within 28 days after receiving the decision, give notice to the other Party of its dissatisfaction. If the DAB fails to give its decision within the period of 84 days (or as otherwise approved) after receiving such reference, then either Party may, within 28 days after this period has expired, give notice to the other Party of its dissatisfaction.

In either event, this notice of dissatisfaction shall state that it is given under this Sub-Clause, and shall set out the matter in dispute and the reason (s) for dissatisfaction. Except as stated in Sub-Clause 20. 7 [Failure to Comply with Dispute Adjudication Board's Decision] and Sub-Clause 20. 8 [Expiry of Dispute Adjudication Board's Appointment], neither Party shall be entitled to commence arbitration of a dispute unless a notice of dissatisfaction has been given in accordance with this Sub-Clause.

If the DAB has given its decision as to a master in dispute to both Parties, and no notice of dissatisfaction has been given by either Party within 28 days after it received the DAB's decision, then the decision shall become final and binding upon both Parties.

The strength of the DAB procedure is that whenever there is any problem between the people on Site, whether it is caused by a difference of opinion on a technical matter, a problem of interpretation of the Contract, communication or simply a misunderstanding, it can be referred quickly to an independent tribunal. The problem can then be resolved, with the assistance of the DAB, whether this requires an explanation, opinion or binding decision.

Sub-Clause 20. 4 lays down the procedure for the DAB and further details are given in the FIDIC Annex: Procedural Rules, including the following. Both Parties make available to the DAB any information or facilities which it requires. The DAB may decide to conduct a hearing to consider submissions on the dispute from the Employer and the Contractor.

20. 5　Notice of dissatisfaction

The parties could accept the decision of the DAB as resolving their dispute, presumably honouring it or negotiating a different but acceptable resolution. If either party does not accept the DAB's decision, that party must serve a notice of dissatisfaction (NOD) in accordance with paragraph 5 of Sub-Clause 20. 4 which states: "If either Party is dissatisfied with the DAB's decision, then either Party may, within 28 days after receiving the decision, give notice to the other Party of its dissatisfaction and intention to commence arbitration. If the DAB fails to give its decision within the period of 84 days (or as otherwise approved) after receiving such reference, then either Party may, within 28 days after this period has expired, give notice to the other Party of its dissatisfaction and intention to commence arbitration."

In order to avoid the DAB's decision becoming "final and binding" either party may serve a notice of dissatisfaction. The notice shall:

(1) state that it is given under Sub-Clause 20. 4;

(2) set out the matter in dispute; and

(3) set out the reason (s) for dissatisfaction.

The substance and form of the notice must be adequate, in that the party serving it must make it objectively clear that it is dissatisfied with the DAB's decision, and why it is dissatisfied.

20. 6　Arbitration: selecting the applicable pathway

There are two pathways to arbitration under the standard FIDIC form. The first (under Sub-Clause 20. 6) is in order to resolve disputed DAB decisions or where no DAB decision has been issued, and the second (under Sub-Clause 20. 7) is to deal with the situation where there has been a failure to comply with a DAB decision. In terms of enforcing a DAB decision this means that the party referring the matter to arbitration has to select the applicable arbitration clause, and draft a referral that reflects the requirements of that provision. The key here is whether a notice of dissatisfaction has been given. The timely service of a notice of dissatisfaction is a condition precedent to the referral of a dispute to arbitration under Sub-Clause 20. 6.

The route to enforcement by way of arbitration in respect of a DAB decision that either party is dissatisfied with, requires a consideration of the interrelationship between Sub-Clauses 20. 4 and 20. 6. Importantly, paragraph 6 of Sub-Clause 20. 4 states:

"Neither party shall be entitled to commence arbitration of a dispute unless a notice of dissatisfaction has been given in accordance with this Sub-Clause." The words are restrictive, in that a prerequisite to arbitration under Sub-Clause 20. 6 is the service of a notice of dissatisfaction (NOD). A failure to serve a notice has other ramifications, which are set out in the last paragraph of Sub-Clause 20. 4: "If the DAB has given its decision as to a matter in dispute to both parties, and no notice of dissatisfaction has been given by either Party within 28 days after it received the DAB's decision, then the decision shall become final and binding upon both parties."

The arbitration agreement at Sub-Clause 20. 6 states: "Any dispute which has not been settled amicably and in respect of which the DAB's decision (if any) has not become final and binding shall be finally settled by arbitration." In order to commence arbitration under Sub-Clause 20. 6, a notice of dissatisfaction must be issued within time. If the notice is not issued, then the DAB's decision becomes "final and binding", and any failure of either party to "promptly give effect" to the DAB's decision can be referred to arbitration under Sub-Clause 20.7.

🔊 疑难词汇 🔊

1. dispute ridden industries 纠纷诉讼缠身的行业
2. US National Committee on Tunnelling Technology 美国隧道技术全国委员会
3. El Cajon Dam and Hydropower Project in Honduras（美国加州）埃尔卡洪水坝和洪都拉斯水力发电项目
4. pushed for a US-style dispute board 力推美国式的纠纷解决委员会
5. reached an impasse 陷入僵局
6. failing agreement 如果没有协议
7. rightly or wrongly 无论正确与否
8. commitment to 投入，致力委身于
9. minutes of meetings 会议记录
10. escalate into 逐步升级为，激化为
11. adjudicate 裁定，宣判
12. interim award 临时裁决
13. discharge 解雇，免除
14. full term 妊娠期，足月，任期
15. impartial 公平的，公正的
16. frivolously 轻浮地，愚昧地
17. substitute 代替，替补
18. reluctant 不情愿的，勉强的
19. within a matter of days 一两天的事
20. opening paragraph 开始部分，开头段
21. repudiate 拒绝，否定
22. allegation 主张，辩解
23. tribunal 法庭，裁决
24. route 路线

🔊 疑难语句 🔊

1. To ensure that the procedure is seen to be fair, and hence to establish confidence in the DAB, it is preferable that names are not accepted or rejected until the Tender has been accepted.

为了确保程序公正，建立 DAB 的权威性，合理的方式是在中标以后再确定（仲裁员）人选。

2. The work of a DAB member requires a commitment to be available to spend time for the project as and when required.

DAB 成员要信守承诺，即任何需要的时候在项目上花费一定的时间。

3. To be asked to allow one's name to be put forward involves some commitment and

208

so the time between the name being put forward and the appointment being confirmed should be kept to a minimum.

邀请某人成为仲裁员并承担一定责任，提名的时间与任命的时间应减到最少。

4. If at any time the Parties so agree, they may appoint a suitably qualified person or persons to replace (or to be available to replace) any one or more members of the DAB. Unless the Parties agree otherwise, the appointment will come into effect if a member declines to act as a result of death, disability, resignation or termination of appointment. If any of these circumstances occurs and no such replacement is available, a replacement shall be appointed in the same manner as the replaced person was required to have been nominated or agreed upon, as described in this Sub-Clause.

在任何时候，如果双方同意，他们可以任命一个或多个合格的人选来代替（或可能代替）DAB 一个或多个成员。除非当事人另有约定，在 DAB 成员因为死亡、残疾、辞职或合同到期等原因不能履行职责时，任命将生效。如何上述情况发生，而替代者没有发生，正如子条款所描述的，替代者将与被替代者的要求一样被任命或者同意。

☞ 中文综述 ☜

一、DAB 的产生与发展

在"新红皮书"出现以前，FIDIC 用来解决工程中争端的方式是以工程师作为裁决者对争议事项进行裁决。该方式在工程实践的纠纷与争议解决中确实起到了一定的作用，但随着该模式广泛和深入的运用，其缺点也逐渐显现出来。这主要表现在工程师与雇主的关系上。由于工程师是由雇主雇用并支付其所有费用的，所以其在工程中的中立性受到了普遍的质疑。自 20 世纪 80 年代以来，在国际工程实践中，产生了一种新的解决争议的方式，即"争议评审团"（Dispute Review Board），简称 DRB，DRB 即是 DAB 的前身。该方式改变了过去由工程师作为解决工程合同争端中间人的局面，开始由工程师以外的第三人对工程争议进行独立地评判。随着世界银行 1995 年 1 月将 DRB 纳入世界银行的招标文件范本，DRB 开始全面进入国际工程领域。FIDIC 敏锐地观察到了这一点，顺应了历史的潮流，果断地放弃了工程师作为争端裁判人的模式，将 DRB 引入了其新版的合同中，建立了 FIDIC 合同下的全新的"争端裁决委员会"（Dispute Adjudication Board，简称 DAB）争端解决机制。该机制是 FIDIC 借鉴 DRB 方式，并适当加以改造，使之适用于国际工程实施的成功改革之举。

二、DAB 的组成

DAB 的成员通常有三名，一名由雇主推荐，经承包商同意；另一名由承包商推荐，经雇主同意；第三名由已选定的两名成员提名推荐，经雇主和承包商同意，并任命为主席。在工程实践中，由于聘请此类专家的费用比较昂贵，因此对于小型项目此类委员会可以由一名专家组成。

在挑选 DAB 委员时，除了职业素质外，还要考虑以下条件：

（1）任何成员不得与争议的任何一方有从属关系；

（2）任何成员不曾受雇于合同的任何一方，没有与任何一方发生过经济关系；

（3）任何成员在担任 DAB 工作以前，不曾介入过此工程项目的重要事务，以免妨碍其独立公正地进行调解工作。

DAB 成员的任命既可以在合同签订后，也可以在争议发生后。FIDIC 的不同合同版本，对聘用此类专家成员的规定也不同。一般来说，若工程较复杂，合同额度较大，在工程开工后即任命此类成员，目的是使这些专家成员早日介入项目，熟悉项目的进程以及争议产生的背景，以便于更好地公平解决合同双方的争议。

对于 DAB 成员的人选，可以由承包商或雇主选择自己了解的相关专家，也可以由一些相关国际组织提供推荐人选。如 FIDIC 就有自己的争议评判员（Adjudicator）专家库，中国国际经济贸易仲裁委员会（CIETAC）也正在积极筹建自己的此类专家库。在工程实践中，对于彼此不同意对方提供的专家人选，FIDIC 合同条款规定：在双方对评判员人选不能达成一致意见时，由 FIDIC 主席来指定。

三、DAB 决定的依据

DAB 决定的依据有很大的灵活性。总的来说，DAB 决定的依据中最主要的依据是技术规范、合同条文和事件的相关证据。但 DAB 决定的依据不仅仅是这些，还有很多社会学、经济学、管理学等方面的原理和知识，以及 DAB 成员自身对于这些规则的认识。在DAB 成员就提交事项作出决定时，要将相关证据进行逐一地清理、比较，并根据工程实际选出最适合的部分作为裁决依据。与审判和仲裁相比，DAB 决定的依据来源广泛，其并不排斥法律以外的规则，如商业习惯或行业惯例，同时也可以是法律以外的法理，甚至是宗教教义。

四、DAB 的有效要件

1. 实质要件

在 DAB 的有效要件中，实质要件是指任何一个 DAB 决定能够发生法律效力所应具备的条件。在这个意义上，实质要件又可以称为 DAB 决定的一般生效条件。只有具备了实质要件的 DAB 决定才能为法律所承认并产生行为人预期的法律后果。否则，就会因为欠缺实质要件而成为无效的或可变更、可撤销的决定。判断实质要件是指是否存在争端，并有明确的利益诉求。争端是 DAB 的裁判对象，也是启动 DAB 程序的前提。如果不存在争端，DAB 将无法作出相应的决定。同时，申请 DAB 应当遵循的是利害关系原则，而不仅仅是法律关系原则，即争端主体之间只要因利益冲突而产生争端，就可向 DAB 申请裁决。

在"新红皮书"合同条件下，只要是与合同或工程实施有关的事项，包括工程师的任何证书、确定、指示、意见或估价等方面的内容，无论涉及合同、法律，或是商务、技术，如果任何一方认为无法通过双方之间的交流和磋商，也无法通过征询 DAB 意见的方式予以解决，均可按 20.4 款的规定提交 DAB 作出决定。

2. 程序和形式要件

DAB 决定原则上要求尽量采用书面形式。虽然根据第 20.3 款的要求，申请裁决"可以"采用书面形式，但在 FIDIC 合同中，书面材料是裁决的初步证据，也是争端解决期间的起算时间的依据，申请裁决的当事人一般均会采用书面形式，即便特殊情况下（诸如紧急情况需要立即裁决）也可采用口头形式，但也应等紧急情况过去后，补充记录相关内容。当任何一方要求 DAB 作出决定时，其提交的文件必须送达 DAB 的主席，并将相关材料抄送对方。同时，申请材料必须声明是按照 FIDIC 合同第 20.4 款所提出的。

五、DAB 决定的生效和执行

DAB 决定作出以后，在可能被随后的友好解决或仲裁裁决改变之前，对双方均具约束力。雇主或承包商任何一方不满意裁决决定，可在收到该决定通知后的 28 日内，将其不满通知另一方，否则任一方无权着手争议的仲裁。在发出表示不满意通知时，同样要表明该通知是根据本款规定发出的。28 日内任一方未发出不满通知，该决定则成为最终的对双方均具有约束力的解决方案。

根据第 20.7 款的规定，如果 DAB 的决定已成为最终的并具约束力的决定，而合同有一方未能执行该决定的话，另一方可以将此事项直接提交仲裁，而无需再次获得 DAB 的决定，也无需尝试友好解决过程。在这种情况下，仲裁的目的就变得非常简单、明确，裁决结果也可通过相应程序得到执行。

根据第 20.8 款［争端裁决委员会任期期满］的规定，如果合同双方因与合同或工程的实施引起的问题产生争议，但 DAB 由于任期结束或其他原因而缺失，那么任何一方可将争议直接提交仲裁。

DAB 的执行分为两种形式：其一是自觉执行。当争端双方均对 DAB 裁决表示满意或接受时，DAB 决定通过争端当事人的自觉行动得到了实现。其二是通过后续程序得到强制执行。DAB 的决定能否如同仲裁裁决那样，可以直接作为强制执行的依据呢？就目前各国立法情况看，DAB 的决定还不能够直接作为强制执行的依据。作为补救，FIDIC 合同第 20.7 款规定，如果 DAB 的决定已成为最终并具约束力的决定，而合同当事一方拒绝执行该决定，另一方可以直接提交仲裁。这实际上是通过仲裁的裁决来赋予 DAB 决定强制执行的效力。此时 DAB 的决定是仲裁裁决的依据，仲裁庭一般不会再对案件另行仲裁，而是直接根据 DAB 最终生效的决定作出裁决。需要注意的是在第 20.4 款规定的时间内，向对方发出表示不满意的通知，是当事一方将争议事项提交仲裁的必要步骤。按本款的规定，如果没有此类通知，任何一方无权将争议提交仲裁。由于当事一方不满意的对象是 DAB 的决定，因此该决定势必成为今后仲裁人关注的焦点。

Questions

1. What are the different methods of dispute resolution in construction disputes?
2. How are DAB members appointed?
3. Is the DAB decision legally binding for contract parties?
4. In case one party is not satisfied with DAB decision, what is applicable pathway for arbitration?

参 考 文 献

[1] 韦嘉. 国际工程合同管理(双语). 北京：中国建筑工业出版社，2010.

[2] 尼尔 G. 巴尼. FIDIC 系列工程合同范本——编制原理与应用指南. 张水波等译. 北京：中国建筑工业出版社，2008.

[3] 吕文学，张水波. FIDIC 设计—建造和运营(DBO)项目合同条件导读与解析. 北京：中国建筑工业出版社，2010.

[4] 田威. FIDIC 合同条件应用实务(第二版). 北京：中国建筑工业出版社，2009.

[5] 李明顺. FIDIC 条件与合同管理. 北京：冶金工业出版社，2011.

[6] 本书编委会. 建设工程施工合同(示范文本)(GF-2013-0201)使用指南. 北京：中国建筑工业出版社，2013.

[7] 王天翊. 建筑法案例精析(第二版). 北京：人民法院出版社，2003.

[8] 崔军. FIDIC 合同原理与实务. 北京：机械工业出版社，2011.

[9] 陈新元. FIDIC 施工合同条款与应用案例. 北京：中国水利水电出版社，2009.

[10] 郝林. FIDIC 施工合同应用技巧. 北京. 中国电力出版社，2008.

[11] 刘文生，夏露. 工程合同法律制度与工程合同管理. 北京：清华大学出版社，2011.

[12] 李德智. FIDIC 合同原理与实务. 北京：化学工业出版社，2013.

[13] John J. P. KROL. Construction Contract Law. John Wiley&Sons Inc，1993.

[14] Peter Hibberd，Paul Newman. ADR and Adjudication in Construction Disputes. Wiley-Blackwell，1999.

[15] Michael D. Robinson. A Contractor's Guide to the FIDIC and Conditions of Contract. John Wiley & Sons Inc，2011.

[16] Theodore J. Trauner. Construction Delays(Second Edition)：Understanding Them Clearly, Analyzing Them Correctly. Elsevier Inc，2009.

[17] Kit Werremeyer. Understanding & Negotiating Construction Contracts：A Contractor's and subcontractor's Guide to Protecting Company Assets. John Wiley & Sons Inc，2007.

[18] David Chappell. Standard Letters for Building Contractors，Fourth Edition. Wiley-Blackwell，2008.

[19] Nael G. Bunni. The FIDIC Forms of Contract (Third Edition). Blackwell Publishing，2005.

[20] Richard H. Clough. Contruction Contracting, A Practical Guide to Company Management(Seven Edition). John Wiley & Sons Inc，2004.

[21] John Van Der Ouil，Arjan Van Weele. International Contracting (Contract management in Complex Construction Projects). Imperial College Press，2014.

[22] Andy Hewitt. Construction Claims & Responses(Effective Writing & Presentation). Wiley-Blackwell，2011.

[23] Brian W. Totterdill. FIDIC User's Guide A Practical Guide to the 1999 Red and Yellow Books. Thomas telford，2006.